THE 6 COMMANDMENTS

The Bible 3.0:

COMMANDMENTS
OF THE CHOSEN LIFE

*A Roadmap to Personal Success
and Enlightenment*

THE 6

The Bible 3.0:

COMMANDMENTS
OF THE CHOSEN LIFE

*A Roadmap to Personal Success
and Enlightenment*

Jonathan A. Hacohen

The Awakened Press

The Awakened Press
www.theawakenedpress.com

For information about special discounts or for bulk purchases, please contact The Awakened Press at books@theawakenedpress.com.

The Awakened Press can bring authors to your live event. For more information or to book an event contact books@theawakenedpress.com or visit our website at www.theawakenedpress.com.

Book editors, Lindsay R.A. Dierking, Angela Heis
Cover and interior design, David Moratto

Printed in the United States of America
First The Awakened Press trade paperback edition

ISBN: 979-8-9891827-5-6

To my brother, Joe. You taught me the differences between being a boy and a man. You provided me with the tools to succeed rather than do it for me. You were always there for me, as a brother and father figure in my life. You led by actions rather than words. I would not be where I am today without you. You gave me the power of determination and the will to succeed. You are the most brilliant person I know with many G-d-given gifts. Thank you for putting the time into me and your lifetime of patience. I love you and I appreciate you.

To yoga: You took a wounded man with ambition and brought clarity to his life. You showed me the pathways to heal my body, mind, and soul. Thank you for embracing me into your community and being there when I need you. You have given me so much in my lifetime and all you ever asked was that I show up.

A special shoutout to Sukha Yoga (www.sukhayoga.ca), my home yoga studio in Thornhill, Ontario, Canada. You are family to me. Namaste.

Contents

—◦◦◦—

PART I:
BUILDING THE FOUNDATION

PART II:
THE 6 COMMANDMENTS OF THE CHOSEN LIFE

PART III:
ENLIGHTENMENT

Introduction

—◦❦◦—

Take a look in the mirror. Are you happy with the person looking back at you? Do you want to keep that person status quo? Or is that person ready to evolve beyond their comfort zone?

Whether you're living a happy or unhappy life, everyone needs to understand themselves and how they are choosing to live. Yes, you want to be more productive and achieve goals, but are you happy doing it? Do you have a good relationship with yourself and with others? Is life a death sentence for you? Or is life an opportunity for daily growth and for your world to evolve?

The Bible 3.0: The 6 Commandments of the Chosen Life is a lifestyle guidebook for designing and living the life that you choose. It is meant to be kept by your bed, on your nightstand, a coffee table or wherever it is easily accessible to you. This will become the ONE book that you can use to shape every aspect of your life and existence. Together we will understand every part of your being, from the beginning in setting the foundations for a fulfilling life to the ultimate appreciation of the meaning of life.

Imagine a world where you get to decide where you go, what you do, and who you get to be. Pretty exciting, isn't it? This does not have to be a fantasy. It can be your reality. Every day you get to make choices. Ultimately, the accumulation of these decisions will be the path that you take. Think of your life as your "Chosen Life."

You get to make the rules. You get to decide how you will live. It is *your* life. Take control of what your life will look like.

The Bible 3.0 is about YOU connecting with *yourself*. Dig deep —figure out what you're doing in your life and how you're going to live it. Ultimately, you are seeking your Chosen Life. You are here for your purpose. It is up to you to discover it.

At the core of *The Bible 3.0* are the 6 Commandments of the Chosen Life. We will dive deep into each Chosen Commandment and how you can implement each into your routine. The building blocks for life are the first four Chosen Commandments: water, sleep, nutrition, and exercise. Once you learn to create a lifestyle that incorporates the first four Chosen Commandments in unison, you will have created a foundation that sets you up for the greatest life you could have ever imagined.

From there, we will go on the road to enlightenment with additional steps and tools that you can learn and practice to take your energy to the next level. This is when Chosen Commandments #5 and #6 come in: yoga and meditation. These are labels that you have certainly heard and may have experienced in some form or another. But whether you feel that you have a love or resentment toward yoga and meditation, we will incorporate these practices into your life to help you break through your limitations and progress to new heights beyond what you ever thought was imaginable.

I will also discuss my own physical, mental, and spiritual awakenings and shifts during this book. However, any stories I share are examples of what can develop within a person when they make the commitment to growth and evolution. I teach it, but first and foremost, I study it. My stories and examples are a roadmap to help you develop your own lifestyle. Anyone can speak it. But ask yourself— how many actually do it?

If you read through this book you're going to have quality and quantity of life—because you're going to be more in touch with yourself and therefore the world. Everything comes back to the systems in this book, which focus on the body and the mind. And by taking care of your body and mind, in turn you're going to take care of your spirit.

Together we will build basic life systems that you can create and implement in your daily routine. You will look better, feel amazing, and create goals and mindsets for yourself that will shift you to the realms of positivity and success. We will look at the relationship between your body, mind, and soul and how they function independently as well as together. There will be work involved, but nothing that you can't handle.

Along the way, you will be completing many tasks and assignments. There will be no grading system. No pass or fail. Quite simply, every step that you are able to reach will lead you to the next path. Some parts may not resonate with you or even feel like blockages. That's okay! Always do the best you can and move ahead in the chapters. You can always return to previous passages and see them in different lights.

While I heavily encourage you to read the chapters in order (as they do flow in a sequence for a reason), you are certainly able to choose to flip back and forth between various chapters and headings as they speak to you or are needed by you at particular times.

Let's also make something very clear from the beginning: there is no perfection. You should not be concerned with making your life perfect. Life is but a series of practices that you get to do daily. If you experience a setback in one or more areas of the Chosen Commandments, that is fine. Do not be hard on yourself. You can try again tomorrow. And the next day and the next day. Some parts you may incorporate immediately. Some may take you days, weeks, months, and even years. But whatever road you choose to get there, you will get there. Because you believe in yourself.

Relationships are such an important part of all our lives. But before you look at how you interact with others, think about your relationship with yourself. If working on relationships is important to you, start by improving YOUR relationship with yourself and others thereafter. We are programmed to be focused on others:

What do my kids want? What does my boss want? What do others want? We're constantly looking for external validation. The person we most neglect is ourself. Begin the journey of internal validation. What do YOU want? What do YOU need? Once you feel that internal validation, you will marvel at how your external relationships begin to bloom and shine.

You have been spending your whole life searching to find out who you are. It's time to find some answers. Right now you have made the decision to change the world—YOUR world and your existence. The physical state of the world will continue to be and evolve as it will. What will change is how you choose to view yourself, the world, the people that surround you, and how everyone interrelates.

I am really excited about our road ahead together. I know that you are too. Get ready to plant seeds in the garden of your mind, and together we will see what will bloom. Enjoy the ride as we jump into the book that will evolve your world. Get ready for *The Bible 3.0*. It's time to start from the beginning. In this bible, the world was created and shaped by love.

PART I:
BUILDING THE FOUNDATION

ONE

Love Is a Lifestyle

—⦿⦿⦿—

Love is the foundation for all of existence. When your world is surrounded by love, everything else will follow.

We can spend a lifetime seeking love from others. From the time we are born, we seek the love of our parents. We search for the respect of our teachers, the admiration and approval of our siblings, friends, and future partners. We essentially seek validation through the eyes of love from third parties. The road to external love will get us nowhere. The journey for love begins within.

I'm sure you have asked yourself this question: Why can't (*insert name*) fully love me? We feel that if we received another person's love in a certain way, we would be complete. Yet no matter how much love another person can give us, we will always feel unfulfilled. If we truly seek eternal and lasting love, we must begin to love ourselves. Then we can begin to give unconditional love to others. Once we truly love ourselves and provide pure love to those around us, we are ready to live.

The world begins and ends with love. We enter the world as babies with all the hope and dreams ahead of us, with the full love of our parents. When we pass, we are usually surrounded by our loved ones who will miss us, think of us, and send us their loving thoughts as we head to the unknown after what we call "death." Life begins and ends with love. But if we do not have a life journey filled with love, then in many ways we exist without being.

As you think about the concept of love, ask yourself: Do I truly love? Do I love the person that I am? Can I provide unconditional love to others? And finally, is my heart open to receiving love without expectations? Be truthful with yourself. You have been programmed your whole life to think about what love is. Changing a lifetime of thoughts will not happen overnight. I challenge you to reconsider everything you envision love to be. It is not a road to travel with an external reward being the final destination. It is an internal review of healing and self-care. I know because I traveled that external road of love most of my life. It was only when I looked within that I truly learned what love meant.

As I will touch upon throughout this book, it wasn't until my thirties that I started to have my awakening. This began with the idea of love. I worked hard from a young age. I was a high achiever through school and as I began my career as a lawyer. Happiness, however, was something that eluded me during this stage of life.

When I reflect, the simple solution was to blame others. Whether it was friends or family, I felt that I was unloved. Those feelings carried through into my future relationships. I settled into connections that were not serving me. I compromised my principles and beliefs in what I valued in a life partner, for I felt that all I needed was a person to love me. Sound familiar? The one person that I was afraid to be with was myself.

Ending up alone was, to me, a tragedy that I did not want to face. As long as I was with someone else, I would be loved. Or so I made myself believe.

That road to love turned out to be a dead-end street. Through yoga and meditation, I worked on myself to reshape my thinking. I learned to be alone with myself and with my thoughts and to begin to embrace who I am. Today I truly love myself. With internal love, I no longer need the love of others. It is a fulfilling place to be, which you will find as well through the work to be done that is outlined in this book. It won't be easy, and it will take time. Ultimately it will be worth it as you build your life on a solid foundation of love.

To move ahead in my own life, I felt that I needed clarity. As part of my personal work, I sought out and began working with a shaman. In fact, I have been working with said shaman for several years now. The greatest gift that my shaman has given me is clarity. By understanding and hearing my thoughts and feelings, I began to see the people around me who didn't relate to me on a positive level. There were relationships in which I was investing myself for no real reason. I focused instead on understanding who I was and building a relationship with myself.

The sessions with my shaman were quite beautiful. The majority of the time, I would lie down on a bed. Music would play in the background as the shaman would chant. I would close my eyes and learn to be in a state of complete calmness, physically and mentally. It is in this state where I would have visions, in meditation through the third eye, where I realized that there is some sort of hidden world "out there" beyond the land of the living. For me, sometimes these were visions of things to come or images of people who had already passed on. I did not ingest any magic formulas or potions. I would be alone in my thoughts and with my visions. Focus through the shamanic sessions provided me clarity at the highest states of meditation possible. It was difficult work, but one that allowed me to let go of the past and work toward my own future. As each session progressed, I would begin to have more clarity about myself.

During every appointment with the shaman, I would return mentally and continue to lie in complete stillness while the shaman played her music and chanted. Sometimes nothing happened. Sometimes visions arose, but they were different from my out-of-body meditation states. During mindful meditation, my spirit would sometimes come out of my body and I could watch myself lying still. I could see beyond the realms of the living world that I knew. It made me assess what I consider living and dying and that a form of life indeed exists after we pass on.

After each session, I would come out feeling refreshed and alive. And from there I began to question: What am I doing on Earth?

What does my life mean to me? One answer was appearing very clearly: I was living a life devoid of love. If I hoped to change my patterns and reverse my course, I would need to learn the meaning of love in my life.

The afterlife has more to do with *how we live* while we are still "alive." Are we truly living a life, or are we simply going through the motions? Love is at the start and end of our existence. So what about the middle?

Whether we are alive for one year, ten, twenty, fifty, one hundred, or more—do we give love? Do we receive love? In the rat race to get ahead, to make money, and to have the most stuff, love is often put on the back burner.

Love is many things to many people. Is lust also love? What about happiness? Passion? Nurturing? Caring? If you feel physical attraction for another person, yes, this can be love. If you care for your family—your elders—that can be love. It ultimately feels that we are too concerned with the label of love and its meaning. Stop putting pressure on yourself to find love and expect that it will provide you with all the answers. Love is what you make it to be. Love is not an end result. Love is a lifestyle.

To truly love and feel love, we do not need to be so concerned about formal definitions. Love is not meant to be restrictive. We do not need to compartmentalize it so that it will fit what we need it to be.

I lived a life where I held onto a belief as to what love needed to be and provide for me. It focused on external validation and for others to fill my cup full of love. Yet no matter who was in my life and the amount of love that they provided, my cup often felt bare. I was relying too much on love to make me happy. At least, not the purest form of love that one discovers within themselves.

If you feel love within you—and then you act with selfless love—then love is actually there. If you act and feel with a void or a lack of a wholesome purpose, then you can question whether in fact love is flowing through you. At this stage, please assess whether you feel that you are living a life with love. Do you feel it inside of you? Let's break down our understanding of love and its flow within your existence.

The three stages of love are as follows:

STAGE 1: YOU LOVE YOURSELF. Regardless of how others speak to you or treat you, the one person you look to for love is yourself. You are comfortable within your own skin. You respect yourself. You believe in yourself. You love the person that you are and care for that person immensely. Internal love without the need for external validation—that is Stage 1 on the road to love. None of the other points in love are possible until you can successfully fulfill this level.

STAGE 2: GIVING LOVE TO OTHERS UNCONDITIONALLY. Once you love yourself, you are able to give love to others. Without being able to take care of yourself lovingly, how could you possibly love others as well? The keys to this stage are to love oneself fully and from there to give love to others—without conditions. If you feel that you will only love someone if they love you back, that is not giving love unconditionally. To be able to care for someone and love someone without expecting any returns—that is a true form of love. Congratulate yourself when you reach Stage 2. You are on an amazing path. To be able to then love others without reciprocation means you have entered a new level of love for yourself. Your mind should be blown at what you have been able to accomplish.

STAGE 3: RECEIVING UNCONDITIONAL LOVE. The highest power of love is when two people provide one another unconditional love. You love a person and expect nothing in return. Now imagine being able to receive love that has no strings attached. Someone gives you love for the simple reason that they care for you and do not expect it back. When you reach Stage 3, it is the ultimate state of being. Because of

Stages 1 and 2, we can be happy within ourselves and give love to others unconditionally. Consider Stage 3 a bonus round. Receiving unconditional love is the cherry on top. To be in a loving relationship where two people give each other unconditional love is the purest exchange and form of energy called prana. With prana by your side, you will be unstoppable.

Now that you understand the three stages of love, let's find your inner love. It is there. We need to nurture it to bring it out. And it will always begin with the search for love from within.

Note that no work is being asked of you at this stage. That work is to come. In the early stages of this book, your job is to simply assess who you are. Mentally, I am helping you understand who you are and where you are at. Together, we will assess the different components that shape you: body, mind, and soul. Then we're going to be working on them individually and simultaneously.

I must also establish for you from the beginning that this is not a book about love. I am not going to review every component of love as part of *The Bible 3.0*. That may come at a different time in a future book. At this point, I want you to have a basic understanding of love and how it works. In order for this book to be the most effective in guiding your journey, you can let go of the second and third components of love for now. It will be great if you are able to give love unconditionally in the future and receive it back from others, but they are not necessary for you to complete the work required in the upcoming sections. The only part of love that I need you to focus on is Stage 1: self-love.

In living your life, you have more than likely neglected number one—you. To assess who you are and what you are made of, you need to build a solid relationship with yourself. You need to begin to love yourself unconditionally. It is through loving yourself that you will be able to put in the work to construct and connect your body, mind, and soul through the 6 Chosen Commandments. Even if the only love that you have within your life is internal, then you will always have the love you need to survive and thrive. External love is great, but it is a bonus at best. Remember to always love yourself unconditionally as you follow the Chosen Commandments and you will have all the love you will ever need.

If we live a life full of love, life doesn't have to end. Maybe it does in the sense that the physical form may cease to exist. But the love we produce and spread in life—that can continue until the end of time. True legacies. Warm feelings for those that have left the Earth. When people speak fondly of those who have departed, we speak of them mostly for the love they spread when alive. Maybe we did not open an orphanage or directly save people's lives, but we led a loving life. Did we care about those around us and leave a positive, lasting impact? It is the love that you produce and give during your lifetime that will determine who you really are, whether people remember it or not.

Perhaps you have made a mistake or several errors. You may have wronged yourself or others, physically and/or mentally. You can choose right now to switch courses. You can choose the path of life and in turn the path of love, which will turn out to be the path of life. That decision is up to you.

Living most of my life without love was not a death sentence for me. When I had my awakening, I chose to change directions. You can, as well. Do not dwell on the love that you have missed out on in your life. Do not live a life with regret. Understand that today is a fresh start. You have the opportunity to rebuild the relationship you have with yourself, first and foremost. You can practice self-love every day, starting today. The change is immediate. And it starts with setting yourself up with a new mindset focused on forgiveness, healing, and love for yourself.

Life is not a contest to see who the winner is. It is a practice run where every day we can try to live the best life we can. And if one day steers off course, we can right the ship the next day. . .or perhaps the next week, month, or year down the road. As a society we are trained to look for quick fixes and solutions. There is so much pressure to achieve everything immediately. Embrace that this is your life. You get to choose the direction. Nobody can decide for you. You are the captain of your own ship and get prepared to choose your chosen course.

Love for you, then, is not a competition or an end result. It is a lifestyle—one that you can and will practice daily. No matter what is happening or what is demanded of you, the focus will remain the same. The person who needs and deserves your love first and foremost is YOU. You may feel that you have to sacrifice yourself to take care of others, but if you neglect yourself in Stage 1 of love, you will not be able to give the unconditional love required in Stage 2. So practice self-love daily. Make it your lifestyle choice. It is a practice. Not a race. There is nowhere to be but in the moment, filled with love; the love you have for yourself.

You may have a list of items you want to accomplish. Perhaps you want to stop smoking? Lose weight? Change your diet? You may have goals you want to achieve. That's great! We will be getting to goal setting and achievements in future chapters. But before we get to the internal work, we have to understand how you are constructed; how the three parts of your existence—body, mind, and soul—work. We need to comprehend what they do and need independently of each other and how they work together. Once you know your construction and makeup, we will dive into the core of this book: the 6 Chosen Commandments required to create the greatest you imaginable.

To choose the path to live, you need to access love from within your existence. Without love in your life, no amount of effort to heal and build your body, mind, and soul will work. You can run the fastest races, eat the cleanest diets, or meditate outside for hours per day—but the work and energy cannot be built and sustained if you do not appreciate and accept love into your life.

Every facet of your being depends on the energy you put into yourself. That work must be framed with pure love for yourself and without the need for external validation. As you read each chapter and consider your being, always come back to love. If you begin at any stage, always make sure you start with love for yourself.

To move ahead, it is time to forgive yourself for your past. Previous mistakes do not shape you or decide your future. So many success stories have been told by people who did not start on top. They failed many times. Each time they dusted themselves off and began again. When I was at my lowest point in life, physically and mentally, the easiest thing would have been to give up. But I refused. Setbacks motivated me to work harder and find new paths to take. So learn from past experiences. Let go of previous burdens. They do not shape you or define you. Embrace the person that you are today and get excited for all the great things you will do in the future. Say to yourself, "I love you." Embrace yourself. That love for yourself will carry you through until the end of time.

I lived most of my life in a haze. From the time I was born until at least my thirties, I don't know how much love was in my heart, if any at all. It is a hard realization when you see that you sleepwalked through your life. I lived physically but really not mentally. I was dialed out. I was unhappy on so many levels. I felt the world gave me no opportunities and that people wronged me constantly.

When you aren't happy in your own skin, then you likely don't love yourself. And if you don't love yourself, how can you possibly love others? I was sad on some levels to realize that I had lost so many years that drifted by, which I could have enjoyed far more. But in the same light, I was happy. The reason? That it hit me at all and not in another thirty years. My missed years were training years that brought me to the place in the world that I am at now. And in this moment and for all the moments to follow, I can further appreciate the life that I have.

Each moment from there on, I learned to love myself and life more and more. And I was able to give and produce more love daily than I ever had. Life has its good days and bad ones. But even the bad ones don't feel so bad anymore. They are life lessons and I use them to appreciate love on higher levels. From bad can come good. From hate can come love. And from love can come completion.

As we learn to truly live, in order to love, we have to make a decision. Life—is it fair or unfair? Say that to yourself now: "Life isn't fair." How old were you when you first uttered those words? And when was the most recent time you said it? If you are saying it and feeling it currently, then guess what? You are right. And you are wrong.

Life, in many ways, is not fair. But it is not meant to be fair. It is not a board game with rules and victors and losers. It is your life. Maybe you received opportunities that did not play out, or maybe you had to work extra hard to get ahead in certain situations. Do not let external circumstances that are out of your control shape you. Do not give up because life is too hard or because you are finding too many challenges in your way. Bring life back down to basics. Appreciate that you have life and that you are alive. Love the person you are. Do not be hard on yourself because you are not the image of who you think you need to be.

Your evolution will come with time. The work you put in through the 6 Chosen Commandments will help you take control of your destiny. No matter what you look like or feel today, whatever you have accomplished or need to get done in the future, always love yourself. Today. Tomorrow. And for all of your existence.

You can't control external factors—but you can certainly control how you view your life. Choose to see yourself and your life through loving eyes. You are amazing. You can accomplish anything you choose. You are a cheerleader for all the people closest to you. Do not neglect yourself. Cheer yourself on. Love the person that you are. That is the energy you will then attract into your existence.

As you begin to prepare yourself for a new lifestyle and thought process, much work lies ahead. In the upcoming chapters, we discuss how you as a person are made of your body, mind, and soul. You will learn how each component works on its own and in unison. As you get to know yourself on new levels, you will get prepared for each of the steps required to bring you to your highest state of being. This is where you live the life you want for yourself and to truly allow happiness to become your state of mind. To be clear: this groundwork can only be done if it is built on a foundation of love. Without pure love within yourself, all the work on your body, mind, and soul cannot come together. Love is the glue that binds all parts of you as one. So whenever you look for answers on life and the direction in which to head, remember to always start with love. Without love, there is no real life. All the work ahead—and your evolution—must always start with a foundation of love.

TWO

The Body

To understand ourselves, we begin with our construction. Each of us is made of three key components: the body, mind, and soul. The following three chapters are not about fixing and healing each part of ourselves. This will come in later chapters, beginning in Chapter 5 when we introduce the 6 Commandments of the Chosen Life. However, to truly do the work, we must first come to appreciate how we are made up and how we function. In this chapter, we dive first into the part of ourselves that is our *mainframe*: the body.

The body is the temple. The body is what keeps you going and cares for the mind. To have your mind and soul intact, you need to take care of your vessel. And that is the body.

G-d gave you your body—in whatever form it is in. You choose how to care for it. The benefits of shaping the healthiest and soundest body that you can have are endless. You will have more energy. You will function better and more consistently day-to-day. Your body will break down less and have fewer health issues. You will feel better and have a better quality of life.

Taking care of your body is a no-brainer. It is all reward and no risk. Imagine taking a bet where you have everything to gain and nothing to lose. Betting on yourself and taking care of your body is the winning lottery ticket. Make that bet immediately and every day that you can.

I will never forget my personal moment of body realization. It was spring 2011. I was on a family hiking trip through a nature course. My oldest niece, Rachel, wanted to stop and take a selfie together. After we took the picture, she showed me the finished product. Looking at the picture, it hit me. I was fat. I wasn't slightly overweight or out of shape; I was at the heaviest that I had ever been in my life. I started to cry to myself. I knew that I had reached rock bottom. Changes were going to be needed or I would die at a young age.

Before I saw the picture that changed my outlook and life, I did not want to accept my physical conditioning. After completing my medical physical exam earlier that year, my family doctor had some news for me that should have been a slap in the face. My cholesterol was really bad. My good cholesterol was low and my bad cholesterol was considered very high. I was in my early thirties, yet I had the cholesterol of someone infirmed in their seventies.

My family doctor gave me a choice: I either had to go on cholesterol meds or make lifestyle changes. *Real* changes. My eating habits were very poor. There was a period in my life when my daily lunch was a hotdog on a stick and pastries! I wasn't exercising. I wasn't sleeping very much. And I never drank water.

For most of my life, I drank a steady diet of fruit juice, pop, and up to five coffees a day! I knew that I needed to fix my lifestyle, but it wasn't until I saw the picture with Rachel that this realization hit me. Change as a lifestyle would not come easy for me.

Revamping lifestyles rarely comes easily for anyone. We tend to want quick fixes; we want the boot camps and workshops that will solve all our problems immediately. But to create a lifestyle, you need to create a core. And the core on which your life—your world —is built, is your body. To get to where you need to go, you need your body in the best condition possible.

You have heard the expression before: no matter what your faith is, *the body is a temple.* There are some religions that believe tattoos are forbidden. For some, even piercings are abolished. Although there are people who think graffiti and holes in the body are a form of desecration, for others it is a form of artwork and sacred to their beliefs and lifestyle. At the same time, I would like to shift your focus to the many other ways that will destroy a temple—ones that can cause permanent destruction in how the body looks, feels, and especially works.

What about hard living? Drugs, cigarettes, and alcohol pop into mind immediately for most. Certainly, when you put poison in your system, you can't expect a positive result. We can debate all day as to the health benefits of one glass of red wine at dinner or a morning coffee. But what about multiple glasses of wine or cups of coffee? What about strong drugs such as cocaine and heroin, or excessive use of marijuana products? The list goes on and on as far as the "do-nots" of what to put into your body. It's common sense (or should be) if you value your life and are comfortable with yourself that you will not put things into your body that will likely ruin it and cut your existence short.

But there is a harsher, more subtle form of evil lurking in the lifestyle of our general population. It's in *how we eat*—from the food that we consume to the drinks that we have. Salt, sugar, processed foods, fried food... All lead to poor health conditions and in many, death. No, *The Bible 3.0* is not a diet book, but it assists in establishing a focused lifestyle. I will explain.

I was never a big guy until my breaking point in 2011. From the time I was born until I became a young adult, I would say that I was in the slender category. Perhaps I had good genetics in that way. Perhaps there was good luck. But from twelve to thirty years old, I had the same waist size. I worked out at different points, I played some sports, but I was not what one would deem to be active physically. So that didn't help.

It was my eating habits that held me back for so many years. Simply put, I ate horribly. Grilled cheese breakfasts were an everyday occurrence throughout my youth. Skipping lunch or eating greasy meals, having huge dinner portions, late-night snacking all the time—it was almost a game to me to see how much I could eat and get away with.

By the time 2011 hit, my daily lunch consisted of a Philly Cheesesteak sandwich on garlic bread, poutine fries, and unlimited pop to drink. My waistline was out of control. My pants size had increased significantly, and I was between forty and fifty pounds over my regular weight. I shrugged off my waistline to pants shrinking in the wash. The same with my shirts; I refused to believe that there was anything wrong with my lifestyle. Yet the picture told me all I needed to know.

The picture with my niece told me the story. Only then did I understand why my doctor was concerned about my medical condition. In addition to my cholesterol, I was short of breath all the time. I had no strength or conditioning. My body was truly falling apart. My body was, in fact, speaking out—crying out to me, begging for changes. It took me so many years, but I finally learned to listen to my body. I started to accept that changes were in store that would carry me for the rest of my life.

My position on cholesterol medications was that they were not an option. Many believed that cholesterol was hereditary and that no amount of clean eating and physical activity could fix it. I disagreed. From all the materials I was reading and researching day and night, I knew in my heart that it was fixable.

Until that point, I had never thought of how my lifestyle affected my health. But it started to dawn on me... Years of allergies and sinus issues. Multiple sinus surgeries. My unhealthy gut and stomach issues. Then the cholesterol issues. I was abusing my body, and it was fighting back. Now it was time to love my body. And then it would love me back.

I had read and heard about the seven-year rejuvenation process. There are those in the science community that believe that your body can, in fact, regenerate itself every seven years. I have never been able to find a concrete study or evidence to support this, yet it's a concept that stuck with me and often gave me hope. I found it interesting and reassuring on a personal level. Whether factual or a placebo, the idea of rejuvenation still allows me to evolve and improve. The thought being that no matter how hard you have lived and abused your body, you can essentially bring your body to a balance and equilibrium through seven years of clean living.

I knew deep down that in order to set forth on the seven-year rejuvenation path for myself, I would have to control my weight and fix my cholesterol. I would not beat myself up over the bad choices I made for my body over my whole life. Rather, I would congratulate myself on the seven years plus that I worked on fixing and healing my body. Little did I know that I would later become like a real-life Benjamin Button, the legendary man who aged in reverse.

At that point in my trajectory, I was deep into baseball blogging. I have loved the sport for all my life. From the moment my father died at a young age, baseball became my escape and release. And as I grew older, I built up a baseball blog that became famous in the baseball world. Forming connections through players, coaches, owners, and reporters was really cool. However, working full time in law and running a daily baseball blog was burning me out. But I loved it so much that I only kept growing the blog bigger and bigger. Yet, I was still at that crossroads where I knew life changes needed to be made. I simply did not know how to get to my desired outcome.

One Monday morning, as I was driving to work, it hit me. Out of the blue, I made a phone call that would forever change my life and world. I called my head writer as part of the blog and told him the news: I was done with baseball. I was done with the blog. The site was now his.

I was walking away from my comfort zone and my first love. I was giving up the baseball blog cold turkey. I was done writing about life. I was ready to go live it.

The head writer was stunned. He asked me what I was planning to do now.

"It's simple," I told him. "I am going to practice yoga."

As I came to the end of the road, my body was telling me I was going to die young. I was aging myself prematurely. I looked horrible and felt worse. I decided to just do it. I was ready to devote myself to fixing my life. I knew that I had reached the turning point… I was either going to stay on the path I was on and die, or I had to revamp it. I had to bring my life down to zero and restart it again. This was not a situation for a quick fix or Band-Aid® solution.

I needed real change and healing. Mentally, I had been preparing for upheaval for some time until I was ready to give the green light and actually do it.

A misconception is that I made a spur-of-the-moment decision to give up the blog. Yes, it happened in the moment of realization, but it came from weeks, if not months of marination. Mentally, consciously, and subconsciously, I was working on a solution to how I could fix my state of being and balance all of my obligations. As with all major decisions, I came to the following conclusion: I had to focus on the goal that I most wanted and what steps I had to take to get there.

The goal of being healthy and happy was obvious. Now I had to create and implement the steps. With *time* being my most limited commodity, I had to decide how to best allocate my time to reach my goal. By working full time, I realized that my baseball blog was essentially a second job. Focusing on my health and learning or adopting a yoga practice would become a third job. My schedule would not allow me to work three jobs. The most precious commodity that we have is time. Time is limited, and we must choose wisely how we allocate this resource.

I would have to put as much, if not more, energy into yoga in order to make it work. So the decision came down choosing between building a successful blog and health and happiness. I chose health and happiness and thus yoga over the baseball blog.

I have read before about lifelong smokers who give up their addiction on the spot and never go back. I always wondered how they did that until I did a version of it myself. Giving up the baseball blog was one of the easiest decisions I had ever made once it hit me. While writing and reading were passions of mine, I felt that the devotion of time for me in those arenas was holding me back from other pursuits that I needed to explore. I needed to invest the time into yoga to really discover the best me.

From the moment that I gave up the blog, I never wrote again until this book. Funny enough, for a lifelong reader, I couldn't even read a book cover to cover from that point until now. From the time

I was five until my early adult years, I was reading close to one book per day. Then for over ten years, I had both writer's block and reader's block. But I could forgive myself because those were mental blocks that would grow over time and would be dealt with in their own time and space. All I knew was that my body was lashing out at me.

The body speaks to you. It is up to you to listen to it. My body was craving stability and transformation. After months of pondering, it hit me on the drive to work that Monday morning that yoga was the simplest and easiest solution I could commit to. Or so I thought.

Wear a pair of shorts, grab a bottle of water and a yoga mat, and let nature take its course. I wanted the stereotypical yogi male body figure, which was lean and toned. And I would stop at nothing to get it. So I started to detach from the lifestyle that I was living and was ready to adopt a lifestyle worth living.

I had taken only one yoga class prior to signing up for my first of many memberships. An ex-girlfriend was ranting and raving about yoga and told me we had to take a class together. We ended up taking a ninety-minute advanced class since it fit into our schedules one evening. I barely survived sixty minutes of it. I walked out of the class and swore off yoga forever. And yet, there I was, signing up to join a yoga studio to get healthy and have a sexy yoga body (as I put it in my application form).

Looking back, it seems strange that I chose yoga as I hated it the very first time I practiced it. And I hated it for several months from the start of my first membership. I stood in the back of the class, feeling out of place, each class feeling like an eternity. But I had a higher purpose: to get my body in shape and be healthy. Little did I know that yoga would, in fact, most nourish my mind and soul. The sexy yoga body was simply the icing on the cake.

As my life journey has evolved, so have my physical routines. In addition to yoga and walking, I eventually took up boxing, CrossFit, and exercising at the gym. I worked on my nutrition and eating regimens. I hired a dietician and nutritionist, who assisted in preparing meal plans. I began to find that my exercise sessions would not go well without clean eating in place. From there, two other key components were needed to tune my body, which we will dive into as part of this book: sleep and water consumption. To build my temple—my strong body—I needed to focus on exercise, nutrition, sleep, and water consumption. And this journey all started for me through yoga.

I write it because I have lived it. I continue to do so on a daily basis. My yoga practice evolved to the point that I once practiced 395 days of yoga in a row. I had another streak of 365 days in a row. Heck, I even showed up to a studio one Saturday morning and stayed to practice all four classes that day. Over six hours of yoga in one single day. Goals that I thought were completely unattainable when I started yoga were achieved through hard work and perseverance. I also hit injuries and bumps in the road—I am only human and I was no longer twenty, so my body did not always react the way I wanted it to. That was okay. I made adjustments as needed and carried onward.

Ironically, the 395-day streak ended by injury. Not from a yoga class, but slipping on black ice in the winter while texting. This goes to show you that the universe will tell you when things must end and then restart.

I refer to the 395 days of yoga as "the yoga streak." But that time in my life ran deeper than just yoga. It was not just 395 days of yoga—it was 395 days of cleansing my body. It was 395 days of celibacy, full abstinence of sexual activity of any kind—including masturbation. Plus I incorporated disciplined healthy eating and only drank water. I decided that by practicing yoga every day and cleansing myself, my body would reach a state of purity, which in turn would allow my mind to discover clarity.

This mental clarity did arise and allowed me to discover my Chosen Life. By building life systems over time, I was able to transform into the person I am today. It all began with rebuilding my body into the strongest vessel possible, which would allow me to push through all other points of my existence.

Now I am ready to help you start your journey, which will include strengthening and healing your body so that you can become the best version of yourself possible.

It all comes down to the notion that everyone is either living the Chosen Life or *wants* to live the Chosen Life. The life that you seek will come down to what YOUR Chosen Life is, not mine. So get ready to discover and live what will ultimately be the life *you* want to live!

I have great news for you: You do not have to do this alone. I am here to help guide you every step of the way. How you look and feel today can change in an instant. As you come to learn and adopt the 6 Chosen Commandments in your life, you will be making the shifts in your lifestyle that will change your composition forever. Your body, together with your mind and soul, will be nourished differently. The purpose of sharing my personal stories and intimate thoughts is to inspire you to listen to your inner voice and to find your chosen path. My story is proof that hard work and perseverance pay off. How I look and feel did not come easy to me. It took years to reprogram myself and work on my goals. Do not expect quick fixes. Rather, know that by making the decision and commitment to evolve, you have already made tremendous progress. Now you will prepare for the steps in your path to being the best version of you possible.

The body was the first point in my own journey and took the most amount of work. Mentally, I want to prepare you for the road ahead. No matter how mentally strong you are and emotionally devoted to your path you may be, your body may have other ideas for you. Inevitably in working your body, setbacks will arise. Injuries can pop up at a moment's notice. Fatigue. Soreness. Failure. Every time you hit a new high, get ready for the possibility of going three steps back.

I have watched people exercise my whole life. I always marvel at how so many people try to go all out when they first train or work their bodies. They burn out. They give up. And they don't go back. That will NOT be you. As you continue to build a foundation of love for your life, you will also build a model of sustainability for your body to evolve upon. You are not striving for perfection. You are creating a consistent and rewarding life routine.

Please do not be hard on yourself when you do encounter physical setbacks. Even professional athletes, with all the available top resources and coaches in the world, encounter them. That is why professional athletes need to work on their minds and souls as much as their bodies to achieve well-rounded success. We will discuss in the upcoming chapters how the mind and soul work within your makeup. Remember that they are connected to your body and work in unison to power you and your life. *None of this can happen, though, without your body.* Thus, the 6 Chosen Commandments will give you the necessary tools to help shape and transform your body to greatness.

Taking care of your body is a full-time job in itself. But with the steps available to you at your fingertips, you will achieve all the physical goals you set for yourself. Be realistic—and make sure to give yourself plenty of time. It is a life journey.

One thing I learned along my own route is that the first step to one's evolution is to work on the body. As a society, we focus on how we look and to better our appearance, yet all the changes and adjustments we make should better our bodies/minds/souls. They work hand in hand.

That's right. We aren't here to work on each part of ourselves in isolation. We can work and improve the entire package in unison. Remember that you cannot neglect any of these three components: body, mind, and soul. Otherwise, you will simply continue to hold yourself back.

If you mistreat your body, what do you think happens to your mind? Can you make good choices? Are you happy with yourself and others? Probably not. If you take care of your body, then you take care of your mind. Your mind needs your body to function. So to be the best you that you can be, you first and foremost need *love*. Be in touch with love. And to love yourself, you must take care of your body. Feed it a healthy variety of foods. Your body will thank you—and so will your mind. With a nourished body and mind, your soul will prosper from there.

Over a decade later, I reenacted the picture with my niece from 2011. We took identical poses, in the same outfits and setting. When people see the picture, they think that the 2011 me is the older one, and the 2022 me is the younger one. I am over ten years older in the later picture, yet I look over ten years younger—without surgeries or medical treatment. A game plan, hard work, and perseverance were my courses of action.

Maybe Benjamin Button was not just a made-up character, but rather an image that can be created. When I see the 2011 me, I don't recognize him. I don't even know him. Yet he was me—a shell version of me. It wasn't just that he was physically unflattering. He also looks mentally checked out. And there is no substance in his eyes. He is there, but not really there. He is not present. He is passing through.

When I look at the 2022 picture, I love the change that I see in myself physically, but I am most proud of the related changes of being mentally strong and having a passion for life. I am now living a mindful life. This is not just a byproduct of physical work. The transformation works together.

In Chapter 5, we will get to the 6 Chosen Commandments. Many believe that the 6 Chosen Commandments are needed strictly to help maintain the body. But far from it. The 6 Chosen Commandments help every part of you in wholeness—body, mind, and soul.

Your body, brain, and heart all need nurturing. If you are to function at the highest levels and live the longest life and have a quality life, you need your body to work at its best capacity. So the next time you put anything into your body, ask yourself: How is this serving me? Do I need pills, or can I simply eat better? I'm unhappy—will more alcohol fix it? Or are there other ways to feel better?

You need your body. And your body needs you. The more you take care of your body, the more your body will take care of you. It's a direct correlation. What you put in, you get out. So to get the most, put in the most. Treat your body like the temple it is and maintain a level of purity within your system that will serve you. From there, it is time to focus on your mind and shift your awareness to within yourself.

THREE

The Mind

———

You control your mind. Your mind doesn't control you.

Your mind works for you. You don't work for your mind.

Ponder that now. Take it in.

Be honest with yourself. Do you let your thoughts, doubts, and worries control how you live? Or do you control your mind and how you want to think?

Your mind. Your angel and your devil. It can calm you and be there for you. It can frighten you to the point of despair. Your best friend and your worst enemy is your mind.

It's incredible how much time, money, and resources we are prepared to spend on our bodies, including personal trainers, yet we hardly devote anything close to that for our minds. Take therapy, for example. Another taboo topic all too often in society. We are okay with having a personal trainer for our bodies. To put in time at the gym for our physical selves. But yet, for many of us, we are completely content to neglect our minds.

The mind is the engine that runs our vehicle. Imagine how your car would run if you never changed your oil or did a tune-up. Your car would implode very quickly. That is, in fact, what is happening to many people. They are only investing in their outer selves, yet not their inner minds.

In sports, working with a sports psychologist is crucial for many athletes. They train hard, work on their bodies and their sports skills. And they learn that to be at the top they have to devote equal time to the psychological side of themselves. Remember: if it works for LeBron James—a legendary athlete who is arguably known as one of the greatest basketball players of all time—there is no reason why it shouldn't work for you. LeBron has coaches to help him be the strongest mentally he can be. And so can you.

There are many people that suffer from conditions referred to as anxiety and depression. I like to think of depression as regret of the past and anxiety as the fear of the future. There are, of course, many more details to these general labels—but they are real things. But please don't worry. We will be covering anxiety and depression further in a later chapter.

Take note that what often separates winners from the defeated, and the happy from the miserable people, is the mind. And the thing is—the mind is simply there. We choose how to use it and what it produces. Our states of being are what they are. It all comes down to how we choose to view ourselves. We can use the mind as a weapon of strength to grow us, or a weapon of destruction to defeat ourselves.

You wake up in the morning. The same start as everyone else's day. YOU make decisions on how to start that day. You begin conversing with your mind. Are you happy? Sad? Worried? Upset? This morning mindset will often set the tone for your whole day.

My mental awakening was at yoga. Back to the yoga studio, the one-stop healing shop, I was in śavāsana (known as "dead man's pose" or "corpse pose" in English) waiting for the class to start. My eyes were closed, I was calming my mind and being in the moment. Then, an image hit me. There was a visual of me lying in the exact same position I was in—but I was in a box. That's when it really hit me for the first time: I was going to die one day. Everything that I was living for and building toward was, in many ways, meaningless. It would be all over one day, and the form that I was currently in would no longer exist. I started to sob uncontrollably. I was so upset that I almost did not start the class. But I was on a yoga streak, so I would make it through that class. This was a profound moment in my life that I want to expand upon further, but that will come later.

Afterward and for several days to follow, I would meditate on what had happened and what that image of being in a box meant to me. One day, it came to me: I was not afraid to die. *I was afraid of not living.*

It was a saddening feeling knowing that I had sleepwalked through over thirty years of my existence. I never stopped to savor life and all that it has to offer. I don't know if I was ever fully present in the previous moments of my life. It's almost like I was a programmed robot. I was designed to work on tasks, one by one, and to keep getting to the next thing and each one after that.

I worked hard, yes, but I was not mentally strong. I lived a life full of self-doubt and low self-esteem. Many of my supposed friends, family, and mentors who should have supported me were in fact feeding into my low self-image. And I let them. Yet, I do not blame any of them. They were feeding off the energy that I was putting out into the universe, and it was one that did not see me in any sort of positive light. It's almost like I was handing others the ammunition to hurt me with. Why was I self-sabotaging myself in this manner?

An example of this self-sabotaging behavior was sports. I loved playing and watching sports. However, I never saw myself as a talented or gifted athlete. Mentally, when I stepped on any field or court, I was always filled with self-doubt. And that negative energy held me back for years. My effort level was never maximized because I felt like I couldn't succeed while I was playing. I was always tense and nervous, trying too hard. I was very critical of every mistake that I made. I was uncoachable and destined to fail.

My mind was never "into" games when I played sports, and I let my anxiety shape me. Again, it comes back to love. I didn't love myself nor believe in myself. So how could I expect others to believe in me when I couldn't do the same?

The easiest approach for my coaches and teammates was to agree with me: that I was terrible at sports. And that negative energy was simply an extension of the vibes I created. Even if there were other people who tried to boost my energy, no amount of external inspiration would have mattered since I did not have the confidence within myself.

I used to blame others for my sports shortcomings. It is the easy route to blame everyone else. It is much harder to look within. Once I realized that the issue was not the other people but rather my own mind, I started to see the world in a different light.

I can tell you with absolute certainty that I lived over thirty years of my life in "game mode." Think of game mode as the scenario when a professional athlete steps onto a playing surface. They are required to be dialed into their activity the entire time at full mental and physical exertion and focus. This was the level I attempted to live on at all times. That was a heck of a lot of pressure which hurt me on all levels. While a person can live in game mode for parts of their life, attempting to keep it going nonstop leads to inevitable burnout. And while I may have succeeded in many facets, I was losing in others, which led to constant feelings of unhappiness. Every day and all day, I masked the despair with constant tasks and roles to fill the void.

Yet, as long as I was working *for* my mind, my mind would not work for me.

Depression hit me like a ton of bricks. I remember sitting at the doctor's office one afternoon. I was there for a physical checkup, yet there I was, all of a sudden, crying uncontrollably. I couldn't stop for an hour. Nothing was working for me. I took on so much pressure and roles and I couldn't deal with it. I felt like I was making everyone else around me unhappy and that I was a failure. I didn't know what to do.

Now, looking back, under the same constraints I placed on myself, I would instead thrive. I now have the systems available to me to cope with the pressures that I faced years ago. I would now tackle these challenges head-on and be excited for the opportunity to grow. But I could not do that back then. I didn't have the tools to succeed.

Life is what it's going to be. It's how you look at it that will create your reality. And my reality at that time was that all was crashing down and there was no way out. So I took the quick fix; the only way I could find to cope. Without the lifestyle choices as a foundation for the strongest possible me, I went on antidepressants.

Back in those days, even now to some extent, I still feel that my admittance of being on meds to control mental mood would be seen as failure or weakness. I knew in my heart that I needed to take them, but I didn't want anyone else to know. It took me three different medications to figure out the ones that worked for me. From there, I was on them for a year. I would take one tablet every night before bed, which made me very sleepy. And within a month or so, I saw a huge shift.

I didn't feel so much pressure anymore. I was learning to be happy. The doctor weaned me off the meds at the nine-month mark, and I was off them completely at one year. Were they a placebo to some extent? Or did they "fix" me? What I can tell you is that they helped me overcome a rough mental patch. That was almost thirty years ago. And every day, week, month, and year since, I can see the red flags miles ahead of me when I start to feel the depressive feelings. For now, I rely on the 6 Chosen Commandments to get me through these tough moments. I use my mind as the medication and my mind now works for me.

Anxiety, on the other hand, is a lifelong battle for me that may never go away entirely. I accept that it is there, and we work together as opposed to against one another. I have been given anxiety pills in the past from my doctor, to be used on an as-needed basis. I am one of the lucky ones that has not experienced anxiety on a daily basis. Some people have it each and every day. Some people have it twenty-four hours a day, to the point that they cannot leave home or they cannot work. Some cannot even function. My anxiety essentially comes up in the mornings, when I first wake up, for the most part. I know that it is there. I acknowledge it and say hello, and we make a plan together on how to tackle each day that comes.

In my experience, staying hydrated helps battle much of the anxiety. Having a nourishing breakfast, getting sound sleep the night before, as well as exercising in the morning before work also helps. Four simple tools. Four Chosen Commandments to follow—and I can combat a medical condition that can cripple me if left untreated. Yet, it is not treated with pills; it is treated with discipline, a system, and lifestyle. As you become familiar with the 6 Chosen Commandments in the upcoming chapters, you will have the opportunity to create a new lifestyle for yourself that will include a strong mindset for success.

If left untreated, anxiety can wreak havoc on a person. The worry of what can and can't get done; the mind diverts valuable energy and resources from planning and achieving, and gives that energy to doubting and worrying. Your mind starts to tell you what to do, how to think, and what can be done. Think of AI, yet the artificial intelligence that has been programmed is now taking over and in control, and it is your own natural mind. However, your mind is no different than a computer. You program it as you feel. And the better the programming, the fewer crashes and errors you will experience.

Yet somewhere along the way, many stop working on their minds. They neglect their thoughts and inner workings. That neglect has caused the mind to take over. In that position, you work *for* your mind. I see those people walking or driving down the road, almost like mindless zombies. They are really lost in their thoughts.

It's time to take control of your mind and your thoughts. Once that happens, you will be in a better position to control your own destiny.

The failure of your mind to grow and develop is nobody else's fault. It is on you. Playing the blame game is a tiring and pointless exercise. Whether we are at home, at work, with friends—when something goes wrong, we look for a scapegoat. Unfortunately, we very often seek to hold others accountable for their transgressions but fail to look within ourselves to that same standard. I made the conscious choice later in life that I would always look within to understand myself and what was happening. I now always ask myself one question when something occurs that I need to assess: *What part did I play in this?* I highly suggest you start utilizing this question in your world. Before you look to place blame or seek revenge from others, look within yourself. Ask yourself what you did or did not do in order to make something happen. It will take reprogramming.

To help yourself grow, first you need to understand how you are constructed and function. The mind plays a big part of who you are. In your current programming, there are two key mental blocks that are holding you back:

1. **BLAMING OTHERS.** Failing to take accountability for ourselves and our actions.
2. **NEGATIVE SELF-WORTH.** Refraining from being our best through poor self-images.

They say that insanity is doing the same thing over and over and expecting different results. Consider, then, your life and mental patterns. Do you blame others for things that go wrong? Or do you stand at the front of the line and take accountability for your actions?

From there, do you have a negative self-image? Are you, in fact, the one holding *yourself* back from pushing ahead? Ponder these questions every time an event comes up in your life that needs assessment. It may not be external factors bringing you down. It could be you!

When I feel depressed, it is because I blame *myself* for what I see as failures. I feel the need to punish myself. I feel the urge to keep myself in a state of self-blame and low self-worth. I fail the first rule of love: I don't give myself unconditional love. Medications may help subdue the pain and help me cope, but they will never fix me. Only I can fix myself, through how I look at myself and my life through my mind.

I make the choice to live in the present and look forward to the future, and I choose not to punish myself for the past. I learn from errors and I move on. I do not live in the past. I choose to not let my past define me. I define myself. I live in the present moment. I am accountable for my actions. I appreciate and savor my high self-worth.

Armed with my strong mind, depression is no longer an option. It went away, not to come back.

Anxiety, on the other hand, is a state that still creeps up on me almost daily. But anxiety can be utilized as a tool to shape us for success, rather than hold us back. It is all in our minds and how we deal with anxiety when it appears. If you think of anxiety at its core, it is the fear of the unknown. When you blame others for when things go wrong, you are putting yourself at the mercy of others to shape your present and future. Since you live a life where you do not take accountability for yourself, then you are at the mercy of the actions of others.

When we stop blaming others, we do not let others control us. No matter what other people do, we can control how we see the world—as our own actions dictate our lives. It is the most liberating feeling when you are the captain of your own ship. But to be accountable to yourself goes together with you having a high visualization of your self-worth. When you believe in yourself, your future worries will lessen. You *decide your course* in your mind.

When a situation comes up that seems scary on the surface, I tell myself that it is an opportunity for growth. I take my anxiety that would have crippled me years ago and use it for energy to motivate myself to accomplish more. Whatever the outcome may be, as long as I know in my heart that I did all I could and held myself accountable, I am happy. Win or lose, I am proud of myself for having the strongest mindset possible.

It takes a lot of time and practice to shift your energy from external validation to an internal focus. It is possible that this is not how you have been living up until now. But past mindsets do not define you. You can change at any point in your life. When you make the commitment to being the strongest person mentally that you can be, you have started a new journey for yourself. But you have to realize that this may not be how you have lived your life up until this time—and major changes are to come.

There are so many tools you can employ for mental strength. An excellent starting point is outside assistance. Professionals, such as therapists, psychologists, psychiatrists, etc., are out there. Speak to your family doctor. Ask for a referral. Attend sessions. See if there is a fit. Do not give up too quickly again. This may not be something that you are likely used to, so it may be challenging for you. Do not give up.

Ultimately, I am not an advocate for medications for stimulation. There may be a time and place when you need them, and that is a decision you need to make with your doctor if it is right for you. If it is, may it be a temporary bandage. The work will rest mainly on the training you do for your own brain.

In addition to external coaching, yoga and meditation were my keys to mental fortitude. Chosen Commandments #5 and #6, as you will discover in this book, are foundational building blocks for much of your life, especially mentally. Quizzing people who have tried and quit yoga, is it because they could not handle the physical demands of the practice? Nope. It is the mental side of yoga. People say they were bored and could not lie still at the start or end of the class, or they complain about the heat in the room. The same thing goes for meditation. Dropout reasons revolve around boredom and the inability to focus, or other fears. If you tried it and couldn't do it, doesn't that mean you need to practice more? Just practice. Keep practicing, and stick with it. It will get better, and your mind will thank you.

I wish that more children could be exposed to yoga and meditation at far younger ages. These practices are heaven as they help shape the mind through a foundation of life with self-love. But unfortunately for most, our minds are not programmed in this manner. How we see ourselves and life often originates from our upbringing. Family, friends, teachers, and all the external people around us begin to shape us—especially our minds. We are accustomed to having to meet the expectations that we feel others have for us, and we seek approval and love externally. By receiving negative energy toward us, we can reciprocate this energy and the cycle continues. We instead live a life of stress and pressure. This is a cycle that can easily be broken if we take away those pressures and live our lives seeking only the fulfillment from ourselves within. Wouldn't that be way more fun?

There was a famous news conference once upon a time with basketball star Allen Iverson of the NBA Philadelphia 76ers. Allen made a decision to skip a practice. And then he was in front of the media. That famed press conference would, in many ways, over-shadow much of the greatness he achieved on the court. For as long as he was on this Earth, he would be remembered for his fateful words on that day: "What are we talking about? Practice. Practice. Not a game. Not a game. Practice." This is one of my favorite rants of all time. Allen said the word "practice" twenty-two times in his speech. While he was vilified at the time and became the butt of many jokes (heck, I can't hear the word "practice" without thinking of him), I believe Allen was right. I believe he was so right that in many ways he was a Zen master ahead of his time. Think about it. You can watch the interview. Allen is calm. He is mindful and living in the moment. He has perspective. "It's not about a game. What were they talking about? Practice."

Let's take Allen Iverson's thoughts now into practical terms from that perspective. Think of your daily life and all you do. Consider how much pressure you are possibly putting on yourself each day, and the expectations you may have built up for yourself. You may feel that you live each and every moment depending on the very next action you take. Every decision can feel like you are taking the final shot in game seven with the whole season on the line. You hit the shot—you are the hero. You miss—you are the culprit. Is that truly how you want to live? I sure don't. And I don't believe Allen Iverson did, either, as he described "practice" that day.

Now imagine a life where everything you do is only practice. Not a game—but practice. If you miss practice, then you can attend another practice. If your session did not go well that day, you get another kick at the can tomorrow. It's only a practice. Nothing is on the line. You are simply practicing to get better, day by day. Feel better? I sure do.

This newfound mentality can shift into every aspect of your life. Let's start with personal relationships. Imagine you have a discussion with a loved one that perhaps got heated and escalated into a fight. Do not carry that fight into the next day and beyond. That was simply one discussion. A practice. That discussion was not a game. You were practicing how to speak with the other person and that particular episode did not go well. You will do better tomorrow. When speaking with them the next day, be open. Let them know the discussion did not go well for you the other day, and you want to try again with a new conversation. You want to keep practicing until you get it right. There is no pressure, as the relationship is not going to be defined by one conversation. By taking away the pressure of a previous fight and starting a conversation on a fresh slate, I would bet your relationship will grow and thrive as a result. It is not a game with the winning shot on the line. It is just practice.

Now let's carry our new mental edge into work. We are accountable for ourselves. Our work functions are not dictated by the actions of others. We have a strong sense of self-worth. And finally, we do not feel pressure. Our jobs are not based on one assignment. We will do our best—and it is a practice. If a given work assignment goes well, we will rejoice. If another work assignment perhaps does not succeed, we will learn from it, grow, and do better next time. But we will not punish ourselves and carry negative energy into our work going forward. Whatever the outcome will be, as long as we know that we did our best and had high self-worth, we will grow and be better always.

When I function well, I often think of Allen Iverson, the Hall of Fame basketball player who played for fourteen years in the NBA. He had unlimited talent provided to him by the universe. He was also the hardest-working player I have ever seen, honing his craft and becoming one of the greatest shooters in basketball history. He was not perfect, as he missed many shots in his career. For all of his accomplishments, he never won a championship. For all of his greatness, he will be most remembered for his speech about practice.

While at the time he was seen by many as lazy and unmotivated for missing practice, his words became a mantra for life perspectives and focus. When something doesn't go right in my life, I tell myself often, "It's okay. It's not a game. It's practice. Just practice. You will get another chance and do better next time."

I wish that I had listened to Allen Iverson earlier in my life. But unfortunately, I did not have the tools for a strong mindset in the past. I knew how to work hard, but hard work on its own was never going to suffice if I was going to break through to the next levels. I could work as hard as I could, up to the point of exhaustion. But if I did not start my function with a strong mental focus and outlook, in many ways I was defeated before I even began. Combining hard work and a strong mental focus would lead me to great things, but it took a lifetime to learn how my mind works and to make it work for me instead of against me.

Imagine every physical activity you have ever done. Wouldn't you have succeeded much better if you were mentally strong while performing them? What about your job? Relationships? Would you have built better connections and achieved more through mental toughness?

What if you had the ability to handle feedback from your boss better? To understand and hear your partner, or every person you interact with?

Every task you attempt to complete and accomplish—every component of your life—becomes better through a mind that works for you. When you combine the body and mind performing at their peaks, you are almost unstoppable.

Yet, there is one final component that is missing: the hidden intangible that separates most winners and losers in life. The component that all world leaders, heads of businesses and industries, and award-winning athletes share—and that is called soul.

FOUR

The Soul

"If it doesn't challenge you, it doesn't change you."
—FRED DeVITO

=ᴑᴑᴑ=

The quote above came from the main yoga studio I have attended throughout my life, in the men's changeroom on the wall near the showers. I would stop and read it almost on a daily basis. Again, yoga left such an imprint on my life; it is not a coincidence by any stretch of the imagination. My awakening and transformation can all be traced to yoga.

Think about it. How many items come up in life that challenge us? Instead, what is our natural reaction? To give up and quit. To say that it is too hard and not for us. We can make a million excuses. And we pick the excuse that suits us best to justify our lack of focus, activity, and commitment. We do this often as humans. It's in our DNA. It is challenging for us. We are satisfied with how we are, so there is no need to change ourselves.

On the other hand, you have made the commitment that you want to change. You want to grow and evolve. So how do you do that? Well, you guessed it: through challenging yourself. By going outside of your comfort zone. Yes, I know that sucks. And yes, you will possibly suffer physically and mentally to get there. But if you stick with it, I promise you this: you will reach levels that you never thought were possible. Thank you for putting this out there, Fred DeVito. You have made an impact in our lives.

I first truly connected with my soul at a Buddhist temple. Before becoming a JewBu, I was living—but without faith. It's not that I didn't believe in G-d or a higher power; rather, I was more drifting in my own world. I didn't believe in myself and I was living a life without true purpose or meaning. I lacked soul. I lacked spirituality. I was not truly living.

It is important at this stage to emphasize that I have a deep respect and love for Judaism. I was born in Toronto, Ontario, Canada, in the Jewish faith to Israeli parents. My first language is Hebrew, in fact. I went to a Jewish school from grades one to eight. But in my younger years, while I took in the teachings of Judaism, I never felt fully connected. At a young age, religion and faith felt more forced upon me as opposed to me wanting to learn them. Especially for younger people, we often do not want to do what we are forced to do. We want to follow our own ideas! To be authentic to myself, religion felt to be an obligation and a burden. As I reached my late teen years, I did all I could to rebel against religion of any kind. What I was doing was closing off my soul. Little did I know that my spirituality would awaken in later years.

I was always fascinated with Buddha from a young age, although I had a curiosity about other cultures and religions too. However, it wasn't until I adopted yoga and meditation into my life that Buddha started to integrate. I noticed the Buddha statues throughout various yoga studios and the talk of mindfulness, deep breathing, and living in the moment. All of this fed my curiosity for more. I had a deep craving to explore myself. My yearning and drive to live the life I wanted resulted in me attending a Buddhist temple and seeing what it was all about.

The first time I entered a Buddhist temple, I took down information and purchased a book. I met the people working at the temple and found out the hours of operation. Over the next few months, I was attending temple sessions weekly. Sometimes I attended two times a week, as my schedule allowed it. I attended classes to learn of the Buddha's teachings. I attended meditation sessions. Sometimes there were combined classes and meditation. I enjoyed them all.

Every time I attended these temple ceremonies and classes, I felt like I was feeding my soul. Physically, I was learning to sit and meditate. Mentally, I was learning and growing my knowledge. But most of all, I was finding purpose in my existence. I felt inspired every time I went to the Buddhist temple. I longed to be a better person, to help others, and to help myself unlock my potential and get past my own limitations. I was beginning to embody Buddha. My soul was awakening for the first time in my life.

I could feel Buddha sitting beside me, watching me, and speaking with me. The more I felt Buddha's presence, I began to process the calmness and happiness of Buddha within me. It's almost like time started to stand still when I was at the Buddhist temple. Each time I was there, I wasn't worrying about the past and the future. The more I practiced meditation as a Buddhist, it was as if Buddha's energy was within me. My mind and soul began to open in many directions, and I felt freer and more alive than I had ever felt before.

I had manifested the Buddhist temple for much of my life. It was a vision within my mind from an early age, where I could see myself attending and meditating with Buddhists. I often told myself that I would go to a Buddhist temple when the timing felt right and I was feeling ready. When we delve later into Chapter 16 of this book, I will review the fine art of manifestation overall. As far as my manifestation of Buddhism, I can make two arguments. One is that I subconsciously manifested Buddha into my life as a child from looking at Buddha statues at home in my youth. My other consideration is the conscious manifestation of Buddhism through my yoga practice and meditation in my mid-thirties. Without both of these life events, I don't believe I would have ever come to attend a Buddhist temple in my life. That is one of the beautiful components of manifestation: various seeds can be planted within you over time. You never know for certain which seed ends up blooming within your soul and mind, but they will come to be—as long as you plant enough seeds and give yourself the time needed to blossom.

The more I attended the Buddhist temple, the more often I was reading and studying about Judaism! I started to also attend a Jewish synagogue again. I felt reborn in my early forties, as my soul awakened through finding my path of learning. Studying the spirituality of Buddhism helped me understand Jewish readings in a new light. I felt a powerful combination of religion and spirituality within me. I was better understanding myself through my connection and relationship with both G-d and Buddha. They both became my teachers by inspiring me.

I soon became connected with my inner self, as well as my thoughts and feelings. From there, once I knew and understood myself better, I could then connect strongly with the people around me. I began making new friends and relationships. I was bonding with people because I was rooted within myself.

We are often born into our given identities. For me, it was the label of being Jewish. Raised in the religious and cultural faith of Judaism, that is how I identified myself throughout my life. When I began studying and immersing myself in the spiritual life of Buddhism, I did not feel that I was being unfaithful to my religion, culture, or upbringing. On one hand, I began to see myself religiously and culturally as Jewish. But in spirituality, I am a Buddhist. Thus, rather than having to pick one over the other, I embraced that I am both. A JewBu was born.

Better yet, a JewBu became alive and was being acknowledged as such. By labeling myself as a JewBu, I feel at home. I am expressing to the world how I truly identify myself, as I am free. The reaction has been overwhelmingly positive. People are curious as to what a JewBu is and how I found my path. I interact with people through being authentic and true to who I am and what I believe. People are generally curious to learn more, and I am open to share my thoughts with them. By knowing myself and understanding myself on an authentic level internally, I am now able to relate with others like I never had before in part because of my JewBu path.

My hope is that by reading and learning about my journey, that you will find your own spiritual path.

So many people are programmed from birth to follow a particular religion that any deviation is seen as improper. I don't understand that. Why can't people be free to learn and experience other thought processes? Even if they will not adopt them, then why not, at least, learn and be aware of other ways of living in our world? Opening our minds to different religions and spiritualities should not be considered taboo. It should be encouraged! Do not be afraid to break out of the norms and cycles that you have known your whole life. You are allowed to find your own path—or solidify the existing path that you are on. *Your life* is not meant to be lived for others. *You need to live for yourself always* as a starting point. It is vital for your well-being that you give your best self to others. To do that, you need to know who you are and love yourself.

I was a relatively shy child growing up, with only a few close friends. I did not talk very much, but I spent my time listening and learning from those around me. I am fortunate to have my core group of friends from grade school but did not make many friends as a teenager and young adult. It was not until later in life that I started to bond with people on a deeper level than I ever had before. It was because my heart was opening, and I was able to really connect with others in ways I did not imagine possible.

By closing off my heart at a young age, I did not have a relationship with myself. By failing to identify with myself and who I was, I was unable to reach other people. It is a scary feeling to live life with a closed heart. It feels like one is living on autopilot, without feeling and purpose. You are going through the motions, but everything feels fairly meaningless. That is how I lived most of my life until I discovered my path. From the moment I found my JewBu identity, I began nurturing the best relationship with myself that I have ever had. I found love for myself, the key step in love from Chapter 1.

Just because you attend religion or religious ceremonies, does not mean you are spiritually connected. The spiritual foundation of understanding myself as a JewBu allowed me to give love unconditionally to others and accept love back. I learned to open my soul and unlock the love for myself that I never thought existed. I cultivated more friends than I've ever had in my life, with deep, meaningful relationships that truly grew my soul.

A great example of a friend I formed a lasting connection with is Steve Karsay. Steve is now one of my best friends on the planet.

We had originally met when I was a baseball blogger over a decade ago. After a telephone and email interview for my blog, we planned to start writing a book together. Heck, we even started to write it! But alas, my life was going in a different direction at that point. I could not continue with the book at that time, as I decided to put writing aside and practice yoga. Steve understood completely and gave me his blessing. While we kept in touch in the beginning, we lost touch over time. Steve was entering a new stage in his own world, having entered coaching after retiring from playing the game of baseball. And I was on a yoga journey, discovering who I was.

Over a decade later, Steve and I reconnected. As luck would have it, I was going to interview him again, this time on my recently formed podcast, the "Chosen Life." Steve agreed and we taped shortly after. Even though we'd spoken on the phone countless times before, we had never actually met face to face—in person or virtually. That interview was our first visual encounter—and it was a recording of two friends who had seemingly known one another their whole lives. It was an incredible experience and that one recording led to a major shift in my life.

Here is a little excerpt from this taping:

> *Jonathan: The funny, ironic part is that we've known each other for a lot of years, yet this is the first time we're actually meeting.*
>
> *Steve: Face to face, yeah, absolutely. You know, we've been talking for a long time. The one interview you did with me a few years back when I got into coaching and we just kept in touch and just have a good rapport with each other. You know we talked a little bit about doing a book together and you know a lot of things so it's really good to see you. It's really good to meet you for the first time face to face.*

As Steve and I were talking and planning for our podcast taping, it hit me: We did not write our book together more than a decade ago for a reason. The universe wanted us to wait and produce our conversations in a different format. I thought to myself how much of a shame it would have been if our conversations had not been recorded; for people not to see, and especially hear, Steve Karsay's experiences as a major league player and coach in his own words, or with his expressions. It was on that note that as soon as the realization hit me, I wrote a lengthy proposition to Steve, for us to create a docuseries, whereby we would record Steve's life story in podcast format. After taking his time to consider my idea, Steve agreed and fully jumped in.

I wanted to title the docuseries, "Steve Karsay: A Baseball Story." But Steve wanted to call it "The Chosen Journey." And thus, "The Chosen Journey" was born. In Steve Karsay's mind, the docuseries was about his life and journey, but on the same token, it was about the life of others—the paths they took and the decisions they made. For the listeners, the premise was to hear about Steve's life, inside and outside of baseball, along with my story as the co-host, as well as the journey of our guests who would come on occasionally. From there, the listeners could think about their own chosen journeys and be inspired to make their best decisions and to live their best lives.

That is the kind of person Steve Karsay is—to take a program that should be devoted to telling his story and instead, create a platform to inspire others. It is no wonder that the universe brought us together. Only by learning to truly open my soul and heart was I able to build a lifelong connection with Steve as an amazing friend and brother. It is through our daily talks that I become an even better version of myself. Steve has taught me many lessons over time, but first and foremost, what it means to have heart.

There is one clip of our talks that always sticks out in my mind. It went viral with over 500K views on social media. Steve explained why he ultimately chose to leave coaching baseball. He picked being a father to his son as the top priority in his life. As a single father myself, Steve's words really hit home and when he was done, I had tears in my eyes:

Steve: I was taking him [my son] to school one morning and he's sitting in the back of the car and I'm driving. And without hesitation, within this conversation that we're having, he goes, "Dad, after December, you're not going to be able to come with me or do much with me because you got to start spring training up again, don't you?" And I was like, "Well, with the lockouts going on," and I explained the lockout to him, and I said, "you know spring training will be spring training." And he goes, "I'm really going to miss you this summer."

And at that point, things just pulled on me and I didn't say anything to him. I dropped him off at school and came home. I had a conversation with his mom and I'm like, "Our son's really missing me. Like I have a feeling that he understands now at the age of eleven what it means to have me at home and what it means to have me away."

Steve left a powerful impact on me that day and I vowed to make my loved ones an even deeper priority after hearing this story. Steve is an amazing human being and I consider myself very fortunate to call him my friend.

Steve Karsay knows what it's like to have a demanding job and role. He was a major league baseball pitcher for eleven seasons. He is one of few people to ever step on a major league diamond and play in the show. You have a better chance of getting struck by lightning or winning the lottery than playing even one MLB game. Steve played in 357 of them. From there, he continued in the game as a coach, both as a pitching coach in the minor leagues in the Cleveland system, and then three years as a bullpen coach with the Brewers. Steve has closed games wearing pinstripes in Yankee Stadium. So, when Steve Karsay tells me what makes a winner, I listen.

In Steve's estimation, there is one intangible you look for from a great baseball player that is rare to be found: heart. Together with heart comes hard work, passion, and a love of the game. Will this player put it all on the line to win the game? Will they play hurt? Will they put their team first? How much do they love the game of baseball to succeed? This is how Steve measured himself when he was pitching, and when he assessed the teammates who he would go to battle with in order to win. It is the same insight he used working with the young players that he had to assess as a coach; those who had soul could reach the highest possible levels. Soul is the most difficult attribute to measure, yet the one most needed, according to Steve, to be a champion.

I remember one day when I went to complete a bench press set with my trainer, Jared Heft. We had done this hundreds of times already. My body was in a fantastical physical shape. My mind felt good. Yet, I faltered on the bench. I asked Jared, "What happened?" He said it was very simple: I didn't respect the bench. I didn't respect the process. I was not putting my heart into it. Without investing my full soul into what I was doing, I was limited in what I could achieve. My body and mind were ready. They needed my soul to complete the process. Once I respected the bench, I would hit my numbers and beyond.

By reading my story as to how I invigorated my soul, I now want you to reflect within yourself. It is your soul that I ask you to assess and connect with on YOUR level.

It is human nature to neglect the soul, or even to fail to recognize its existence. To understand and incorporate the upcoming 6 Chosen Commandments into your life, you will need to connect with yourself on a level you have likely never reached before. You need to find YOUR soul. Your energy. Your heart. And once you do, you will then be ready to put in the work to transform yourself to being *the best you* possible.

I have a little bit of homework for you as we end this chapter. It is fun, though! I am going to ask you some questions. Think about them. Answer them at your own pace. And once you complete this book, feel free to revisit them again and see how your answers shifted.

THE SOUL QUIZ:

1. What are important things in my life?
2. What drives me to work hard and succeed?
3. What is my identity? How do I see myself?
4. Who are the people closest to me? How and why do I connect with them?
5. Do I have passion in my life?

If you are struggling to answer some or all of these questions, then it is time to take a deep assessment of your life. I can tell you that the younger version of me would have received a failing grade. I was working hard, but I would not have been able to tell you why. I didn't really have people who were close to me, or passion in my life. It is okay to admit this; in fact, coming to terms with what is real for you is liberating. You have done nothing wrong by answering the Soul Quiz truthfully. What is revealed to you should open your eyes to how you are built. Without being connected with your soul, you will be unable to live a life with love, the key foundation of your existence.

The most amount of work ahead for you is to repair and build your soul—to discover who you are and what will make you tick. Only then can you reach the highest levels you never thought were possible.

Some of the gateways to the soul include meditation and yoga: Chosen Commandments #5 and #6. To reach these foundational elements, you will need to get your body and mind aligned through Chosen Commandments #1 through #4. There is a pattern and systems in place outlined for you. Do not worry. We will be taking baby steps to get you there. And you WILL get there. I am here for you.

Once you accept that you have a soul and need to connect with it, you will already be halfway there. You cannot work on what you do not believe exists. Thus, knowing your soul and working to connect with it is the name of this game.

My yoga and meditation practices brought me to the identity of being a JewBu. I feel at home with this connection. I also wish for you to feel at home with your connection. Whether you want or need to find a religious and/or spiritual path, it is time to discover your unique composition. What do you believe? What do you identify with? What drives you? What ignites passion within you?

To connect with your soul, you will be spending a lot of time alone with your thoughts. Don't be scared. This is *you* we are talking about—the person you must love the most in the entire world!

I encourage you to read lots. I spend much of my free time reading many different texts. Not just Jewish and Buddhist books, but a multitude of books on all sorts of subjects. Somewhere along the line, by spending time with yourself and acknowledging your thoughts, by reading and opening your mind, my hope for you is that you start to discover your inner self, whomever that may be. Learn to love and embrace it all. Every part of you is important. I discovered my inner JewBu and my world exploded for the best. Now, let's find who you are and shape your journey to the highest levels beyond what you ever thought was possible.

Later, I will also be sharing with you how I explored my Jewish roots and developed a Buddhist lifestyle and mindset. It was on that road that I became a JewBu. Until I realized that I was a JewBu, I never fully understood or could appreciate who I was. I never fit perfectly into any particular religious or spiritual label. So I stopped looking and focused my life on incorporating and fulfilling all 6 Chosen Commandments into my lifestyle. I needed to look inward and discover myself—and once I did, I felt at peace with who I was and the road to learning who I would be as I continued to evolve.

My wish for you is that when you read of my JewBu journey, that this will inspire you to find your motivational source, which can include your religious/spiritual path and what that means to you. May you feel that there are no right or wrong answers in this regard. May your body and mind be at such a strong equilibrium level, that they combine with your soul and create a balanced you.

Your days of neglecting any part of your existence are now over. It is time to put in the work and create the lifestyle that will balance you most. *Your Chosen Life.*

We have started our journey through *The Bible 3.0* by establishing the building blocks. We understand that love is the beginning and end of life. Without love, one cannot have a true existence. From there, we come to understand as humans how we are constructed. The body, mind, and soul are the three parts that shape who we are. Each work together and must be trained and appreciated.

You are now ready to discover your lifestyle and build your systems. I hereby present to you the greatest gift I can give: the 6 Commandments of the Chosen Life.

The 6 Chosen Commandments are the gift I gave to myself, which continue to help me discover the life I want to live. By learning to implement these principles into your lifestyle, you will explore your life purpose and the existence that you wish upon yourself. You will be unstoppable. You will be the best you that you have ever seen and experienced.

It's time to shift life into a new gear and see what we really *can* do and accomplish.

PART II:
THE 6 COMMANDMENTS OF THE CHOSEN LIFE

FIVE

The 6 Commandments
of the Chosen Life

⋙⊙⋘

I LOVE to eat. I'm sure you do, too. In understanding the foundation of love in your world, combined with how your body, mind, and soul operate and are connected, picture that you just finished the appetizers at your favorite restaurant. You came in hungry—in this case, for knowledge—and I provided you with delicious morsels to whet your appetite. Your belly and mind are happy, but they crave more.

With that being said, you are ready for the main course. You are ready to do the work—the meat and potatoes of our journey through *The Bible 3.0* and your path to an awesome life.

It is my honor and privilege to bring forth the keys to life which have been shared with me by the universe and all my education, experience, and life evolution. I call these keys to life the 6 Commandments of the Chosen Life (or the 6 Chosen Commandments, or Chosen Commandments, for short). You are envisioning the life you always wanted and dreamed of. Now get ready to build it and live it!

Chapter 1, "Love Is a Lifestyle," was designed to build your life foundation; to help you become aware of the importance of self-love and how loving yourself unconditionally is the building block for your existence. Love is a powerful tool for success, but as you learned, it should not originate from external sources. *All the love you will ever need will come from within yourself.* It is vital that you keep this in mind as we dig into the future work that you will be performing

53

in the 6 Chosen Commandments. All your work must be done with the thought of loving yourself and building your own lifestyle and systems that will produce the greatest version of you in the end. You will work hardest and most productively if you feel the love for yourself that you deserve.

Chapters 2–4 were building-block chapters to help you understand and assess how you are constructed. You have a body—the physical vessel that carries you through life. You have your mind that contains your thoughts. And your soul is your passion, motivation, heart, and drive. You cannot function to your full capacity if all three components of you are not aligned. Again, the intention was to establish that we are made up of three components and all must work together as part of our work to come. You may have tried to improve your body, mind, and/or soul individually during the course of your life, but I am here to tell you that this will not work. To achieve *the greatest you*, with your body, mind, and soul in sync, we must work on all three parts together. They feed off each other and work together to thrive. Recognize this and remember it. As you go through each of the 6 Chosen Commandments, remember two key points:

1. **Always practice the 6 Chosen Commandments with unconditional self-love.**
2. **Remember to always nourish your body, mind, and soul. They work together and feed off one another.**

The 6 Commandments of the Chosen Life are called "Commandments" for a reason, much like the way that G-d delivered the Ten Commandments to Moses to deliver to the people. I feel that way about the 6 Chosen Commandments. The universe delivered me the 6 Chosen Commandments through my life experiences and education, and *The Bible 3.0* is my gift back to the people—to you as the readers. The universe instilled the 6 Chosen Commandments within me, and I am now placed on the journey as a guide and facilitator to deliver the message of the 6 Chosen Commandments to you.

For me, as a JewBu, I live my lifestyle by practicing the 6 Chosen Commandments daily. In whatever religion, faith, and lifestyle you identify with, I know that the 6 Chosen Commandments will benefit you in creating your daily systems for success.

Sustainable long-term evolution will only occur for you if you are truly motivated to see the 6 Chosen Commandments on the road ahead and if you commit to following that path. The 6 Chosen Commandments are in place for a sole purpose: they are life systems that you will choose to incorporate within yourself if you wish to discover the best you possible. These are not religious obligations or requirements from anybody else put onto you. The 6 Chosen Commandments represent your roadmap to not just get by in life, but to get ahead and thrive.

The 6 Commandments of the Chosen Life that are the foundation of your lifestyle as part of *The Bible 3.0* are as follows:

Chosen Commandment #1: The Effective Sleep System
Chosen Commandment #2: Water Is Hydration for Life
Chosen Commandment #3: We Are the Nutrition We Eat
Chosen Commandment #4: Physical Activity
Chosen Commandment #5: Meditation
Chosen Commandment #6: Yoga

The 6 Chosen Commandments are placed in this order for a reason. I want to simplify your journey and make it as easy to access and maintain as possible.

I started my journey in a different order. I took the more complicated route by beginning with yoga, before following any of the other Chosen Commandments. You can feel free to begin in any order— and you may, in fact, already be practicing one or more of these 6 Chosen Commandments.

To keep things very simple, start reading each of them in order. Begin with the first four Chosen Commandments for an easier and more sustainable journey. And then slowly incorporate meditation and yoga into your lifestyle.

I spent a good three- to four-year period working on the 6 Chosen Commandments, getting the first four down as part of my lifestyle. So, for your first read-through of *The Bible 3.0*, as you review the 6 Chosen Commandments chapters in their given order, you can always mark and return to a particular chapter later as you see fit to relearn any and all systems.

I have given seminars on lifestyle in the past, which have emphasized how the 6 Chosen Commandments have revolutionized my life and inspired others how to recreate theirs. Usually I have shared these values with a group of professionals, including lawyers and realtors. I would give a survey asking my audience how many of the following six items they regularly incorporate into their lifestyle:

1. A regular sleep schedule of approximately seven hours, but as much sleep as needed to be able to wake up without an alarm clock.
2. Consume water regularly, a minimum of two liters per day (about half a gallon, or 12–15 cups per day). Coffee, tea, pop, juice, and alcohol do not count.
3. Nutrition: not a fad or a crash diet. Do they regularly eat clean, with purpose, and with regularly scheduled balanced meals each day?
4. Physical activity: Do they exercise regularly? At least three times per week?
5. Meditation: Have they ever meditated during the course of their life?
6. Yoga: Have they ever tried yoga and incorporated yoga into their routine in addition to any other physical activity?

I would poll my audience to see how many of the 6 Chosen Commandments they were already incorporating in their existing routines before attending the seminar. I found it shocking and saddening to see the number of people in the audience that were incorporating zero to two Chosen Commandments into their lives out of the six. Rare was it to see anyone reach four or above. Much of my audience at seminars relayed that they felt overwhelmed without a workable routine and the solution was simply to give up, rather than figure out how to improve their current lifestyle.

I have a better solution for you, so that you do not lose your way in developing your routine. It is not about a quick fix and crash diets, boot camps, or other extreme measures. It is about building sustainable systems for yourself. They will not change your habits tomorrow or next week, but by utilizing them over time consistently, your lifestyle will evolve and grow.

The 6 Chosen Commandments are for everyone wanting a better life, including you. They are not newfound secrets that are being uncovered for the first time. These are all areas that have been with us for years. We know that they are there. But we simply refuse time and time again to incorporate them into our lifestyle.

When people approach me for tips on lifestyle changes, one of the first comments that I receive is that they are "not like me." They also state that the 6 Chosen Commandments don't come easy to them like they did for me. For some reason, many people assume that I understand the 6 Chosen Commandments because I have lived them my whole life. WRONG! Guess again. I was probably the worst offender that I knew of when it came to the 6 Chosen Commandments. Up until my thirtieth birthday, this is how I stacked up as being 0/6 on the list:

1. **SLEEP:** Irregular sleep patterns. I averaged maybe five hours per night.
2. **WATER:** I drank NONE. I mostly drank fruit juice and pop.
3. **NUTRITION:** My lunch in high school was regularly hot-dogs on a stick, a pastry or two, and a slushie from a corner store. Enough said.
4. **PHYSICAL ACTIVITY:** I was one extreme or another. I either worked out daily or not at all. I would say that most of my physical activity came between fourteen to nineteen years of age with a huge drop-off after.

5. **MEDITATION:** Did not exist.
6. **YOGA:** No chance.

So, reading my words, know that I walked in your shoes. In other words, I know what it is like to laugh and roll my eyes at the thought of incorporating any, let alone all of the 6 Chosen Commandments. I had my reasons as life caught up to me. For my own health, physically and mentally, I knew that I needed to evolve. You will have your own reasons.

Note that it is never too early to incorporate the 6 Chosen Commandments into your life. If you have children, you can get them started as soon as possible. Making wise and concrete choices for yourself is the only way to go.

I completely evolved my body, mind, and soul through the incorporation of the 6 Chosen Commandments. Most importantly, after I reached what I thought was my peak, I continued to rely on them to maintain myself and keep going for a balanced and happy lifestyle. Now I want to help you reach your new levels of glory.

It is very important that you remember that there is NO timeline when it comes to incorporating, refining and creating YOUR systems within the 6 Chosen Commandments. It is, after all, YOUR Chosen Life. You are the one who chooses how to best live it and create a foundation that works for you.

Remember: this is not a race, it is a practice. There is an evolution to the process. So please find the pace that you are comfortable with and insert gradual shifts that work for you and are sustainable over a long period of time. If you move too quickly, then you run the risk of crashing and burning. And that could happen one or more times. You may have to restart at ground zero. There is no shame in resetting your journey. Remember as a practice you can try and try again as many times as needed!

You have currently built up a system of routines and habits. Some are good and some need improvements. *That is okay.* You cannot erase a lifetime of negative routines and habits overnight. So please move slowly. Do not give up. You are not alone in this. We are all in the same boat as you. You are human. You are not perfect. You are not going to change who you are and your current systems all in one shot.

The results will not matter. All that will matter is that you are trying your best and that you are going to keep practicing over and over. Eventually, you will find the balance between the 6 Chosen Commandments that work best for you.

Some people may be able to get the 6 Chosen Commandments down fully within six months. Some may take one year or longer. Again, there is no rush or competition. Every incremental change you make today is better than what you were doing yesterday. Savor each victory. And know that you are building a solid foundation for your life.

Remember as well that there are so many variables when it comes to our construction as people. Gender, age, and medical conditions are three crucial factors that can affect so much of how we live and function. So a shift in what you do in your life may not work for others, based on what they need. In working with your doctor and other professionals, be truthful about any factors that are out of your control that may limit parts of the systems that you implement into your life. And if some parts of the 6 Chosen Commandments are more difficult than others for you to follow, then try to figure out the reasons behind the roadblocks. There are always options and modifications available to you if needed. Consider every possibility as to how you will make your shifts and systems. It is time to begin your life again! To be reborn. Giving up is NOT an option.

The Bible 3.0 is here to help you create a lifestyle. You are certainly welcome to create for yourself short-term and long-term goals, which we will discuss. But do not limit yourself to reading this book in the hopes of achieving one limited outcome. Focusing your concentration on a small-picture goal takes away the energy from the other aspects of your life. You are focusing on your *lifestyle*. There is no pressure when it comes to working on a lifestyle. Your Chosen Life is the biggest factor that you could shift your energy toward. When your lifestyle is in place, everything else will follow from there.

As a bonus, to help eliminate any barriers that you may have in your mind, I have provided in Chapters 6-11 the top ten excuses as to why you are not practicing each of the 6 Chosen Commandments. If you have ever made an excuse for *why* you are unable or unwilling to follow through with something, it is likely in those top ten lists. Not only have I listed the top ten excuses, but also the reasoning of why those excuses are simply that—excuses. They are not concrete reasonings based on logic, but rather misconceptions or limitations that you have created for yourself in your own mind. Remember we discussed the power of the mind in Chapter 3. Your mind can power you to greatness, or it can hold you back indefinitely. Only YOU can decide to follow the 6 Chosen Commandments. It is up to you to make that determination.

Let's first eliminate some words from your vocabulary if you are debating whether to start incorporating the 6 Chosen Commandments:

1. **MAYBE OR NO**
2. **CAN'T**
3. **WON'T**
4. **SHOULDN'T**
5. **COULDN'T**

Any word associated with negativity or hesitation tells your mind that this is not an option. Failure is not an option. You do not have to be perfect. This is not a competition. There is no pressure or stress. Any change you incorporate into your life today is better than what you were doing yesterday.

Instead, let's incorporate these words into your vocabulary:

1. **YES**
2. **CAN**
3. **WILL**
4. **SHOULD**
5. **COULD**

Do you see the shift in mindset we did?

For example: If I ask, "Are you thinking of drinking a glass of water?" it will not be beneficial to you to say, "Maybe I will." Instead, say, "Yes, I will."

Did you say that you can't practice yoga? Now say, "Yes, I can." A shift in mindset from negativity or passivity to positivism is powerful stuff and all you need to do is simply shift the direction where your mind is going.

Now imagine I came to you today and asked you to make six simple tweaks in your life. Baby steps. For the purpose of this exercise, we will assume that you are currently following zero of the 6 Chosen Commandments. Therefore, assuming you are starting at ground zero and from a fresh slate, the changes would look as follows for the upcoming Monday to Sunday:

1. **SLEEP:** Go to bed earlier thirty minutes every day. Try to get fifteen more minutes of sleep every night.
2. **WATER:** Drink one extra glass of water per day.
3. **NUTRITION:** Cut out one unhealthy food you eat per day and incorporate one additional piece of fruit and veggie into your meals daily.
4. **PHYSICAL ACTIVITY:** Commit to one fifteen-minute walk per day.
5. **MEDITATION:** Sit down and meditate for five minutes ONCE this week.
6. **YOGA:** Turn on a yoga class online and practice one class for fifteen minutes this week.

By following the above six tweaks from Monday to Sunday for seven consecutive days, we have now successfully incorporated all of the 6 Chosen Commandments into your life in just one week! Together they may seem like a lot, but in actuality, these were not drastic at all. You started with little incremental changes every day and built toward great results after just one week. This example represents a little taste of what you have to look forward to in the chapters ahead.

Slowly over time, you will learn about each of the 6 Chosen Commandments and find your routine that will fit your lifestyle. Perhaps you will choose to work all six of them together, or on each one separately. Remember, you are under no timeline or pressure to complete a "test." You are working toward achieving your Chosen Life and the lifestyle that will best work for you in order to achieve it.

At this time in our journey, you do not have to make immediate changes to your lifestyle. I have simply highlighted for you what lies ahead so that you can mentally prepare yourself. Once we dig deeper into each of the 6 Chosen Commandments, you will slowly over time make your choices as to how you wish to evolve these systems into your life routine. You will choose the speed you will take when you travel your life road. I am here to give you the map for when you are ready to begin your journey. Do not think of this as an upcoming race. It will feel like a scenic drive, as we view the key sights along the way, which are the components of your being.

Now that you are familiarized with our trajectory, it's time for you to learn to practice the 6 Commandments of the Chosen Life daily. The work begins now.

SIX

CHOSEN COMMANDMENT #1:
The Effective Sleep System

———◆◆◆———

When viewing the 6 Commandments of the Chosen Life as a list, ponder as you begin your journey which area of your life you are most neglecting. When I speak to people who approach me in the quest to make life changes, the one area that consistently comes up short is sleep. It's a fundamental part of life and our being, yet we seem to come up short in this area all too often.

I feel that many people have a love/hate relationship with sleep. It feels like sleep has to be one extreme or another. We either get too much sleep or too little. As we get older, I find that most people suffer from sleep deprivation. Choosing to forego sleep is a dangerous game, one that can alter your mood, health, and overall well-being.

Sleep is a no-doubt pillar of the Chosen Commandments. It is in the initial four of the 6 Chosen Commandments for a reason; there are no coincidences here. I will put it to you bluntly: if you want to have a happy life, I suggest you make quality sleep a priority. Not just sleep on the surface, but *quality sleep*. There is a difference.

I have seen people who sleep for five hours and look refreshed and energized. And people that sleep for ten hours and look tired and weak. On the surface, my first question is to look at whether each of these individuals had quality sleep. That is the dealbreaker.

As you will learn throughout this book, I personally developed benchmark systems through failure and reprogramming myself throughout my life. If you are not sleeping enough or enjoying solid nights of sleep, know that I have been there. I was one of you. For the first thirty-plus years of my life, I did not sleep very much. I did not set up a path each night for a good night's sleep. And I paid the price dearly. I suffered for years from health issues, anxiety, and depression. I won't begin to tell you that lack of sleep caused my ailments, but it certainly contributed to them. Through experimentation and research I realized over time that the less sleep I had (especially quality sleep), the more my body and mind were breaking down. Yet when I was obtaining more consistently daily sleep, my health issues lessened.

I knew I had to create systems for myself to fix my issues, and sleep was at the top of the list.

From my early teens until my early thirties, I was lucky to average approximately three to five hours of sleep per night. And it was not even a great night's sleep. It would take me forever to fall asleep and I suffered from restless sleep. Sound familiar? Until I envisioned the 6 Chosen Commandments and made sleep a priority, sleep was really an afterthought for me. Deep down I knew that I was not functioning at my best and that my lack of quality sleep was essentially killing me. So I slowly but surely invented my own systems that would fix my sleep.

People normally focus on the sleep portion, while they miss the benefits and need to have an effective *wake-up system*. To function at your best daily, you need both your sleep and wake-up routines to function equally well, together. We examine both in this chapter, not to worry. I have you covered.

Have you ever felt that you are making your life better by replacing sleep hours with more work? It can feel like you are better off by putting in more time at the office, but the contrary effect is happening. The damage that you are doing to your body, mind, and soul by ignoring sleep is substantial.

Imagine a life where you can fall asleep almost at will and wake up each morning refreshed before your alarm. Imagine being able to use sleep to rejuvenate yourself and get ahead.

As you will learn by putting together your life goals and systems, the 6 Chosen Commandments do not work in isolation. They work in unison and feed off one another. As you start to follow the other Chosen Commandments, your sleep will get better. Even without the system in place for sleep, by default you will improve your sleep by having the other Chosen Commandments in place.

- If you drink lots of water, you will be hydrated. You will sleep better.
- If you implement regular physical activity, your mind and body will benefit. You will sleep better.
- If you bring clean eating into your life, you will sleep better.
- If you practice meditation, your mind will be calmer. You will sleep better.
- If you practice yoga, your mind and body will benefit. You will sleep better.

Let's now examine your top ten excuses for not sleeping:

1. **I can't sleep very much.**
2. **I don't need a lot of sleep to function.**
3. **Falling asleep is too hard.**
4. **I wake up in the middle of the night a lot.**
5. **Sleep is for the dead. It is a waste of time.**
6. **There is no comfortable way to sleep.**
7. **I get nightmares all the time!**
8. **I'm too hungry/thirsty to sleep.**
9. **There is not enough time to sleep.**
10. **Health issues affect my sleep.**

There are many, many reasons why you may not be sleeping. Some may be valid; most are flat-out excuses. Sorry, *you* may believe them. I don't. If you are not sleeping much/enough/soundly, there are more than likely reasons behind your neglect. And make no mistake—you are neglecting yourself! If you enjoy prematurely aging, feeling "blah" and unhappy, as well as digging an early grave for yourself, please go ahead and continue not sleeping. Have I caught your attention? Great! That was my purpose.

I will give you the cold hard truth: Even if you are following the other Chosen Commandments (eating well, performing physical activities, drinking water, meditating, and practicing yoga), you are limiting yourself to ground zero if you do not get the proper quality sleep you need. *Remember: the Chosen Commandments work together in unison, not in isolation.* Picture sleep as the glue that holds your life together. Without that glue, everything will fall apart. Your body, mind, and soul do not stand a fighting chance of operating at their best without sleep. So let's get past the excuses and envision what our lives could look like with a proper night of sleep every night.

I love referring to LeBron James, the legendary basketball player. Part of his process is the use of a hyperbaric oxygen chamber. I don't expect you to seek out and purchase or rent the use of such a chamber, but consider for a moment why LeBron, and other athletes and celebrities, utilize these products, including float in water tanks. It is to heal and regenerate their bodies. Daily activities, life, aging—these factors are all hard on our bodies. We need *recovery* to avoid injuries and stay our freshest. Think of your bed as YOUR rejuvenation chamber. Every night you have the opportunity to heal your body and get it to the best condition it can be in. If you want an added bonus, you will also be caring for your mind and soul as well—a triple package of goodness for yourself—and all you simply have to do is sleep.

A lack of sleep will mean a tired body. A tired body leads to an exhausted mind. A body and mind without energy cannot fuel the soul. You will lack the capacity to be energized and inspired without adequate sleep. Why are you doing this to yourself? Please do not make excuses. Think of how important life is and how you are given the opportunity to live. Don't throw that away by prematurely aging yourself. Sleep is around for a reason, embrace it!

During my ongoing therapy sessions, even today, my doctor always asks me in the first five questions what my sleep average was since the last time we spoke. I was not oblivious to why he was asking the question, but I did not always make a conscious effort to improve it. I told myself all sorts of lies. "My personal life is too hectic. Work is too busy. Sleep isn't important." Whatever I needed as a crutch to justify my failure to look after myself, I took it. But I was only fooling myself in the process. To have the best life possible, I needed to be refreshed each and every day. This meant making a commitment to have the best quality sleep possible and creating the systems to make this happen.

To best maximize the quality and quantity of your sleep, there are many factors you need to look into. You need to be honest with yourself as to how you set up your sleep system. Your task will be to create for yourself a list of the sleep steps that you can commit to within your new sleep system and then fully implement them. As with every system, all the steps work in unison. Knock one out, and the others will drop or suffer.

I will now walk you through the setup of creating your Effective Sleep System. There are several parts, but do not get intimidated. Work through them slowly, step by step. You know all of this! You simply need the reminder and the list so you can effectively follow through. Creating a sleep system is a process, but one that you need to survive and thrive.

1. SLEEP HARDWARE

It is not very difficult to put the sleeping environment together. But make sure you are conscious of the choices that you make so that you can put yourself in the best position to have great sleep:

BED: Do you sleep alone or with a partner? What size works best for you—single, twin, queen, king? Separate beds? Separate rooms? Be honest with yourself and make sure that you are using the right size bed that fits you. Maybe there is a better room location for the bed? Also make sure where the bed is located in relation to the window or door. Adjusting the location of your bed can make all the difference in the world.

MATTRESS: From the size of the mattress, firmness, pillow top, foam or coils, adjustable... The list goes on and on. Make sure you have the best mattress that works for you.

PILLOWS, SHEETS, BLANKET/COMFORTER: Don't kid yourself; changing pillows could make a world of difference. Think of every option, such as how many pillows, and their size or firmness. From there, review the material for the sheets, comforter types, etc. Your options are endless, so don't be afraid to try different combinations until you find the right ones for you.

SHADES/WINDOW COVERINGS: Some of us need complete darkness in our bedrooms to sleep (most of us do). Note how much light comes into your room in the morning. Is that a good thing for you? Does light come through your door and/or window at night and is that distracting you? The darker your room, the better your sleep will likely be.

LIGHTING: Yes, we need to think of every detail, even the small ones. I like having easily accessible bedside lighting, including lamps if I choose to read and get ready for bed. It will make your room less bright, and your brain will know that sleep is coming. If your bedroom is lit like an arcade before bed, you are overstimulating your senses. Dimmable lighting is your sleep's friend. Some lamps can even be programmed to turn on gradually in the morning to help you awaken. Not necessary—but a plus. You may want to look into it.

ALARM CLOCK: I know your smartphone/tablet has an alarm clock feature. That's fine. But I recommend a physical alarm clock in the room for a number of reasons. Mainly, to keep you accountable to wake up and as a backup alarm. There is nothing worse than sleep-ing through an alarm, or worse—the alarm sound *not* coming on—when you need to get up. So for my own peace of mind, I like hav-ing two separate alarm clocks set: the one on my nightstand and my phone's alarm.

NIGHTSTAND: Not having a nightstand is minimal, I get that. But I still advocate for this piece of furniture. It is a place to store your lamp, alarm clock, and the charger for your smartphone/tablet. Boom. It's the command center for your sleeping aids. Try to find one that is not bulky, and fits well in the flow of your room and with your bed. There is no one type of solution for everyone—find a convenient nightstand that works for you.

BOOK/TABLET/E-READER/PHONE: As part of your nighttime ritual, you will need to decide what your falling asleep routine will be. Are you planning to read? If so, you may use a physical book, an e-reader, or a tablet/smartphone (please try to avoid the tablet/smartphone—too many distractions possible). The only time I advocate for the use of a tablet/smartphone at night is if you are using some form of a sleeping meditation guide. In that case, turn off all notifications and only play your meditation sounds/talking. When I was at my worst point of sleeping, I relied on meditation to help me build up my ability to sleep. Then I slowly weaned off the meditation guide and was able to fall asleep on my own. Books can be quite effective as well, but note that you should only have to read a few pages at a time before bed. If you are reading endless chapters, then reassess your bedtime routine.

SLEEPING MEDICATION: Some people need/want to use melatonin or some form of a sleep aid to help them fall asleep. Please make sure to speak to your doctor before using any form of medical-type sleep-ing aids. At best they should be temporary starting points, but ones you would stop using that allow you to become self-reliant. Try to avoid having your body depend on a pill or medicine to sleep when you can use meditation to train your brain instead.

PJS: You pick what works for you. Full layers, pants, shorts, tanks, undies, commando. Whatever works for you on a given night, make sure you are comfortable when you sleep and have a good body temperature.

2. BEDTIME ROUTINE—MAP IT OUT!

A friend of mine with a PhD in psychology really helped me out with this one. When I was having issues sleeping, he helped me create a list and a chart. In my case, we made the chart in great depth, noting my timing from the moment I went home until I went to bed. For all of the remaining items you see listed below, we mapped them out and gave them timelines. I created a "bed schedule." That way everything would get done, nothing would be missed, and I would feel relaxed and in control and create a solid pattern for sleep. Here is an example of a bedtime schedule:

6:00–7:00 p.m.:	Get home, make dinner, eat
7:00–8:30 p.m.:	Take dog for walk, practice yoga at home
8:30–9:00 p.m.:	Go over calendar and to-do list for next day
9:00–9:30 p.m.:	Pack up lunch for next day, lay out clothes for morning
9:30–10:00 p.m.:	Meditate for ten mins, shower, brush teeth
10:00–10:30 p.m.:	Put on PJs, set alarms, read, go to sleep

Feel free to use this above schedule or similar, or develop your own timeline. Every day may be different and schedules may need tweaking. You may not be able to follow your schedule perfectly. That's okay. Having an idea of a schedule leads to structure. Structure leads to routine. And routine is the system of which you will have the best chance to capitalize on great sleep, night after night.

3. BALANCE FOOD/WATER SCHEDULE

If you are eating huge meals before bed, please stop it. If you are drinking vast amounts of water before bed, please stop that, too. When you go to sleep, *all* parts of you need to go to sleep. This includes your mind and your body. If your body is using a great deal of energy to digest food, it will be hard for you to fall asleep and stay asleep. If you are drinking huge quantities of water before bed, you are likely going to have to relieve yourself during the night. So be realistic. Set yourself an eating schedule. Likely dinner and then a final night snack. Try to make the last meal before bed one that is light and easy to digest. Space out the timing so you have lots of digestion time before bed and keep your water consumption heavier earlier in the day, and lighter in the evening. Your body will thank you. The trick is also not to go to bed hungry or thirsty. Those late-night cravings turn into second dinners and cheat meals. Speak to a nutritionist/dietician and figure out what foods will fill you up before bed but also be easy to digest. Play around with it—this is your life. Find the meals that are best for your body and conducive to sleep.

4. PLAN CLOTHES, FOOD, AND SCHEDULE FOR THE NEXT DAY

Please do not leave these items until the last minute. The last thing we need for you to feel is stressed and rushed before bed. Early on in your evening, lay your clothes out for the next day. Take your time. Pack up your lunch and snacks for the office. Bringing your food with you will mean you won't cheat or fail to eat altogether. And finally, figure out what your calendar is for the next day. Note where you have to be in the morning and what time you need to wake up. Know your day ahead of time. The last thing I possibly want to see is you stressing about these items the morning of. Plan your day beforehand and you will wake up to an organized day ahead.

5. FINISH YOUR TO-DO LISTS, EXERCISE, AND SHUT OFF ELECTRONICS

Many of us are guilty of a bad habit of cramming too many activities immediately before we go to bed and get ready to sleep. These are items in our minds that we think are very important, yet we choose to leave them to the last minute as we end our day. The effect of dealing with these things too late in our day is that our sleep will be adversely affected.

To maximize the quality of your sleep, you will need to begin a winding down process well in advance before you get ready for bed. You will get these items done early on so that you will prepare for your sleep properly.

Below is a list of additional items you must complete well before you begin your bedtime routine:

- Look at your to-do list for the last time for the day. Please get all those final little items out of the way, or move the due dates. Your to-do list for the day should read zero by the time you are done for the day.
- If you are planning to do any exercise—whether at the gym, walking, running, or even sex—please get it done earlier rather than later in the day. We do not need you all hyped up right before bed. High energy does not translate to great sleep.
- One tool that does not get enough credit is television. If utilized in moderation and limited scheduled times, television can become a great de-stressor and encourage you to relax and enjoy entertainment as you finish up your day. Whether you enjoy watching sports, reality TV, news, dramas, comedies, or any type of programming, television can help relax your mind when used effectively. The keys here are to limit the amount of watching time per day (one to two hours should be your maximum goal), the time of day that you are watching, and limit snacks or bad eating habits when

watching TV. If you plan your routine smartly, you can make television become a good relaxing part of your schedule.

- Finally, get your last emails, texts, calls, or whatever you need out of your system. Once you are ready for the bedtime routine, notifications should be off and your phone should be put away for the rest of the night.

6. SHOWER/BATHE, BRUSH TEETH, GET INTO PJS

There is nothing worse than waking up on the couch the next morning, with lights still on and you're still in work clothes. Yes, I have been there many times before—maybe you have, too. If you value your sleep and you want to get into a sleeping frame of mind, then let's create a sleep setting for the body and mind. This means taking a nice shower or bath, to begin. Let's feel nice and clean when we get into bed. You may prefer to do this in the morning and not have to take two showers/baths; that is fine. But there is something to be said about being clean, feeling clean, and going into bed clean. From experience I can tell you that all of my best sleep nights came from a shower/bath beforehand. From there, practice nightly grooming routines. Brushing your teeth, flossing, etc. Perhaps you want to add additional grooming now or in the morning. Whatever your habits, know the more you have a grooming routine, the more likely you will follow it and you will feel clean and on top of your game. Finally, figure out your choice of PJs and start making your way to bed.

7. MASTER YOUR TIMING: SHUT-DOWN TIME, WAKE-UP TIME

This is not a drill. It's your life. As you begin to make preparations for sleep, be honest with yourself. Set the ideal amount of sleep you want for that night. What is your hard-set deadline to try to fall asleep by? And what time ideally do you want to wake up the next morning? Keep these timelines in mind. They will help you co-ordinate how much space you have left to finish the rest of your nightly routines. When you set your wake-up times, please be realistic. Do not leave everything to the last minute. Build yourself buffer time when you wake up to allow for possible snoozing and for gradual waking up and slowly getting ready. Buffer time means less stress for you and a better feeling in the morning.

Mastering your timing is a key point about your sleep pattern and one that you need to put a lot of attention toward. If you are currently sleeping for two hours a night, then setting ten hours as your sleep goal will likely be unrealistic. Set a realistic time frame—maybe then it is three hours for you, or four, five, or six. You pick. When you wake up in the morning, take note of how long you slept. Feel free to keep a sleep log to yourself. Then by the end of the week, you will be able to note how much sleep you have obtained each day. If every week or so, you can show any improvement in sleep length, you are already ahead of the game. You may want to increase the amount of sleep by thirty minutes per night, once a week, or go up by one hour a night once a month. Set yourself little incremental increases over time.

A key starting point is to analyze approximately how many hours you sleep per night currently and how many you ideally want to obtain. You may be several hours off, or very close. Work on the quantity of sleep to build over time. The quality of sleep will improve for you when you keep solid bedtime routines at night and wake-up routines in the morning. Quality will follow quantity—so work on the quantity first. And note to yourself each day approximately how many hours of sleep you plan to obtain each and every night.

8. SETTING ALARMS, SOUND, LIGHT, AND ROOM TEMPERATURE

Again, we need to think of all the final details as we move forward to sleep. If you do not set alarms for the next day, you are creating stress and chaos in your mind. You will be too worried about not waking up in time and asking your mind to store too much information. We have technology for a reason—use it. You need your mind to shut down when you prepare to sleep. So make sure you have your dual alarms ready to go so that your mind knows there is insurance set up in case one alarm fails. So now you have peace of mind to get ready for a good night's sleep.

Consider what type of alarm clock that you are using, including the wake-up sound. There are so many options these days to use music and tones: soft-sounding alarms that gently increase, or even the use of lights turning on within your bedroom rather than a sound-type alarm clock altogether. Try as many alarm variations as you can that will help you wake up routinely and feel good in the morning.

In addition to the sound of your alarm in the morning, the background sound/noise while you sleep is very important to pre-determine ahead of time. If you are like me, then you like to sleep in complete silence. The only sound that has ever effectively worked for me is a low-volume guided sleep meditation playing in the background. This still took me weeks to get used to and put into effect. If you like background noise and know this about yourself, then start to plan what type of noise you like. Some people like to have the window open and listen to traffic as they sleep. Another option can include background music or calming sounds playing in the background. Try different ways. If you think you NEED noise to sleep, try sleeping in complete quiet for a few nights and see how it works. Similarly, try background sounds if you only sleep in complete silence. Experimenting will find the ideal amount of noise that you need around you so that you can optimize your sleep.

When it comes to light, it is fairly accepted that a pitch-dark room is key for sleep. So consider investing in darkening shades in your room and setting lights on timers if you read so that everything will shut off by a certain time and allow for your sleep. Light comes into play as you fall asleep and when you wake up. To wake up gently, there are lights you can buy that gradually turn on over time so that you have a peaceful and calm wake-up routine. Don't discount the setup of your bedroom. Light, as well as sound, can affect how you fall asleep, stay asleep and wake up.

In addition, please be mindful of the temperature in your room as you prepare to sleep. Too hot or too cold does not work for most of us. Create a room temperature that will allow for a peaceful, comfortable feeling as you fall asleep and then prepare to wake up. If you have a smart thermostat, you can program your room temperature to change depending on night vs. morning.

9. SLEEP RITUALS: READ, MEDITATE, COUNT SHEEP, GRATITUDE

Congratulations, you are almost ready for a great night's sleep. You got this!

To fall asleep, *thinking about having to fall asleep* may not be your best course of action. Therefore, consider what routine you want to utilize when you are in bed before you drift off to sleep.

Perhaps you want to read a book? Have a form of music or guided meditation playing? (If you choose that route, I suggest putting it on a timer so that it doesn't play indefinitely and risk waking you up in the middle of the night.) Or maybe you want to lie in bed and count sheep in your mind? Whatever you choose, note that not all methods will work on any given night. What worked for you yesterday may not be your best method tonight. So if you need to evolve the final sleep routine, go for it. Have options available at your fingertips. Don't focus too much on the method. Envision that amazing night's sleep that is to come. Hold on to that image and make it happen!

One item you may wish to incorporate as well is *gratitude*. As you start to fall asleep, think about all the great things that happened to you during the day. Focus on positivity; the successes that happen in life. Say thank you to one or more wonderful things that happened to you. You can write them down or make a mental note. Falling asleep with gratitude sets you on a path of positivity where you appreciate the day you had and acknowledge it, thereby preparing yourself for great things to happen the next day.

Very often, the last thought of your day will become the first thing you think of when you wake up in the morning. Thus, it is key to have positive thoughts as you begin to fall asleep so that you can create a solid foundation for yourself each morning as you start your day. Our last thoughts at night also have an interesting way of resonating within our dreams and falling into the next day as well. So be mindful that positive energy, especially feeling gratitude as you drift to sleep, can flow through your dreams and into your next day. It's a wonderful continual cycle which you can build for yourself every night and all you need to do is think happy and wonderful thoughts as you go to sleep. Easy, and yet so rewarding!

10. SLEEPING POSITION AND SHUTTING DOWN THE MIND

We all sleep differently. Some of us are back sleepers, others prefer their side, some on our tummies. Find the position that allows you to best fall asleep and wake up feeling refreshed.

I prefer sleeping on my back in the "dead man" pose (śavāsana). For any of you non-yogis out there, this pose is the position that every yoga class begins and ends with. All you do is lie on your back, with your legs and arms spread out beside you for any amount of spacing that feels comfortable to you, with your palms always up. I figured that if the "dead man" pose can work so well to relax me at the start and end of yoga classes, then why not try it out for sleeping as well? And guess what? It worked!

I find that stomach sleeping cuts off my air too much and side sleeping hurts my joints and creates soreness. If you can't figure out your right position, consider working with a sleep doctor or professional to help develop the right sleeping positions that work for you.

No matter what sleeping position you choose, never forget to shut down your mind. Now is not the time for planning, thinking, and worrying. *It is time for sleep.*

If your mind does not shut down, tell your mind, "Hi Mind. You work for me. I don't work for you. It's time for us to go to sleep. I will deal with you in the morning." This may sound corny, but it works really well. This is part of reprogramming your brain and making your mind an effective tool for you rather than a hindrance.

Your body, mind, and soul are all parts of you. They need to work together in unison for you, not against you. Be your best supporter, not your internal enemy. That's why the final work you should allow yourself to do before having a peaceful night's sleep is to bring your mind to peace. Your body, mind, and soul all need a good night's rest to recharge and rejuvenate. The time for work is done. So let it all go at this last stage.

* * *

Having completed the above steps for a good night's sleep means that you have successfully completed half of the routine. Well done! The Yin to the Yang for a good night's sleep is to have a great waking-up feeling the next morning to match it. But that does not happen by accident. Nope—it means more systems and routines. But not to worry, I've got you covered for this one as well. Once you feel comfortable in the process of having a bedtime routine, let's work on your morning wake-up routine. Note: once you get the routines down, they are a combined system that work together as a team. You cannot have one without the other.

An effective wake-up routine consists of the following points:

1. TO SNOOZE OR NOT TO SNOOZE?

I'm guilty. I played the snoozing game most of my life—seeing how long I could sleep until I had to press the snooze bar on my alarm clock, how many times I could press it until I had no choice but to wake up. No matter how many times I played that game, the results were the same: horrible, restless sleep. I was sick of it and needed a change.

I learned an interesting trick over time which took me much patience and practice until I got it right. I would go to sleep without setting an alarm clock to see what time I would wake up naturally. My sleep while doing this was all over the map. Sometimes I slept for five hours, sometimes ten hours plus. As I developed my bedtime routine and my ideal sleep time, a curious thing started to happen: I would usually wake up a few minutes before my set alarm time. Not only would I wake up before the alarm, but I woke up refreshed and alive. So when it comes to waking up, remember, when you snooze, you *do* lose!

2. WAKE UP REFRESHED

Once you are done with the snooze game, you will learn to wake up on your own. Your mind and body will tell you when it is time for sleep and when it is time to wake up. So, wake up feeling good. Smile. Tell yourself a great day is ahead of you. Get out of bed slowly and get ready to start your day. Get ready to live your life with purpose and wake up with positivity.

3. DRINKING WATER AND BATHROOM TIME

You might feel groggy when you wake up. I do all the time. The mind could sense that there is an anxiety-like feeling in the early waking hours. However, it is possibly just *dehydration* talking.

As we sleep, we get dehydrated. That is a reality of life. Because of this, plan how much water you ideally want to drink when you wake up. Perhaps keep it by your bedside. Maybe you want to drink lemon water first thing to cleanse yourself or add in apple cider vinegar, as well. Whatever your plan is, make water a priority first thing. You need to hydrate and also get your body in motion for cleansing. We will discuss water more in Chapter 7, but as the Chosen Commandments are interrelated, it is at this stage that water and sleep/waking up work together.

A morning poop a day gets the groggy feelings away! It may not be a pleasant thing to think about, but being regular should be a regular routine for you. If you are at all concerned with the quantity or quality of your bathroom feces, speak to your doctor immediately. What you release in the bathroom can speak volumes on your health and any medical concerns. For most of us, a good morning water and/or coffee can jumpstart us. For others, there may be other underlying issues. Listen to your body—stay hydrated and do your best to be regular in the morning.

4. MEDITATE/YOGA/EXERCISE

Physical activity is to come in Chapter 9, with meditation in Chapter 10 and yoga in Chapter 11. So no need to worry, we will be breaking down these Chosen Commandments in greater detail soon. At this particular phase, note that some activity to start your day is amazing. I personally love either an intense session at the gym or a yoga class first thing in the morning. This gets the body physically active and loose, the mind calm and focused, and the soul energized and inspired.

Are you one of those people who come into work every morning dragging your butt, lifeless and with no energy? Then you of all people MUST get active first thing every morning. Look up successful world leaders and heads of businesses. What do most of them have in common? They wake up early and are physically active to start their day. Try even a ten-minute meditation and then a fifteen-minute walk to start your day. It will be THE difference-maker in making you feel good, having a sharp mind, and an activated body to kickstart a fantastic day.

5. THE IMPORTANCE OF BREAKFAST

Yet another Chosen Commandment, this one is coming in Chapter 8. For now, think of the word *breakfast*. Break-fast. Breaking the fast. Your first meal of the day is the one that breaks the fast you had from your sleep. Make it light enough so that it is easy to digest but also gives you energy to start your day. Make breakfast a priority, not an afterthought.

It is alarming how many people I have met who skip breakfast altogether and go straight to lunch. They are, in fact, not doing themselves any favors in that way. It causes a chain reaction to a delayed start to the day, which carries forward through the whole day, including sleep.

If you want your sleep to go well, then make sure you start your day just as strong. And that includes a solid healthy breakfast.

6. MORNING SHOWER/BATH

If you exercise in the morning, please make sure to take a shower or bath before work. Your workmates will thank you! A morning shower or bath also washes off sleep and gets you energized for the day. Perhaps you want to start and/or end your day with a shower or bath. Try both and find the ritual that makes you feel the best.

7. GETTING DRESSED/PACKING UP

You have already set out your clothes the night before, packed up your lunch, and got yourself ready. In this way, the morning should be a snap! This is such a great example of time management and prioritization. When you plan ahead and have systems in place, ANYTHING is possible.

8. ELECTRONIC-FREE, PLEASE!

The last key point at this level: Presumably and ideally, you have not been on your phone. You had a great night's sleep. You woke up refreshed. To make both of those happen, electronics needed to be put away. While waking up, the last thing on your mind should be to check your phone. Give the morning wake-up routine to *you*; your body, mind, and soul. Do the things that will make your morning the most productive and feel the best. Television, tablets, and smartphones can wait. Your morning time is for you.

* * *

We have now started the process of creating *your* Effective Sleep System. You want to live for as long as you can and have a quality of life—you have made this commitment. This is important to you. Thus, this chapter has mapped out for you how all the other Chosen Commandments are interconnected with sleep. Without sleep in your life, the other Chosen Commandments will not be sustainable. Sleep is a core Chosen Commandment and was intentionally placed as number one for a reason. To make all the other Chosen Commandments work, you need to have sleep quantity and quality in your life. Sleep is not simply about getting by or doing the bare minimum possible, sleep is a tool for the rejuvenation of life— YOUR LIFE! Embrace it.

Your day ends with the start of sleep, and your next day then begins with the end of sleep. Your existence revolves around sleep. So make the choice today to start your process of having the best possible sleep in your life. You won't regret it.

* * *

Now that you also understand the tools and processes necessary to get the sleep systems in place for yourself, let's look back and debunk those excuses that were previously holding you back from sleep:

I CAN'T SLEEP VERY MUCH.

You can't? Or you won't? Look at the steps above to get a good bedtime routine in place. How many of them are you currently following? Unless you answered all of them, then it is not a question that you *can't* sleep—it is simply that you are *not allowing* yourself to sleep. You do not have the systems in place for effective sleep. Don't tell yourself that you "can't sleep." Tell yourself that you need to sleep and WILL create the systems to make that happen.

I DON'T NEED A LOT OF SLEEP TO FUNCTION.

Fair enough. Right now you are likely getting by on minimal sleep to function. Good for you. Is that what you want for your life? Do you want to get by, or do you want to get ahead? By sleep rejuvenating your body, mind, and soul, don't you think you are much better equipped to plan and conquer each day?

What if I also told you, that as a rejuvenated person, you could be far more productive and perform tasks in less time? *Get ahead in less time*—all because you devoted more time to quality sleep.

FALLING ASLEEP IS TOO HARD.

Once again, check out the bedtime routines. How many are you following? Did you set yourself up for a good night's sleep—or a restless sleep? The answer could be as simple as changing your mattress or pillows, changing your sleeping position, or turning off electronics earlier in the night. Go through the Effective Sleep System outlined above step by step and, somewhere along the way, you will develop better nighttime routines and systems. Falling asleep will no longer seem impossible—it will become a given result because you set yourself up for success.

I WAKE UP IN THE MIDDLE OF THE NIGHT A LOT.

Go through the bedtime routines again. If you are waking up in the middle of the night, it is usually the result of drinking too much water or poor eating habits before bed.

Don't even get me started on alcohol or coffee before bed. We will cover that as well in the water chapter coming up.

At this moment, simply note that if you cannot stay asleep, it is likely that you have done something before bed that is triggering the intermittent or frequent waking up. And if you feel that it is a medical concern, speak to your doctor immediately. Your body and mind are not happy if you cannot stay asleep soundly at night. Listen to yourself, respect yourself, and find out what is triggering it.

SLEEP IS FOR THE DEAD. IT IS A WASTE OF TIME.

If you have read through this chapter and still feel that sleep is a waste of time, then I suggest you go back and reread this chapter again. Again and again. Rejuvenating your body, mind, and soul is one of the most—if not THE most—important gifts you can give to yourself. Sleep is a gift. Cherish it.

THERE IS NO COMFORTABLE WAY TO SLEEP.

Sleep should feel amazing. You should look forward to it every night. If you cannot get a comfortable sleep, go through the checklist above for the bedtime routine. It is structured in a particular order on purpose and one or more items you're applying may be out of sequence. Once you find the processes that work for you, I can almost guarantee you blissful nightly sleep. A struggle can turn into ease almost overnight and it's how you see it and set it up that will decide the outcome.

I GET NIGHTMARES ALL THE TIME!

Nightmares suck! I used to get them all the time. I noticed that my nightmares were most prevalent if I had a big meal before bed or consumed a jittery drink such as alcohol or a caffeinated beverage.

Watching excessive television or reading on my phone right before bed didn't help, either. I was going to bed with a nervous and stressed brain rather than a calm one. The more I felt relaxed and peaceful setting up my nightly routine, the more nightmares went away. In addition, when my stomach was not working hard to digest and I didn't have sugar or stimulants in my system at night, I was calm enough to fall asleep. If you create peace and tranquility when you fall asleep, then you should have that same peace and tranquility as you sleep throughout the night.

I'M TOO HUNGRY/THIRSTY TO SLEEP.

We will get into that in Chapter 8, "Chosen Commandment #3: We Are the Nutrition We Eat," as promised. However, there is such a thing as overconsuming food/beverages before bed, as well as under-consumption. It sucks to feel hungry when we go to sleep. When you work on your meal plans and timing for eating, you have to recognize that certain foods work depending on what stage of the day you are in. For example, the foods you consume before a work-out are far different from, to be on the safe side, those that you have before bed. If you are finding that you are continually hungry/thirsty before bed, don't be afraid to adjust your meals and water schedule. You will find the optimal point where you feel nice and saturated for good sleep, without being bloated during the night or in the morning. It's all a question of having a plan when it comes to food and water while finding your optimal balance.

THERE IS NOT ENOUGH TIME TO SLEEP.

This one goes along with all of the Chosen Commandments. "I don't have time to work out. I don't have time to eat well," etc.

I will simply ask you at this point: do you have time to live? Because once you die, you may not return. If you want to live, and you want quantity and quality of life, then you have NO choice but to make sleep a priority.

I don't care if you need to cut out a television show. Or cut out of your emails early. It's not a question of a lack of time. It's a lack of priorities.

Given that sleep is likely the most important activity you will do in any given day to stay alive and live a quality life, it deserves to be right on the top of the list of priorities. You have all the time in the world to get quality sleep. Schedule it—make it a system—and it will happen.

HEALTH ISSUES AFFECT MY SLEEP.

I certainly hope that this is not the case. I am not going to discount the fact that many people do suffer from medical conditions that affect their sleep. But before you go looking for pills or quick fixes due to what you believe to be a medical condition affecting your sleep, answer this:

- Are you following a bedtime and wake-up routine as outlined in this chapter?
- Are you consuming water as per Chapter 7?
- Do you have a solid basis of meal plans noted in Chapter 8?
- Are you following Chapter 9 and have a regular routine of physical activity?
- Are you meditating as per Chapter 10?
- Is a regular yoga practice outlined in Chapter 11 part of your lifestyle?

By all means, I am not stopping you and actually encourage you to consult with a medical professional if you feel that any health issues are limiting your quantity and quality of sleep. I will also dare say that unless you are following all six steps I just outlined above, then your sleep deprivation or whichever medical condition you have or feel you have may actually be a result of failing lifestyle choices.

The 6 Chosen Commandments are in place for a reason and are intertwined as I have been telling you throughout the book so far. If one is out of place, then the others will suffer as well.

I have given you the tools to best work on your sleep rejuvenation. But for this to happen effectively, we need the other parts of the systems to click. And for sleep to receive its benefit, it needs its next closest ally. We progress to water—another building block for life.

SEVEN

CHOSEN COMMANDMENT #2:
Water Is Hydration for Life

—◈—

Welcome to the simplest Chosen Commandment of the six. Yet, this Chosen Commandment is perhaps one of the most challenging for people. Isn't it interesting that we struggle with the simplest things in life at times?

For those of us living in developed and modern cities or countries, we sometimes forget how lucky we are to have easy access to the seemingly simplest resource for us—water. It is too easy to take for granted how accessible water is for most of us. Depending on the city you live in, tap water may even be considered safe for consumption without additional filters. For others, between add-on filters and filtration systems, to water coolers—the options for water access can be unlimited. However, there are many people throughout the world who struggle to drink water, for the reason that they do not have the means to access it.

As you go through and internalize the second Chosen Commandment, ponder this thought: *I am so blessed and fortunate to have readily available drinking water for my consumption.*

You may also wonder, *Why am I not taking advantage of it more often?* There are many people on Earth who would be so grateful to have the water sources for drinking that some of us do. Let's utilize water better, out of respect to those who wish they had this resource and do not.

Considering the above thoughts, for many of us it comes down to the consumption of water is a struggle - not because we can't access it, but for the simple reason that we refuse to drink it. We know it is there and that it's good for us. So why do many of us fail to implement systems to regularly consume water?

Let's start with the top ten excuses for not drinking water:

1. I don't like the taste of water.
2. I drink other beverages including coffee, tea, juice, pop, etc.
3. I don't need to drink much water.
4. I simply can't do it.
5. I only drink water when I'm thirsty.
6. Sparkling water is the same as flat water.
7. I keep forgetting to drink water.
8. I can't drink hot, room-temperature, and/or cold water.
9. I use sweeteners in my water, so I'm good, right?
10. Less water means less urination.

So many excuses, so little time.

Right now, do not focus on why you are not consuming water. Instead, let's discuss why water is one of our Chosen Commandments.

Thankfully, *The Bible 3.0* is NOT a scientific textbook. As a result, I will not be throwing at you all sorts of statistics behind the reasons to drink water. If you have lived on this Earth for any amount of time, you know you need water to live. Over half of the human body is made up of water. There is a reason why we were constructed in this manner.

Your body without water is like a car without oil. It can only run efficiently for so long. Hydration is a top Chosen Commandment because your body needs and craves water on so many levels.

Think about how your body reacts when you wake up in the morning and go hours without drinking water. What about when you're exercising or playing sports without water? How is that working out for you? I am looking here at a concept called *dehydration*, which is the state when your body is lacking water and craving it.

Mentally and physically, we are functioning far below our best if we are dehydrated. I should know. I went thirty-plus years of my life without drinking water!

I know that you have read the above and probably said to yourself, "IMPOSSIBLE! There is no way that this man went so many years without water." Okay, I may have had the occasional glass here and there. But even with sports, I added as many sweeteners as I could to make my water tastier. In my earlier years, I would not consume water unless it was sweetened. But I learned to cut out the sweet drinks and go cold turkey. There was no choice.

As a baby through my toddler years, my drink of choice was apple juice. As I grew older into an adolescent and a teenager, I drank tons of pop and fruit juices. Through grade school and high school, I did not drink anything at all during school hours. In university, I drank mostly pop, fruit juice and coffee. At one point I was up to approximately five coffees a day. Sound familiar?

I faced so many health issues throughout my younger years that I have lost track of them all. While I don't directly blame my lack of water intake for my issues, this certainly didn't help. When I got to the point in my early thirties when I was at my lowest, I had no choice but to overhaul my diet. The nutritionist I was working with made it very clear to me: water was going to be part of my life. It's something I resisted forever. I simply could not get over the fact that I hated the "taste" of water. But I came to accept that I was now at the point in my life where I had no choice—I was going to consume water whether I liked it or not. Perhaps, I thought, over time I could even train my brain to appreciate and like water.

Think about your own water consumption. How many actual pure glasses of water are you consuming per day? Now think of all the other liquids you are likely consuming in reality:

1. **Coffee/tea**
2. **Alcoholic drinks**
3. **Soda pop**
4. **Fruit juices**

5. Sparkling/flavored water
6. Energy drinks
7. Other misc. drinks: yogurt drinks, coconut water, etc.

All of the above types of drinks—and any other beverages that are not pure water—are, in fact, NOT water. They are treats. Think of them more as dessert than water consumption. I want you to assess how many non-water drinks you have per day. And over the course of developing your system, you will need to decide how many non-water drinks you are going to consume.

I understand and appreciate the need/want/benefit of consuming coffee and/or tea. The same goes for red wine. If you feel you need it or want it, then don't deny yourself that pleasure. But I ask that you find a balance. If you are a five-plus coffee per day drinker like I used to be, find a way to wean yourself down to one to two cups. And please also watch what you put into your coffee and/or tea. If you are using white sugar, STOP IT! We will discuss this more in the nutrition chapter, but white sugar is a no-no in the Chosen Commandments. If you cannot drink your coffee and/or tea plain, then find substitutes. Use milk or a non-dairy creamer. Find healthier sweet additives such as monk sugar.

Every incorporation of a Chosen Commandment is a gradual one. Slowly learn to take something out, while slowly putting something in. The art of lowering your bad drink choices (and this fits any of the non-water beverages you consume) is simple. Each day, make the commitment to how many of this choice beverage you will have during the day and make a schedule.

An example: Let's go back to the five-plus coffee per day drinker. Let's say they are putting 2 creams and 2 sugars in each of their coffees. Let's say we are good with the cream. I would ask that you look at your body's level of tolerance toward dairy and if dairy is in fact working for you. Try skim milk sometimes or non-dairy creamers—they are delicious and can saturate your need for a thicker and sweeter coffee. But if you insist on the cream, go for it. But slowly try to move to 1.5 creams per coffee and then 1 cream. Make the change every week or two; start to lower the intake slowly. Do the same with your sugar intake. Every week or two, lower the amounts you put in. Instead of 2 sugars, move to 1.5. Then 0.5. And eventually 0. As you decrease the sugar intake, try a healthier sweet additive—my personal favorites are monk sugar or coconut sugar. Just 0.5 teaspoons of monk sugar is sweeter than 2 white sugars, and it is far better for your body.

So go ahead and play around with the coffee additions. From there, begin to wean yourself off the five-plus coffees per day. Make the commitment, for example, that for the next week or month you will only consume four coffees per day. Make a schedule!

Let's say right now you are consuming a coffee every three hours: 9:00 a.m., noon, 3:00 p.m., 6:00 p.m., and 9:00 p.m. Let's make a schedule for four coffees per day. 9:00 a.m., noon, 4:00 p.m., and 7:00 p.m. See what we have done there? We kept your first two time slots the same and then paced out the other two cups of coffee. If 7:00 p.m. is too early, move the last coffee to 8:00 p.m. You can also try decaf for the last one or two cups. There are so many gradual fixes and adjustments. In this case, you are still consuming a lot of coffee, but less than before. You will start to watch what goes into each coffee. The art of making a change is to create a goal, and from there, a plan. In our case, you will select how many cups of coffee you want to drink, what type of coffee you will choose, and what you will put in the coffee. Finally, you will make a schedule for when you consume each one. Drink them slower—sip on them if you have to. Gradual changes lead to big results.

In the following Chosen Commandments, nothing would work if water was not part of the equation:

- Physical activity without water? Simply not going to happen! To be physically active, you need to consume water to replenish your body. If not, welcome to dehydration city.
- Sleep without water? You can rest assured that you will sleep less, have less fulfilling sleep, and be in a constant state of dehydration without water.

- Nutrition without water? How do you plan on eating clean and healthy if you are not providing your body with water to assist it with the digestion of food? Water and clean eating make a great team together.
- Yoga without water? If you plan to make it to the hospital with dehydration, this is your best ticket. If you didn't consume water before yoga, you will surely learn at this stage.
- Meditation without water? A body without water leads to a mind that is scattered and unsettled. To assist your meditation practice, your body needs to be in alignment so that your mind can stay sharp and focused to meditate.

As you can clearly see above, the 6 Commandments of the Chosen Life work in unison. If you want the Chosen Commandments to work, you must make water a foundation of your daily routine. It is *not* an option to forgo it.

As I personally incorporated water into my life, I made two drinking schedules. Each schedule was the daily/weekly/monthly chart measuring my planned beverage intake. One schedule focused on the bad beverages I was consuming and how to slowly wean myself down to one coffee per day with NO OTHER beverage, besides water. The other schedule was how to slowly incorporate pure water into my drinking schedule so that I could incorporate a dozen glasses of water into my daily routine. With a schedule, timelines, and thus a plan, the pressure was off. I did not have to think about it anymore. All I had to do was follow the plan and I knew that I could do it. And so can you.

* * *

Now, provided that you have accepted that you NEED to consume water, the next question is: HOW do you consume the necessary water? As with everything in this book, you do not need to be (or should not be) extreme in your actions. This is not a case of going from no water drinking to five liters (about half a gallon) the next day. Baby steps will build your foundation to a solid lifetime ahead of water consumption and hydration.

Here are steps to incorporate pure water drinking into your lifestyle:

1. **WATER SOURCE:** Select your source of water. You can use bottled, tap, a kettle; whatever fits your needs and budget.

2. **UNFLAVORED FLAT WATER:** No sparkling or flavored waters! You can use these initially when you are starting to create your system of water consumption. But you will slowly need to wean off these and move to unflavored flat water. It's not sexy—but it is the most effective for your body.

3. **WATER TEMPERATURE:** You might enjoy hot and/or cold water, which you can still indulge in on occasion. Yes, they count! But try to stick to room-temperature water as much as possible as it is the easiest on your system.

4. **WATER CONTAINER:** How do you plan to consume your water? In a glass? Cup? A sealed container? Pick a container that you will readily use and be consistent with. I like the idea of having a glass or plastic travel water container that I can take everywhere. If you have it with you, then you will consume it.

5. **WATER APP:** You can set up a system for water consumption to keep track of what you're drinking and set goals for yourself. There are water apps for your smartphone that can do this. Find the one that works best for you and download it today. Then set your goals every day and week, and get ready to adjust them.

6. **WATER ROUTINE:** Creating a sustainable target for water consumption is key. Let's say that you are at the point now that you consume no water whatsoever. If that's the case, I want you to add one glass of water to your routine today, then one glass tomorrow and every day for the next week. Think about it. You only need to consume

one glass per day as an extreme. Then you can make it two glasses per day in the second week, three glasses per day in the third week and four glasses per day at the end of the month. By three months you will be up to a dozen glasses. If you need to go slower, then you can make it one glass of water per day for an entire month. Then incorporate a second glass per day during month two, three glasses per day by month three, and so forth. At that pace, you will reach a dozen glasses in one year.

THE KEYS:

- Do not get bogged down by a time deadline and feel pressure.
- If you miss a glass on a particular day, you do not need to add it the following day. Practice and try hitting your target the next day.
- If you are seeing over the course of time that the goal is unattainable, then lower the goal. Create a schedule that you can meet sustainably over a period of time. Be honest with yourself. Make a schedule that is realistic and doable.
- Stay at it—and incorporate the water slowly.
- Have a smartphone app to remind you can make all the difference.

Consider having a water buddy. Ask your spouse, friend, co-worker, etc. to join you on your water journey. You'll be surprised to find how easy it is to find someone close to you who is suffering from a lack of water in their life too. Having a friend to keep you accountable can make things more interesting and fun. But don't rely on any other person—this is YOUR thing first and foremost.

* * *

Now that we have analyzed the need for water in our lives, let's discuss *practical solutions to overcome your ten excuses not to consume water!*

I DON'T LIKE THE TASTE OF WATER.

There are many things in life that we do not like. It doesn't mean that we do not do them.

If most of us worked at jobs that we only liked, how many of us would be unemployed?

Let's pull up our big boy and big girl pants. If you don't like the taste of water, let's slowly, at least, get you to *tolerate* water. Perhaps you prefer hot or cold water. Try any temperature at the beginning. Over time you will accept room temperature water, which will work best for your body.

Try cheats at the beginning. You can buy fancy cups or containers where you can add fruit to your water. Perhaps find a decent/not-bad additive that you can add to it. I used the flavored squeeze bottles and added a squirt at a time, and then slowly I weaned off those additives as well. Speak to a dietician/nutritionist. Find bottled waters you like. I gave you the tools earlier on selecting water. Make the conscious decision to find water that you will agree to consume.

A secret: The more you perform physical activity and yoga, the more your body will crave water. When you take plain water with you to your exercise routines and yoga, then you will/should naturally accept water. There is nothing like sips of water after a hot yoga class. So stay active, find ways to make water taste great for you, and mostly, learn to slowly sip and drink plain water. Turn something you hate into something you love. The water is the same: it all comes down to *how* you see it.

I DRINK OTHER BEVERAGES INCLUDING COFFEE, TEA, JUICE, POP, ETC.

Congratulations. You and most of the population. If you drink another beverage in excess, that is okay; you have the tools in this chapter to create a schedule to slowly wean yourself off the other beverage choices. If you enjoy consuming sodas or energy drinks, for example, your goal should be to drink *zero*. Speak to a health expert like a dietician or nutritionist. There are no health benefits that come from drinking sodas and energy drinks, while these forms of beverages can be dangerous to your health, depending on the frequency they are consumed and their ingredients. As for coffee and tea, perhaps limit yourself to one or two per day. These beverages are more beneficial if used in moderation, and neither are substitutes for water.

Assess the drink choices you are currently making. Are there any perceived health benefits at all for the drinks you consume, or are they simply a guilty pleasure? Think long and hard about the health goals you want to reach. Decide for yourself how many of each of these beverages you are comfortable with consuming and then make a long-term and short-term schedule to get you there. If you are currently drinking six beers a day, for example, and you want to get down to two beers per day, then great. Ideally you would want to be at zero to one beers per day, but two is surely better than six. Don't focus on what you are *un*able to do—focus on the progress you are making. Rome was not built in a day. Even if it takes you two years to get yourself down to two beers from six, then I salute you! Knocking off four beers per day means that you are consuming 1,460 fewer beers a year. Process that for a moment. Looks like a victory to me! So set your goals and schedules, be honest with yourself, and practice each day building YOUR new beverage routines.

If alcohol consumption is an issue in your life, please do not be afraid to ask for help if needed. Any form of alcohol, including beers, wines, and spirits can be highly addictive and difficult for many people to reduce or eliminate from their lifestyle. If you suspect that this may be the case for you, please remember that you are not alone. Feel free to reach out to your family doctor for guidance or a referral. There are many support groups and forms of treatment that are available to you. Taking such a step could save your life one day. It can feel with addiction that there is never a good time to begin a lifestyle adjustment. If my words apply to you, then I highly encourage you to begin today or as soon as possible. Healing begins the moment you recognize that change is needed within you.

I DON'T NEED TO DRINK MUCH WATER.

Please go back and reread this chapter. That is simply false. Perhaps you are functioning without drinking much—or any—glasses of water, but you are certainly not functioning at your best. You would not drive your car without filling up gas or changing oil (if it is not an electric vehicle). You know what will happen to a gasoline car if it does not receive fuel—it will stop. A car that does not have regular oil changes will have an engine that will seize and die. Similarly, your body needs and craves water to stay hydrated and operate at its best. Don't deny your body what it needs. You will look better, feel better and give your body the best chance to operate at its highest levels by consuming water. You do NEED water. Accept it. Live it.

I SIMPLY CAN'T DO IT.

You can't—or you won't? Do not use defeated language when speaking to yourself. You purchased this book. You were inspired to make life changes and build systems that will elevate you to new levels. So, what does it mean when you say you can't do it? It's not that you *can't* do it, *you are choosing not to do it.*

Talk to yourself. Have many conversations with yourself. Let's keep this in perspective. I am not asking you to go into the boxing ring with Mike Tyson or run the Boston Marathon. I am asking you to pick up a glass of water and consume it.

If you are consuming no water at all, then what I am asking you to do is commit to drinking one glass of water per day. From there, increase the intake to two glasses per day, and so on. You can do that! Today, tomorrow, and for the balance of the week, you can start by simply consuming one extra glass of water per day. Do you get up in the morning? Do you get yourself dressed? Do you go to school and/ or work? Do you pay bills? You are functioning. You know how to do things. Picking up a glass of water should be the easiest part of your day. Take that extra glass of water right now. Gulp it down. Sip it over thirty minutes, one hour, or two hours; I don't care. But consume it. By consuming that extra glass of water, you have already shown yourself you CAN do it. And you will continue to do it, as you incorporate this Chosen Commandment into your daily routine.

I ONLY DRINK WATER WHEN I'M THIRSTY.

Drinking when you are thirsty is fine. We all get thirsty—that is our body's way of telling us we are dehydrated and need more water. So why do you need to wait to the point of dehydration to consume water? Let's get proactive instead of reactive! Do you fix the windows and roof in your house over time, or do you wait until they break to fix them? Do you do regular oil changes for your car, or do you wait until the engine ceases? If you regularly consume water, you may never feel thirsty (or at least not often) and that is not a bad thing, that simply means you are hydrating your body regularly. Be proactive—give your body what it needs. Your body, mind and soul will thank you.

SPARKLING WATER IS THE SAME AS FLAT WATER.

If you are consuming little to no water to start, I have no issue with you drinking sparkling water (at least you would be consuming a *form* of water). Use sparkling water as an initial gateway into water consumption if you are lacking water at this point; and long-term, you can keep it around as a treat. But I would prefer you limit the intake to one or two glasses maximum per day. Talk to your dietician or nutritionist. The bubbles and fizz you are adding to your body are not the best things to consume. Flat, plain water is ideal for you—for all of us—for our systems and digestion. Bloating is a real thing. Sparkling water increases bloating and can be holding you back. So no, you do not have to give it up if you like it. But if you are not a sparkling water person, please choose flat water if you have to make the choice. Not all waters are created equally.

I KEEP FORGETTING TO DRINK WATER.

Schedule, schedule, schedule. Routine, routine, routine. Welcome to your new best friends. There is no right or wrong way to get water consumption done in a day, as long as the totals are there. My goal is to drink three liters of water per day, which is about a dozen cups. Therefore, I use a water container that holds 750 ml of water to accommodate that. I know I need to drink four of these containers per day, so I create a schedule. I finish one container by 9:00 a.m. Another by noon. From there, I finish containers by 3:00 p.m. and 8:00 p.m. Easy!

You can do the same. Find the water containers that work for you—perhaps having a larger container means you will finish more water sooner. If you are relying on using a small glass and having to fill it up each time, that is where the forgetting can begin. Having a sealed water container with you—everywhere you go—means you are more likely to get the water consumption done.

If all else fails, get a water consumption app for your phone, as discussed. Program in the app how much water you want to consume over certain time intervals and set reminders. If you follow the app, then you can't miss it.

Being forgetful generally means that there is no schedule, routine, or plan. Create your system and you will stay on track.

I CAN'T DRINK HOT, ROOM-TEMPERATURE, AND/OR COLD WATER.

I absolutely despise the word *can't*. It is so limiting and defeating. It's time to shift your mindset. It's not that you can't do something, it's that you *won't*. You are not trying. You have given up. You have painted yourself in the negative from the start. Why are you doing this to yourself? You love yourself. You believe in yourself. So you can and will do anything that you set your mind to!

When I started drinking water regularly, I found that I only liked cold water. I couldn't stand hot or room-temperature water. But I encountered an issue: Cold water is hard on the teeth and my system, so I couldn't consume much water if it was ice cold, even though I loved the taste. What did I do about this? I didn't change overnight. I am not a machine! I adjusted and made gradual changes. Instead of freezing-cold water, I would leave my water out until it was a lukewarm temperature. And I started getting used to drinking less cold water, little by little. I would keep leaving my water out over time until I got to the point that I got used to drinking room-temperature water. Gradual shifts led to major shifts. Now when I'm at a restaurant I ask for water with no ice. Sometimes I will even squeeze a lime in there.

Try creating your shifts. It's not that you *can't* do it—it's that you are not used to it. So get used to it, little by little.

I USE SWEETENERS IN MY WATER, SO I'M GOOD, RIGHT?

Please see the discussion on sparkling water above. Using these additives is great for gradual shifts or to have as occasional treats, but they are not substitutes for the real deal. If you are drinking no water right now, I would rather see you drinking a glass of water with a little sweetener in it than a bottle of beer or a coffee with cream and sugar. But it is not the solution; it is the better choice of the not-so-good options. Don't accept anything less than the best for yourself. These are temporary, but not final, solutions.

LESS WATER MEANS LESS URINATION.

And more water means more urination! Ladies and gentlemen, we are not in first grade anymore. Why is there such resistance to urination? I've worked and gone to school with people who feel that not going to the bathroom all day is like a badge of honor. Really? If you do not have a regular pee and poop schedule, please go see your doctor immediately.

I remember what it was like not to poop for almost two weeks. I ended up in the hospital taking medications to relearn bowel movements. There is nothing more satisfying than one or two poops per day at least—especially in the morning—plus frequent trips for urination. Now, if you are urinating more than twenty times per day, that should be of concern. But I can tell you that urinating easily eight to ten times on an average day is not a bad thing. Urination means you are flushing toxins out of your body; that the water intake is working. If you want to get *really* technical, the color of your pee and the consistency/look of your poop also says a lot about how your body is digesting and working. Study it, feel free to perform your own research online as to different types of poops, and talk to your doctor.

There is no shame in going to the bathroom. This is a healthy part of life. If you are consuming less water to avoid going to the bathroom, then please start reprogramming your brain immediately. More water consumption will lead to more urination and better pees and poops. Take in what you *do* need so that you can release what needs to go, as well. It may not be pretty, but your body will thank you. And having your body functioning well by being regular will calm your mind. You will feel more at peace and at ease, which will lead you to be energized and soul inspired to accomplish more. By going to the bathroom regularly, you are nurturing your body, mind, and soul. Win, win, and win.

Now that we have increased your water intake, we have set the foundation for your body's consumption of fluids. Drinking water will also assist your body to take in and break down nutritious food.

Nutrition and water are like love and marriage. You can't have one without the other. As you look at your water schedule and feel really good about your increase in water intake, it's time to focus your mind on the next part of your journey... To feed your body nutritious food and get your system healthy and functioning at its best capacity.

EIGHT

CHOSEN COMMANDMENT #3:

We Are the Nutrition We Eat

—◦◦◦—

Welcome to one of the hardest, if not THE hardest, Chosen Commandments to follow and maintain: eating. Nutrition. The food chapter.

Most, if not all of us have a strange relationship with food. There tends to be a love/hate cycle that never seems to stop. For most of us, we seem to be so focused on consuming as little food as possible or a lot. There are also so many diets and regimes to follow. It can get so overwhelming!

Do not despair. What you have done in the past with food does not define you. Today is a fresh opportunity to evolve. We will continue to build gradual and manageable life systems for you and nutrition is no different. The keys will be to find your goals and develop plans and routines.

We are all guilty of it at some point in our lives: barely eating or eating poorly. The starting point is how we *view* food. *At its core, do not look at food as either a chore or an escape.* You do not eat just to get by or fill empty voids. Food is energy. Food is fuel. Food is not a punishment.

It's time to embrace the role food has in your life and utilize it for glory. Eating affects how we look, and as a result, how we feel. Make food work for you—not against you.

As you start to work with this chapter, please assess at what point you are at. There is no shame as to what your eating habits have been up to this point. But please recognize that there are many different eating disorders out there. They are debilitating and can take over your life. Consider as you read my story about your own relationship with food over the course of your lifetime. Is it a healthy or unhealthy one? If you are intentionally overeating or undereating and feel that you have no control over how you consume food, please consider speaking to a medical professional immediately. Once you have a difficult relationship with food, it is often very challenging to break out of it without external help. Mental health is at the forefront of key discussion topics in our society today. If you feel at all that you are trapped in any sort of difficult cycle in your life, including any issues with food/eating, feel strong enough to stand up and ask for help. Know that you are special and that asking for help shows strength and determination.

Outside of medical conditions that require assistance or treatment, there are so many reasons why we do not eat properly and why nutrition is not a priority for us. I can write a book for you about the excuses or reasons why people do not have nutrition in their lives, but let's stick for now to *ten common excuses why people are not into nutrition:*

1. The needle on the scale never moves down regardless of how little I eat.
2. I love food too much to give it up.
3. I am not skinny, so I need to eat lots.
4. I can't eat a lot in order to stay skinny.
5. Healthy eating is boring and not for me.
6. I am going to die one day anyways. What's the point?
7. Healthy eating is a myth. It doesn't matter what you eat.
8. I am so confused and don't know where to begin. I'm giving up!
9. No matter what I eat, I look the same.
10. Healthy eating is a lie to make you spend more money.

Don't forget as you are going through the 6 Commandments of the Chosen Life that they are interrelated. They work together. If one element falls off the map, then the other Chosen Commandments suffer. Take nutrition in this case. Picture how this fits within the remaining Chosen Commandments:

- By having a regular nutritious eating schedule, you will sleep better. Your body, mind, and soul will be better prepared for a good night's sleep and you will wake up more refreshed.
- If you eat cleaner/better, then your water consumption will follow suit. Healthy eating and drinking water are a marriage made in heaven.
- You will be better equipped to follow a consistent physical activity routine if you have nutritious food in your system. You will also see long-term improved results as far as how you want to look if you are eating right.
- To effectively meditate, your body, mind, and soul need to be aligned. If you are eating poorly, your body will be weak, your mind and soul will be scattered, and you will not be able to sit still and focus. Clean eating leads to a clean body, mind, and soul. Remember that.
- If you plan to have yoga in your life, you will learn that what you eat before and after a yoga practice is very critical. Yoga on a heavy stomach is a no-go. Eating a lot after yoga is not recommended either. Yoga, in many ways, can help you balance your eating schedule for more gradual shifts, rather than consuming large meals. The moment I started to practice yoga, my road to nutritious eating also took off.

Nutrition is the most difficult area to create a program for someone because there are so many factors that go into the equation. Gender, age, height, weight, allergies, digestion, medical conditions, body preferences, and tolerances... The list seemingly never ends. If the time is right that you are ready to bring nutrition into your life and create systems for yourself, your first step is to get help. I did. For much of what you need to get done in terms of your journey, it is very difficult to do it alone, especially when we do not have training in this area.

Speak to your family doctor and make a game plan to start. Is a dietician or nutritionist right for you? Make appointments for consultations with medical professionals. Get referrals. Read their websites. Call with questions. If you feel ready, get to work with professionals, and know that any step of the way you can always change the professional or start to work on your own. You are never limited or stuck. Put yourself in the best possible position to succeed!

My professional was Linda McCharles, a registered dietician based in Toronto, Ontario, Canada. When I first met Linda, I was approximately thirty-five years old. I had not attended a gym in about fifteen years. I had started a yoga practice that was going very slowly for me. I was not drinking very much water yet. I was still sleeping maybe three to five hours per night. My eating habits were very poor, and I was not meditating. At this time I had no recognition of the 6 Commandments of the Chosen Life at all. I simply knew that I needed to make changes to survive. I was fat and out of shape. The pictures did not lie. I was the heaviest I had ever been in my life. That was my wake-up call. Combined with the fact that my doctor wanted to put me on cholesterol meds, I felt like I had hit rock bottom.

When I met Linda, I had started what I thought was healthy eating. I had put myself on a salads-and-fruits diet. I decided that eating three salads a day and fruits for snacks would clean me up. I knew that I was eating poorly, and my waistline showed it, so I invented a quick-fix cleanse to get me off my bad eating. I gave up all my bad foods overnight. But this was not sustainable nor was it a solution; I needed help to create a manageable lifestyle when it came to eating. Thus, I spoke to a colleague who highly regarded Linda. I then made an appointment immediately and went to see her.

With Linda, I discussed my eating habits for most of my life. I was ashamed to admit it, but I had a bad relationship with food. In my case, I ate whatever I wanted with no consequences. I know what it's like to eat twenty chicken nuggets in one sitting. I also used to purchase a large bucket of fried chicken on a Friday night, peel off and eat all the skins from the chicken throughout the night, and eat the chicken for every meal from Saturday to Sunday until it was done. I had done this on many weekends—it was not a one-time deal. I was a regular at all the fast-food restaurants—you name it. I loved soda, slushies, cakes and pastries, and any snack I could get my hands on. Nothing was off-limits for me. I ate and drank whatever I wanted, whenever I wanted, for as long as I wanted. The fact that I had severe stomach and sinus issues was not a deterrent for me. I felt those were hereditary traits that were beyond my control.

I stayed the same size and waistline from eighteen to thirty years old. I looked fine, I felt okay, so there wasn't an obvious need for me to make any changes. It wasn't until I ballooned in my mid-thirties and developed deadly cholesterol that I woke up. Linda took all of this in with patience and understanding.

I expected to be scorned and put on a strict diet. Instead, I was met with compassion and understanding. Linda had seen my story thousands of times and was ready to equip me with the tools to succeed.

She left me on my first day with some homework. I was to write down all the foods that I ate for one week. I was to go back to "regular" eating, to be honest with myself, and to write down every piece of food that touched my lips with the approximate quantities and time eaten. I kept doing this homework for approximately two months, keeping track of my food intake. In the meantime, Linda started to develop a list of all the foods I *did* like. Her job was not to limit or punish me for enjoying food. Rather, it was to develop sustainable plans and systems that I could utilize and create a lifestyle that worked for me. I was surprised! I was allowed to eat bread. Rice pudding. Coffee! Linda developed meal plans for me that I would agree to and utilize between our sessions. And then we would meet, review my progress, and adjust my meal plans as we went along.

As we worked together, Linda gave me reading materials on nutrition and eating. I was also doing my own research and incorporating supplements such as protein and creatine into my diet. As each week went along, I was feeling better and better. I was developing a daily yoga practice. I had meal plans that gave me the proper sustenance and a routine. I didn't have to think about it, which made eating so easy. I prepared everything the night before and would have my meals set for the following day. I knew what I was eating and what time I would have it. This slowly became my lifestyle.

After working together for a few months, Linda fired me one day during a session. I was overwhelmed. I couldn't understand how the woman who had helped me develop such a great life routine would not be working with me anymore. She explained that she felt I had the tools and desire to continue on my nutrition journey solo. She told me that she was so proud of me and that I was a top student of hers. However, I had learned the tools from her to build a foundation and now I was equipped to continue on that path—to move forward with my evolution and growth, as well as one day helping inspire others to make their best food decisions. I embraced Linda McCharles and thanked her for all she did for me. When I walked out of her office that day, I was determined to continue eating healthily while maintaining and growing my newfound lifestyle.

It has now been over ten years since I last saw Linda. I am proud to say that I am healthier and happier than ever. I never went back to my old ways. I discovered the 6 Commandments of the Chosen Life along the way and adopted them daily ever since.

I've definitely had a very interesting time evolving my eating routines over the past decade. There are so many buzzwords that are thrown around when it comes to nutrition—feel free to adopt as many (or as few) as you wish. It is not about the labels; it is about the outcome. Nutrition, healthy eating, clean eating—whatever you want to call it, that's fine. Note that they all lead to the same page, so do not get fixated on the words and definitions.

I have tried many different diets and eating patterns over the past few years, not to search for a quick fix, but to experiment and learn what is good for my body and better understand what my body needs.

The main regimes I have tried and incorporated are the Mediterranean diet, the ketogenic diet (otherwise known as keto), intermittent fasting (IF), and being an ovo-pescatarian (quasi-vegan). As far as keto goes, I went heavier on the protein and lightened up on the carbs. For the Mediterranean diet, I incorporated more grilled chicken, olive oil, and salads into my lifestyle. I still use parts of the keto and Mediterranean diets to this day. I eat fish approximately one to two times per week. I love eggs, but they do not always agree with me. When I was a teenager, I couldn't eat eggs as I would break out into hives after eating them; I developed a food allergy. That came to pass, though, and I did fall in love with eggs again. Sometimes I still find that my body has a hard time digesting them, and the same with some other foods. If that is the case, there are digestive enzymes or other supplements to assist with the digestion process. If you have not supplemented before, speak to your doctor about taking food allergy tests and find out what foods your body does not like or has a hard time digesting. You can save yourself a lot of time and aggravation learning this information.

Around the time I went into bodybuilding and fitness competitions in 2019 is when I was deep into intermittent fasting. That type of dieting was all the craze at the time, and I found the concept intriguing as I was looking to achieve very low body fat (I made it down to eight percent or so at my peak) and intermittent fasting sounded like a great ticket. I did two twenty-four-hour fasts every week, and then the 16/8 schedule for the remaining five days (sixteen hours fasting with an eight-hour eating window). Using IF made my life much easier. I ate much less than I ever had before and had a very easy eating schedule for five days. I really enjoyed it, and it was a great route for me to lose weight and tone up. Nevertheless, I eventually made the decision that for my physical strength in the gym that it was hurting more than it was helping me. I became tired, weak, and was unable to hit my numbers on weights. I was not concerned about being too bulky, but I wanted to feel strong and lift a good amount of weight. I decided that IF was no longer my ticket to my desired route, so I let it go shortly after my competition. Again, like anything, it is a great tool that is available, just not for everyone.

* * *

As I warned you earlier in this chapter, creating one eating program that will suit everyone will NOT happen. At least not in this book—or in reality, in my opinion. Who you are and what you need will depend on the many factors that work to shape you, but I will not leave you stranded. I know that as part of learning and following the Chosen Commandments, you do need a roadmap to get you started along the way. In which case, I am happy to share with you *the items that you should/must follow to develop a nutrition program that will work for you, no matter what the method:*

1. **WORK WITH PROFESSIONALS.** We have touched upon this already. So get cracking! Speak to your doctor. Look into dieticians and nutritionists. Consult with trainers and/or people who are fit and that you respect/admire. By speaking to enough people and asking many questions, you will eventually discover a professional who will work with you. Do not do this alone if you can avoid it. Depending on where you live, health plans or insurance may help cover you. Find out your options; you may be covered, and this will be a free benefit. Otherwise, if you can afford it, please hire a professional. If you have to sacrifice other expenses to make this happen, please consider it as it's an investment in your life and well-being.

2. **MAKE A LIST OF YOUR CURRENT FOOD AND BEVERAGE INTAKE.** I have worked with several different professionals on preparing meal plans and they all wanted to see what I was eating and drinking for an extended period before working together. Therefore, get mentally ready to make your list of every piece of food and all the beverages that touch your lips for at least one or two weeks. Write

down the day and time of consumption, and approximate quantities. Seeing that list is an eye-opener for most of us and will start your road to food accountability. Knowing that you need to write down your consumption, you may think twice about that extra soda or a late-night snack. Just remember that list is there to help you, not to create pain or mental setbacks.

3. **READ, WATCH, AND RESEARCH. THERE IS SO MUCH INFORMATION OUT THERE WHEN IT COMES TO FOOD.** Do your homework! Do not rely on one person to make your choices. *You* are the person who ultimately decides your fate. Be accountable to yourself. Again, ask for references from people you trust. Read books, watch videos, and study online articles. These days, information is widely accessible more than ever. Make notes when it comes to nutrition. You will learn about trends, foods to utilize or avoid, and possible meal plans and schedules. Take it all in but do not get overwhelmed; anything you do better today is already ahead of where you were yesterday. You are looking to learn and grow. One step at a time. This will be based on baby steps and building a sustainable system that works best for you.

4. **WRITE DOWN YOUR GOALS.** Be honest with yourself. What do you hope to achieve? Do you want to lose weight? Gain weight? Do you want a bigger or smaller butt/ thighs/chest/arms (insert body part)? Would you like to adjust medical items such as blood sugar or cholesterol? Do you want to just be healthy overall? Have more energy? When it comes to nutrition, if you have your ideal lifestyle and meal plans, what would you like to achieve? Write down your goals and then the steps you think you need to take to get there. Look at your goals

daily and consider if you have a strong grasp of your required steps. Get ready to adjust that list. And know that an important goal to you today, such as losing weight, may be meaningless in the future. Your goals may shift, but the hard work and determination should stay no matter what.

5. **MAKE A CATEGORIZATION LIST OF FOODS.** This will help you and/or your professional to make your meal plans. Create a list of all foods that you hate, food allergies, sensitivities, and foods that you love or cannot live without. You can make as many lists as you want. You can put down foods that you like occasionally. Foods that you don't hate but simply prefer not to eat. You decide. In developing meal plans, you will then try to incorporate as many of the foods you love and look for substitutes for those you hate or have allergies and sensitivities to.

6. **A MEAL PLAN IS COMING.** There is no working around this. If you are committed to effectively eating nutritious food on a consistent basis, then a game plan will be your best friend. This meal plan can be as lax or rigid as you want it to be. It can have specific times, foods, and quantities for you each day of the week. Or you can go as lax as having time intervals and approximate categorizations of food where you choose what to eat. But please note: the more rigid you are, the more disciplined you will be. The laxer you are, the more likely you will not stay focused. It will not be forever, and the plan can evolve. But try to make the commitment, as long as you can, to stick to a set food schedule—timing and foods—so that you stay on track. Be prepared to evolve that list each week, with a professional or on your own.

7. **FOCUS ON LONG-TERM PROGRESS ONLY.** I know this is hard to hear, perhaps, but the scale is not usually your friend. Weighing yourself daily or even weekly will not get you results; it will cause you stress and pressure. This is not what you need right now if you want to develop a long-term nutrition lifestyle. If you follow a nutrition schedule, know that your weight may go up or down. You may look the same to yourself as the days go by. However, you should feel better. Healthier. More motivated. When it comes to nutrition, we are so focused on our bodies that we neglect our minds and souls. When I was eating solely for my body, I lived and died at every weigh-in. When I started to eat for my body, mind, and soul, the pressure was off. I knew that my food intake was working since I had energy, my mind felt clear and sharp, I was motivated and inspired, and my body looked good as an added bonus. Therefore, please know what your goals are, but always maintain a long-term focus. Remember: we are concerned about a lifestyle and not a quick-fix diet.

When I reflect on my past, my biggest regret is about the way I abused myself for close to thirty-five years through poor eating choices. Not only did I cause hurt and damage to my body, but I can also see my lack of mental clarity and spiritual awareness. Every part of me was damaged by the food I consumed. But I choose not to focus on those thirty-five years of hurt. I made choices that I could not take back. However, I did use them as a learning experience to make better decisions going forward.

I have been eating clean for over ten years now. I look and feel younger than I did in my early twenties. My body is stronger than ever. My mind is clear and active. My soul is inspired and connected. I wish I had started my healthy eating routines ten years earlier, but thank goodness I started when I did, rather than ten years later. If I had waited any longer, I don't know if I would have made it to today.

As you have been reading this chapter, think about your own food journeys. Where are you at? Have you eaten well and cleanly your whole life? Do you indulge in many cheat meals? Why do you eat food—because you have to? To escape pain? To seek temporary happiness? Or is it because you need fuel and energy to live? What stage do you feel you are at: are you in a good position, or do you need help to build better nutrition systems for yourself? Whatever you feel, *know that you are not alone.* I have been there, as millions of people have, as well. You do not need to figure this out alone. There are solutions for you to build the best nutrition lifestyle you thought possible. It is up to you to be ready for your evolution.

* * *

Now, let's reevaluate those ten excuses that you may have had when it comes to nutritious eating. These excuses are, for most of us, just that—excuses. *It is time for you to focus on solutions and not these excuses that are holding you back:*

THE NEEDLE ON THE SCALE NEVER MOVES DOWN REGARDLESS OF HOW LITTLE I EAT.

Sometimes we assume that we are doing the right things in life. Maybe we have been following a pattern for so long, that we justify that our choices make sense. That is where the creation of a list of current food intake is so key. *Don't eat to justify your recording.* Make the list as discussed in this chapter and see visually all the food and beverages you are eating each day for at least a week, including the quantities and times. Once you see outright what you are consuming, it will likely make sense why you are not losing weight.

Aside from your water intake, sleep, and physical activity, the food you consume helps factor into your waistline. Know that better food choices will shake up your physical appearance, but this is only one of the 6 Chosen Commandments. If you have truly decided, for instance, that weight loss is important to you, then know that only focusing on food will limit how far you get. The 6 Chosen Commandments working in unison will guide you to much better results.

I LOVE FOOD TOO MUCH TO GIVE IT UP.

I remember once sitting in a lunchroom when one of my bosses came in. He asked me what I was eating with a disgusted look on his face. I told him it was a quinoa and kale salad. He was very overweight with diabetes and was known in the office for his very poor eating habits. He looked at my lunch and told me that he would rather die than eat like I do. I looked at him and told him that I would remember that when I was sitting at his funeral. Grim, yes. But I love life too much to prematurely die. Decide if unhealthy food is more important to you than quantity and quality of life.

I AM NOT SKINNY, SO I NEED TO EAT LOTS.

I love how people determine that they are a certain size which justifies eating large quantities of food. This typically becomes a self-fulfilling prophecy. I've heard this many times: "I am big, so I am hungry all the time, so I need more food." We are not our own best judges. That is where I recommend you sit down with a professional. Let them work with you and develop meal plans based on your height and weight. If you weigh twice as much as someone, that does not necessarily mean that you need to eat twice as much as them.

I CAN'T EAT A LOT IN ORDER TO STAY SKINNY.

I have heard this one often. Even though we are in the age of body positivity, there is a large part of our population wanting to be "skinny" or to look like a bathing suit model, or to get down to a size 0 jeans or skirt, or to be whatever arbitrary size a clothing company puts out there. Do you want to be skinny? Why not be muscular, or toned? How about looking and feeling healthy? It becomes a huge mental barrier when we have to hit targets on the scale and the clothes that need to fit us. Focus on more long-term health benefits rather than arbitrary numbers to hit and you will feel a lot less pressure and stress. You will also build a better relationship with yourself. Whether you are skinny or not—*you are you*. Learn to love yourself, no matter what size you are.

HEALTHY EATING IS BORING AND NOT FOR ME.

We have already covered this in previous chapters. Not everything in life is exciting. What things are is how you perceive them to be.

I now see healthy eating as exciting. I have trained my pallet over time to crave delicious, healthy food. I find greasy, salty, and overly sweet foods no longer to my liking. The food did not change. What changed was how I perceived the food in front of me.

Healthy food may not be for you because you created a roadblock for yourself in how you see it. Write down a new message that will assist you in seeing this differently: *Healthy eating is fun and is for me*. Read it to yourself daily. Create a mantra. You can program yourself to do anything you want to. Try a variety of foods. Create fun meal plans. Incorporate foods you love in healthier styles. You can learn to love healthy food and be motivated to eat it if you look at it through a positive lens.

I AM GOING TO DIE ONE DAY ANYWAYS.
WHAT'S THE POINT?

I've heard this one thousands of times. We don't know what tomorrow will bring, I get it. But having a healthy eating lifestyle gives you a better chance at quantity and quality of life. You are hedging your bet, so to speak.

But even if there is no assurance of the quantity of life, why not enjoy every moment that you are here as much as possible? You will feel better with every day you incorporate healthy nutrition into your way of living. Your body, mind, and soul will all thank you. To live in each moment in a happier and more meaningful way—isn't that a reward in itself? Yes, you will die one day. We all will. But do you want to live a life with meaning each and every day? Or do you want to simply get by and go through the motions? Decide today what meaning you want to give to YOUR life.

HEALTHY EATING IS A MYTH.
IT DOESN'T MATTER WHAT YOU EAT.

Whoever sold you that one has clearly not read this book. Please go back and read this chapter in its entirety, and then try to sell me on how it doesn't matter what you eat.

If someone is telling you that eating healthy is a myth, then they are likely trying to sell you a crash diet or quick-fix pills. There are no easy answers in life. True solutions are built through hard work and solid foundations. Everything else is a myth, to me.

Every component of your life will be better if you eat nutritious food. You will also be more equipped to follow the 6 Commandments of the Chosen Life and improve every other aspect of your waking, breathing moments.

I AM SO CONFUSED AND DON'T KNOW WHERE TO BEGIN. I'M GIVING UP!

I marvel at how many people give up before they even try. When I ask folks why they don't practice yoga, they often tell me they don't like it. When I ask them why they don't like it, they often answer that it's not for them. So they have given up, even without trying!

People are usually scared because of the fear of the unknown. If you do not know how to approach nutritious eating, then chances are you have never done it before. I have given you the roadmap to start your journey of eating healthily. Start with a professional to help guide you. Think about it—I don't perform my own surgeries. I don't change the oil in my car. I don't fix my refrigerator. Why? I don't have the experience or training to do it. Chances are, you do not have the experience or training for eating in a healthy way. It's not your fault—you don't know! So get educated. Hire a professional with the experience and training to guide you. Do your research. Start practicing eating healthily. Practice every day. Everyone has to start from somewhere. Let someone else show you if you do not know how. Ask for help. You will learn the steps to get there. But never, ever give up! We will never learn anything until we are taught, and we get to practice repeatedly. That is the only way to get better...including nutrition.

NO MATTER WHAT I EAT, I LOOK THE SAME.

Everyone has a different metabolism. Just because your body looks a certain way, does not mean that you are eating healthily.

Some people can eat junk food all day and they do not gain a pound. Even though they look the same as they once did, their body may not have much energy. Is their mind sharp? Is their soul energized and full of spirit? Looks can be deceiving.

View food as fuel and energy for your body, mind, and soul. Regardless of how you look, focus more on *how you feel* and your outlook. Nutrition is in place for every part of you, not just how you look in the mirror (see a theme?).

HEALTHY EATING IS A LIE TO MAKE YOU SPEND MORE MONEY.

There is another myth that healthy eating has to be expensive. I've heard this one from many people, including those who are wealthy.

To those people, I ask: how much money do you spend every week or month on eating out? Junk food is not as cheap as you think. Healthier food options are more readily available than ever before at most supermarkets. Even if an item is not organic, it could still be healthy. Do not get wrapped up in labels. Do your research. Shop around. Find grocery selections that fit your budget. Most stores have sales all the time—stock up if needed! But do not let money be the excuse for why you do not eat healthily; cooking at home using healthy ingredients will save you money in the long run compared to eating out at unhealthy, cheap fast-food restaurants and the like. *Your health is more important than money. It is not about money; it is about financial prioritization.* Create the choices that make the most sense for your health and wallet. They will involve more home cooking and packing your meals rather than eating out. There are ways to save money and eat healthier, so be conscious of your options and make the best choices you can.

With plenty of water and nutritious food in your system, you are ready for the next Chosen Commandment. Fuel is needed to get your body moving. Whether you like it or not (and trust me, you will learn to LOVE it), physical activity is critical for your physical and mental health and well-being. Get ready to learn to adopt physical activity into your lifestyle and benefit from the water and nutritious food that you incorporated as part of your newfound daily routines.

NINE

CHOSEN COMMANDMENT #4:
Physical Activity Is a Lifestyle

—⎓⎓⎓—

We have come to a portion of the book that is very near and dear to my heart: physical activity.

Physical activity has been part of my life on and off for many years. It is a subject I am extremely passionate about, for it has been ingrained within me since my youth.

I've always loved Arnold Schwarzenegger. For as long as I can remember, I wanted to be Arnold. I remember getting Arnold's bodybuilding encyclopedia and studying his exercises. I created a mini gym in my family basement and cut out pictures from the encyclopedia, which I plastered all over the walls.

I began weight training when I was approximately twelve years old. Before then, my physical activity centered on tennis, walking, and running. I was never a star athlete and I gravitated toward independent rather than team sports. I had the mindset that I wanted to train and perform physical activities, but I did not have the physique or ability for it, nor was my spirit in the game. I gave up very easily and had a low opinion of my athletic worth. Without determination and heart, my physical activity was in a constant cycle of start and stop, until I essentially abandoned it almost entirely for over a decade.

I gave up easily. I made excuses. My *mind* wanted it deep down, but my body and soul would need to catch up.

Keeping this experience I have shared with you in the back of our minds, let's look at ten of the most common excuses why people do not perform physical activities on a regular basis:

1. **I have no time to train.**
2. **I am already fit, so I don't need to exercise.**
3. **I eat well, so training is useless.**
4. **I don't want to get injured.**
5. **I walk/run/go to the gym on occasion. So I'm fine.**
6. **I have no athletic talent, so I'm hopeless.**
7. **I can't find a physical activity that works for me.**
8. **My health issues are holding me back from physical activity.**
9. **I don't want to be skinny or muscular. I'm happy with how I look.**
10. **I tried physical activity in the past and it did nothing. So, forget it!**

I find it incredible how we allow excuses to become concrete barriers to our development and growth. We lie to ourselves, believe it, and then find it difficult to turn back. When it comes to physical activity, there tends to be a never-ending line of excuses. I only listed ten, but I could have easily listed a thousand more. Yet, as with the other Chosen Commandments, physical activity does not work in isolation. Once you integrate physical activity into your life routine, the other key components of our program will grow:

- If you perform physical activity, you will have a much better sleep every night.
- When you train regularly, you will drink more water.
- Physical activity leads to better nutrition habits.
- If you perform physical activity, you will feel more connected to a yoga practice.
- Physical activity leads to strong and deeper meditation.

One point of discussion some people have is whether yoga fits into the physical activity Chosen Commandment. I can see when one practices a sixty-minute standard yoga class in a studio, that there is physical exertion, no doubt. However, I am a strong believer that yoga needs to be supplemented with additional physical activities.

I have tried different activities over time: weight training, boxing, tennis, walking, hiking… Anything works, it simply depends on your goals. Are you looking for strength? Cardio? Conditioning? All of the above? Do not rely on only yoga to get your conditioning in. Yoga is a full practice of your body, mind, and soul; it incorporates some physical activity and some meditation. I love practicing yoga to help deepen the other aspects of the 6 Chosen Commandments, rather than relying on it as one all-encompassing activity. Your body needs more stimulation than yoga alone. As a result, find what works for you and get your body moving even more.

Your body is your vessel. Let's get it into top shape to carry you through life.

Having our bodies break down because we don't care for them is not an option. When you accept physical activity into your life, you will look better and be more capable to take on greater roles. Plus, you will *feel* better! Physical activity is as much, if not more, about mental shifts than physical ones.

I think back to all the physical activities I performed over my lifetime and the amount of start and stop to all these activities that were involved. This may sound very familiar to you in the activities you pursued over your lifetime. Make a mental note or write down your chosen activities. This list will serve you later in this chapter. Notice also that we are in the same boat: we start, and for some reason or another, we tend to drop off. I sure did.

TENNIS: I played this sport rather consistently and aggressively from the ages of eleven to eighteen. I then gave it up as I got "busy" with school and then work. I was lucky to play one or two games per year from there.

I only got back into tennis at the age of forty-four. Sad, considering that it was the sport that I loved most in my life. But I could not devote the time to make games happen. To understand how much I love tennis, I played it daily in the spring, summer, and most of the fall for the eight-year period spanning most of my adolescence. Most rallies and games lasted three hours per outing. That is a ton of tennis! I went to tennis camps, had private lessons, and overall I became very strong at the game to the point that I could serve powerfully and with accuracy. My forehand and backhand were equally as strong. I could hit the ball at any point on the court that I wanted, with as much spin or power that was required. And I let that flush away simply because I could not fit it into my life and schedule. Now I am busier than ever and still have all the time in the world to play a tennis game. It is never a lack of time. It is a lack of priorities. Think about that.

RUNNING: At the age of twelve I realized I had a knack for long-distance running. We had a race in grade seven. As our run progressed, I was keeping up with the person in the lead, while everyone else was falling far behind.

However, I was not exerting myself by simply keeping pace with the leader. I told myself that as long as I stayed right behind him, he would exert himself and set the pace; that I simply had to follow him closely and not overdo it. I felt I had the stamina for this, and it was a ton of fun. I finished in third place that year.

I kept up practicing long-distance running right through high school. I joined the track and field team and competed for one year. From there, as we graduated, my running buddy moved away to another city. I did not like how hard pavement was on my knees and ankles, so my track career was done. But even when you discontinue performing an activity, remember the lessons that you learned from it. They can guide and assist you in future activities.

Running played a key role early in my life in being physically active. It taught me that I can be good at something active, even if I didn't believe that I could be. It was a great transition activity to get me fit and train to be active. And while running itself was not a long-term activity that fit my needs or preferences, I used the training habits and drive that I learned in future activities that I would take on and practice. I am grateful that running came into my life when it did and provided me with strong skills. It set the tone for my future physical routines, especially weightlifting.

WEIGHTLIFTING: I started lifting at home at the age of twelve, approximately two to three times per week. Once I turned sixteen, I purchased a club membership and started going to the gym with my friends. I trained at the club for approximately four years before hiring a personal trainer for a period of time, and really got into it.

When I moved to a high-rise condominium in the city at the age of twenty, I gave up my club membership and used the gym at the bottom of the complex. Later as I moved into a ground-floor house at the age of twenty-seven, I built a home gym in my basement.

At the beginning of this venture, I used the house gym all the time. Then my workout routine started to drop off. By the time I sold the house, I barely used the home gym at all. What happened? From the age of twelve to thirty I was a steady gym-goer, working out usually three times per week, and up to almost daily at my peak. However, I dropped off at thirty years old and did not pick up a single weight until I turned forty-one.

Imagine after many years of weightlifting, there were over ten years of not lifting at all. Why did I give up? It was for the same reason as dropping tennis.

In my mind it was about a lack of time, but in reality, it was a lack of priorities. I restarted weightlifting later in life. Once I took up boxing and made strength and conditioning a priority, having a consistent weightlifting routine only made sense. I not only understood the benefits of weightlifting, but slowly I was also connecting with trainers who helped teach me the right form and create weightlifting programs that would be sustainable for my schedule and physical abilities. This started in 2018 by lifting weights as part of boxing sessions with one of my trainers. From there, I used several personal trainers until I found the right fit. Since 2019, Jared and I have been training together, and there is no end in sight.

Along the way I competed in a bodybuilding/fitness event in October 2019 and won two medals: silver and bronze. Weightlifting is a success story for me because I started it young, gave it up, and then came back to it stronger than ever.

No matter what stage you are in life, *it can be done*. Sometimes we need to give it time before obtaining the right advice and training along the way.

BOXING: It was one of my lifelong dreams to become a boxer. I started boxing in early 2018 and have kept up with it since. I originally planned to compete in a charity boxing match, but I figured out early on that I did not have the necessary skills to make that happen. And that was okay; I still spent hundreds of hours training with trainers, as well as on my own. I hung up a boxing bag in my home and practiced every chance I got.

Boxing was on my mind for many years, but it was only once I made the plan and commitment that it happened. I will never be Mike Tyson, but I don't need to be. I get a good workout and learn a sport that I love.

When you pick up any physical activity, you do not have to learn it in order to become a world champion. By simply learning and training, you are feeding your mind, body, and soul. Your body gets the workout through physical activity. Your mind stays sharp and focused. And you learn to work hard while having passion and determination to get better, learn, and grow. Boxing did this for me later in life. May you find the activity that does the same for you.

BIKE RIDING: At eight years old I received my first bike as a gift and was an active bike rider until the age of sixteen. Living in Toronto, Ontario, Canada, there is no bike riding between November to April most years. But for approximately six months out of the year, I rode my bike almost daily, sometimes for hours at a time. Once I earned my driver's license, my bike riding days came to an end. What a shame, since I loved it so much.

When I ponder about bike riding, I still to this day think about it with a hint of regret. I wonder why I choose to make excuses and not take it up again. I even have a bike sitting in my garage that I can pick up and ride anytime. Yet, I don't. A big part is likely a scooter accident that I had many years ago. Fortunately, I escaped the accident with some bumps, bruises, and cuts. I was lucky. It makes sense why a part of me is gun-shy about jumping on a bicycle. Being on the open road on a bicycle can come with safety risks. But that being said, I know that I can choose to take precautions. I can bike only during daylight hours. I can wear my helmet. I can choose to only ride my bike on trails or within my neighborhood, to avoid major streets and intersections. So while I have developed such a strong routine of physical activity, there is always room for improvement.

I now feel inspired to add to my to-do list to take up bicycle riding in the spring. As soon as the weather warms up and the snow, ice, and salt are gone, I am ready to take up a familiar activity. I am feeling inspired to make a new change for myself. My hope is that this will inspire you to think of such an activity for yourself and to create that change for positive improvements in your own routine.

WALKING: If there was one activity that I have always kept up with, it's walking. Since I could walk, my mom walked with me every night. She encouraged walking as a daily activity. When I had various dogs as part of my family, they also encouraged me to walk daily.

Walking is a very underrated activity, but as long as you are physically capable of doing it, walking is always available to you. I never focus on what I wear or the pace I keep when walking. Simply putting on a good pair of shoes and walking for as long as you can every day can be the easiest physical activity to start and keep up with. That is why you see so many elderly people walking in the malls early in the morning. It works!

HONORABLE MENTIONS: At various life junctures, I tried swimming, judo, karate, and hiking. I recently picked up pickleball as a sport, which I hope will turn into a regular activity for me even as I enter my golden years, in addition to keeping up with tennis. But these sports started and stopped at such an infrequency that they do not get their own mention; however, they were part of my journey to note.

* * *

Something to keep in mind is that it is never too early or too late to learn and participate in a physical activity. Even if it's an activity that does not stay with you long-term, it can still provide you with tools and knowledge that you can transfer to other activities that you participate in, as well as your life in general. It comes down to the realization that *this is your life*. You can try anything that your heart desires. Maybe you will develop a long-term routine and become very strong at the activity. Or you may practice it on occasion for pleasure or to supplement other physical activities. But it is better to try and see than never try at all. Not every activity will become a staple in your routine. But they will contribute in their own way each time.

As you develop more of a relationship and trust in your physical vessel—your body—you can create and incorporate a system similar to the one listed in this chapter to regularly implement physical activity. As with all things you are doing to follow the Chosen Commandments, take it slow. Do not be hard on yourself. If you do not progress or if you relapse, that's okay. Tomorrow is another day. Keep practicing. Please make sure to refer to the list of activities you have prepared as often as you can. This list represents your journey and will inspire you to start getting more physically active over time. Simple, tiny changes will lead to huge progressions over the long haul. So don't focus on the mountain you need to climb. Simply look at each little step as you start to make your ascent. We will get there together.

Now I present to you ten key steps to incorporate physical activity into your life:

1. GET WALKING

I have always been a big fan of walking. I love the art of walking on all levels; of being outside and engaging in motion. I firmly believe in the benefits of walking for the body and mind. In engaging in this activity, you are making your body work and you are calming your mind. As they start to work in unison, they will eventually invigorate your soul to receive inspiration and energy.

Physical activity in general quiets the mind and lets you get your thoughts out and processed. I can tell you with absolute certainty that many of my best ideas come to fruition during moments of movement. I would be working my body and have the result of an open, clear mind… Then, ideas would naturally flow.

If you need a starting point for physical activity, then most definitely start with walking. This is good to do daily. But if you cannot for whatever reason get out daily, then start with three days a week. You will notice that when I refer to almost any physical activity program, three days a week is the sweet spot. Any less is too infrequent and will not achieve ideal benefits, and any more is a bonus, but not mandatory.

2. MAKE A LIST

As you start to incorporate walking as your first physical exercise, you will get the flavor of being active again. I hope that you enjoy it, as you should!

When you transition into the mindset of being active, start making a list. Think of any and all physical activities you have ever done over your lifetime and then add the activities you think you want to pursue to that list. Any activities you've done before and enjoyed will be easier to get back into. Those activities that you dreamed of trying will be exciting to learn. So, let's keep all options open and have a starting point for all physical activities you have done or are willing to try.

3. PICK AN ACTIVITY

As you review your list, I need you to now pick ONE physical activity in addition to your walking routine. I know you may be pumped up and want to start them all. But let's go with one.

Pick the one that you most crave to do and think is most *sustainable* for you currently. I really want you to think long and hard about this. Take your time; take as long as you need. The activity you choose may not be your forever activity. But you should not start an activity, give up after a few tries, move on to the next activity, and keep repeating. The activity you pick should ideally be tried out for at least six months.

Unless the activity is causing you injury and/or extreme heartache, three months or less is giving up way too soon. So go ahead, think of the physical activity you wish for. As long as it is getting you physically active, let's use that as your starting point.

4. WHERE AND HOW ARE YOU GOING TO TRAIN?

Now that you've picked your physical activity, think of *how* you are going to train.

Will you get a trainer? Are you going to train at a facility? If so, it's time to scout out trainers and/or facilities.

Many facilities offer free trials. Take advantage of this! Or will you train at home? Are you going to use videos or online classes?

If you are going to perform your activity, *make a plan of where and how you will train.* I am a huge fan of personal trainers, as well as group classes. If you can swing it, please get personal sessions to start off. It will give you the best foundation for form and technique. You can also look at group classes in addition to private sessions. Having people in the same boat as you will motivate you to keep coming and putting in the work. Plus, it will make it more fun. In short: we need to know the activity that you are picking, as well as the plan of where and how you will train.

5. MAKE A BUDGET

Nothing in life is free, especially physical activity. You may already have all the equipment you need at home and will train on your own; that is fine, especially if your income or budget does not allow for expenditures. *Do not let a lack of funds stop you from physical activity!* You can walk and run, for example. There may be public tennis courts you can go to. You may have gym equipment in your garage or basement. You can own a bike. You can use videos. *Whatever it is, do not let money stop you!*

That being said, when you do create your budget, please write a list of expenditures for your chosen physical activity. Let's say you want to get into boxing, for example. Review the monthly cost options for a membership, private lessons, group classes, and purchasing equipment. Now look at your overall spending and budgeting in life and see if there is a gap, such as funds that you have allocated for expenditures that could be frivolous or unnecessary and could be better allocated to physical activity.

No matter what our incomes look like, we all have our spending habits. Your issue may not be a lack of funds, but rather a lack of prioritization. Make physical activity a priority and see how magically the funds appear.

6. PURCHASE ALL REQUIRED EQUIPMENT

As part of creating your budget, you will need to have all the equipment required for your physical activity. Don't go too "spending happy" right now. Instead, speak to people in the store and at facilities who run the activity you choose. Find out what equipment you MUST have and what is optional.

If you are training at a facility, they may provide some equipment or have rentals. It is better to get into your activity and see what equipment works and what doesn't work for you. In some cases, the inexpensive equipment may be of poor quality, and you will have to upgrade quickly, resulting in a waste of money. In other cases, the expensive equipment may not be necessary. You can always buy or upgrade equipment over time. Make sure you at least have the bare minimums you need to get started.

7. CREATE A SCHEDULE

Now that you have picked the activity, know how and where you will be training, and have your equipment, it is time to make a schedule.

As with all schedules, go as light or as heavy as you wish. While once a week is the bare minimum, schedule three sessions per week to start if you can. The key here is to make your schedule the week before and stick to it.

Your physical activity is like a doctor's appointment. You will keep it. Do not deviate from it unless an actual emergency comes up. If you schedule and honor it, you will show up. And showing up is most of the work. Remember, a good workout leads to a good day.

8. REVISE YOUR SCHEDULE OVER TIME

Compared to all the other Chosen Commandments that you are incorporating into your new lifestyle, I would say that physical activity is the one you need to be most conscious of in terms of scheduling. Time, injuries, willpower, budget, life circumstances, and so many factors can come into play that can wreck your ability to consistently perform physical activities week to week. Reassess your ability and schedule EVERY week.

If you feel an injury or tingle, do not immediately give up. Talk to a trainer. See if there is a modification or another activity that you can perform. Do not constantly start and stop. Learn which injuries need rest and time, and how to find other ways to keep your body active throughout.

Perhaps you will never perform your physical activity more than three times a week. Perfect. Nothing wrong with this!

You can also get ready to increase the amount of physical activity you perform every week. However, as you get more into your activity, fight the temptation to train daily. At least one rest day per week is needed, perhaps two. Schedule and incorporate rest and recovery days.

If you want to and need to max out, try not to exceed five times a week (depending on the activity). There is something to be said about overdoing it and risking injury. I have been there myself many times. Do not feel guilty about rest days as they are part of the process. Enjoy them. And make sure you are assessing where you are every week and get ready to revise your training schedule as you want and need. Your body and mind need time for rest and recovery. Adapt to your shifting needs as you go along.

9. INCORPORATE ADDITIONAL ACTIVITIES OVER TIME

Never be stagnant and complacent. Your body, mind, and soul will always crave more, or something different.

To combat this, add in new activities occasionally. Perhaps they will replace your current activity or supplement them. In this way you will challenge yourself and not get bored or quit. Variety, after all, is the spice of life. So don't think you are "cheating" on your current physical activity by trying something new. Over time you may want to do both or shift courses to a new activity altogether. You may pick certain activities depending on the seasons. Whatever it is, as long as you are performing physical activities consistently each week and maintaining rest days, feel free to switch up activities over time or perform several different ones each week. Be careful not to burn out by overexercising beyond your limits. Keep track of your calendar so that you stay consistent and maintain a balanced life schedule. Finally, don't forget to maintain a budget so that you will not face financial hardship.

10. **CONSIDER WEIGHTS EVENTUALLY**

The elephant in the room: weights. No matter how active you are physically, I really want you to consider adding some form of weight training to your physical activity routine at some point. No matter what other activities you are performing, you will benefit by having weights in your life.

Regardless of your age and abilities, weight training will help you. I will caution you that compared to any other physical activity, do not go at this one alone. Weights can most benefit you if done correctly, and can hurt you if you do not have proper form. You may need to invest in a personal trainer and/or group classes to learn proper techniques. Do not go from zero to one hundred overnight; learn weights slowly and steadily. Build up your muscles over time.

Weight training will help you get stronger, look younger, and feel better. You will help the quality and quantity of your life. As you progress in having physical activity as part of your lifestyle, please ensure that weight training becomes part of the program. You will be so glad you did.

* * *

A cautionary note: If I was in your home and you were trying to lose weight, I would take away your scale. I am not saying that you can't set a goal of losing weight as part of your physical activity, but please do not make losing weight your be-all and end-all reason for exercise. You should be performing physical activity for life and health. Losing weight and looking good, for example, can be added bonuses. The scale can form a mental barrier for you; it can actually set you back rather than benefit you.

I can tell you from experience that when I was performing at my bodybuilding/fitness competition, I weighed myself daily for several months and kept a spreadsheet of my results. Every week I focused on my weight. The numbers on the scale affected what I ate and how I trained each day and week. I formed a very unhealthy addiction and attachment to my weight and that affected many other parts of my life.

So yes, you can own a scale, and you can check it once in a while. But do not become a slave to the scale. Do not judge yourself about how much you weigh—at any point. Allow yourself to feel good about the physical activity you are doing. If you keep a consistent schedule and pattern, your body, mind, and soul will all feel better over time. And if you have any health concerns about items such as your weight, then consult with your doctor. But do not let that stop you from keeping a regular exercise routine you can sustain.

Overall, please be very careful of the long-term and short-term goals you set for physical activity. What you think is an important goal may be so in your mind, but not in reality. Do not be afraid to work with professionals to set your goals. Your doctor, trainer, friends, self-education—think about what you are doing when you exercise and what goals you want to achieve. The goals should be attainable and motivate you to want to continue long-term, as opposed to holding you back or making you feel bad. Think of your own reasonings when you made your list above for the activities you were considering for training. Were they activities you did in the past for nostalgia, or ones you have always wanted to try? When you consider your physical activity, try to have the child's mind, otherwise known as the beginner's headspace. Perform your physical activities not for artificial goals, but because you truly want to do them. Live in the moment each time you train. Enjoy the training for the training itself, not for what goals it will bring you. Goals and results come and go over time, but physical activity will become part of your lifestyle because you *want* to be doing it, not because you have to.

* * *

Now let's take a look at why the ten excuses to avoid physical activity do *not* work!

I HAVE NO TIME TO TRAIN.

Across the board, this excuse seems to hold for almost everything in life. Physical activity is no different. We covered this already: *it is not a lack of time, it is a lack of priorities.* If you commit to, let's say, three training sessions per week at one hour each, then you are committing to three hours per week for physical training. There are 168 hours in a week. Are you really able to tell me that you cannot find three total hours minimum during that time? I don't think so.

I AM ALREADY FIT, SO I DON'T NEED TO EXERCISE.

You are not exercising for the pure goal of being physically fit. You may look great. Fantastic. You are training for your life and health. Regardless of how you look—or how you *think* you look—you are moving to benefit your body, mind, and soul. Every part of you will win from physical activity. So, yes, you must train regularly as part of the Chosen Commandments. *You need exercise in your lifestyle. Nobody is above this, no matter how you look in the mirror.*

I EAT WELL, SO TRAINING IS USELESS.

I love the ongoing debate as to what is more "important" to health: eating well or exercising. How about both? People need to accept that having each is great on their own and combining the two is even better. Nutritious eating and physical activity are two of the six Chosen Commandments for a reason. If you eat really well, then amazing. I'm proud of you! Physical activity, then, is not "useless"— it makes your physical body fit. It keeps your mind sharp. And it invigorates your spirit. By having physical activity in your life, you will eat better. And the better you eat, the more likely you will want to exercise. They feed off one another. Win-win.

I DON'T WANT TO GET INJURED.

None of us ever want to get injured. Did you ever consider that *not* having physical activity in your life would actually lead to *more* injuries? Without exercise, your body will be slower and break down faster. Physical activity will lead you to being stronger and more athletic, and if you do get injured, you will heal faster. Your body is ALWAYS better off by having physical activity in your life. Being afraid to get injured is an excuse. Get past it! If you get injured, then you will modify your routine and heal over time. If you are getting injured repeatedly, there could be many reasons for it; perhaps improper equipment, bad form, or you might be overdoing it and not resting enough. Whatever the reason, do not make injuries the reason to hold yourself back. The fear of the unknown is anxiety. Do not let the anxiety of what could go wrong hold you back from physical activity or anything else in your life. Live. Seize the day. And make sure it includes regular exercise.

I WALK/RUN/GO TO THE GYM ON OCCASION, SO I'M FINE.

If you do those things, then I agree you are heading in the right direction. But never settle. Ever. Performing physical activities on occasion is a starting point. Let's make an occasional occurrence into a regular thing. If you are not exercising regularly, look at the ten key steps for physical activity listed earlier to see why. Chances are that you are not scheduling your activities (that is the usual culprit) or saying you will "do it tomorrow," or "very soon." Tomorrow will likely not come simply from hope. Look at your calendar a week in advance and find the days and time slots that make sense for you. Then make them happen. You will then be more than fine. You will be exercising regularly and will be GREAT!

I HAVE NO ATHLETIC TALENT, SO I'M HOPELESS.

If we only exercised according to this logic, then only top athletes would train. Many sports teams have athletes without actual athletic talent. But they still play professional sports. Do you know that many only have a strong work ethic? What about piano players—do you think they were all instantly gifted? Doctors? Accountants? Lawyers? Plumbers? This is a metaphor for life, not just sports. People are in their chosen professions and doing what they do because they studied, worked hard, and practiced. Not everyone is born with G-d-given natural talents. In fact, very few people are. But that should not stop them. And that should never stop you.

Once you choose your physical activity, guess what? You may not be good at it right away. In fact, you may suck! That's great. Be happy about it! Remember, you now have the opportunity to learn and grow. Do not look at your lack of athletic talent as a roadblock. It means you have to study from a teacher who can train and mold you. From there, you will practice and slowly improve. You will never need to be an Olympic champion (unless you want to be). As long as you show up regularly and enjoy it, that is all that matters.

Even if you are taking classes and feel that you are the worst in the bunch, so what? Everyone has to start somewhere. You are never hopeless. By simply SHOWING UP to the activity, you are already a winner. You have accomplished more than many other people did that day. Anything you do physically at this stage is a bonus. Any activity you practice is better than none at all. Tell yourself that all you need to do is *show up*, then you will practice slowly. And the less pressure you put on yourself, the better you will feel and be.

I CAN'T FIND A PHYSICAL ACTIVITY THAT WORKS FOR ME.

Impossible. Sorry. That is another weak excuse. If all else fails, there is always walking. Even if you hate walking, then make a game of it. Put on some headphones and listen to music or a podcast while you walk. Try walking on different streets, parks, or trails. Stimulate yourself to make it more fun.

Are you training on your own, or with a trainer/partner/class? You will have a much more difficult time trying to push yourself on your own as compared to the motivation you can receive exercising with a trainer or other people. Perhaps you have not picked the right setting for an activity. Try different facilities, classes, and trainers. Mix it up! Perhaps you will like an activity much better if you did it in a new place. Perhaps you are not using the right equipment. Again, speak to a manager of a facility and/or a trainer to make sure you are using the correct equipment. If all else fails, perhaps you are falling into the trap that you are giving up too easily. Give activities time. You may not love them right away. It takes time to learn and grow.

Bottom line: I recommend at least six months of trying before switching. If you cannot find an activity that works for you, keep trying a greater variety of activities and don't give up right away.

Rome wasn't built in a day. Neither was your physical activity level. And if you don't like it and/or aren't good at it right away, then you are human. Give yourself room to grow and learn. BUT NEVER GIVE UP!

MY HEALTH ISSUES ARE HOLDING ME BACK FROM PHYSICAL ACTIVITY.

Health issues are no joking matter. I understand and sympathize with you.

Have you watched the Paralympic Games? Now let me ask you: are you able to walk? Do you have full use of your arms and legs? If not, then you should watch the athletes in the Paralympic Games to inspire you to remain active despite your disability. And if you are not disabled, then ask yourself: do I really have a health issue? Or am I giving myself an excuse? Only you will know. No one is watching to see if you are lying to yourself. This will only benefit you.

If you fear that your health could impact how physically active you could be, please start with your doctor, as they can refer you to a sports doctor if needed. Together, you and your doctor can review your health condition and make a list of physical activities that you could consider. From there, again I recommend having a personal trainer to work with you when you pick your activity. Let them know any health ailments that you suffer from, and the trainer can work with you on modifications and workarounds.

There are many people who do suffer from serious health issues, and they still find ways to exercise and become fit. In many cases, physical activity can help *improve* their health issues.

Many people I have met over the course of my life have made their health an excuse. They felt that age and ailments made it impossible for them to perform any physical activity. I simply let them know that they can continue to hold themselves back and create a self-fulfilling prophecy, or they can push through and inspire themselves to become more physically fit—and happier and healthier in the process. The choice was theirs as the choice is yours. Do not let limitations set you back. There are professionals who can help you break through. Find them and work with them.

I DON'T WANT TO BE SKINNY OR MUSCULAR.
I'M HAPPY WITH HOW I LOOK.

Fantastic. You have an amazing self-image. This makes me so happy to hear!

Now, let's get past the idea that physical activity is about changing your body.

Yes, you can choose to become skinnier or muscular as *part* of physical activity. That can be an added goal for yourself—but not the ultimate purpose of exercise.

What you look like in the mirror is irrelevant. If you have health concerns with your bodily form, such as obesity, that can be dealt with over time. You can work with professionals, such as your doctor and trainer, to look after any real health concerns with your body. But obsessing over how many muscles you have or how skinny you are is a road to NOWHERE. Those are superficial goals that become unhealthy obsessions over time. Obsessing over your body image will take you away from the *real* goals you have to achieve and can lead to depression, anxiety, and failure.

Chapter 1 focuses on creating and cultivating self-love. This includes every part of you, including your body. If you indeed have that self-love where you are happy with how you look, I am giving you a huge hug. With this self-love, you are far ahead of the game. There are so many people on Earth who lack your confidence and are working hard to get to your stage. That being said, do not take your self-love as a reason not to exercise. You are, in fact, in the best position to learn and perform physical activities because you are doing them for the right reasons—to take care of yourself and not for empty, superficial goals. You will perform physical activity to become fit, take care of your body, feel good about yourself, and become healthier, among other added benefits. When you exercise your body, remember that you also exercise your mind and in turn, inspire your soul.

I TRIED PHYSICAL ACTIVITY IN THE PAST AND IT DID NOTHING. SO, FORGET IT!

I also ate healthily for a week and it achieved nothing. I did not lose any weight. I tried yoga once and hated it, so I gave up immediately. If we continued that logic, I would have never walked, rode a bike, drove a car, or performed almost anything in my existence.

There is very little that ever came easily to me. Activities take time to learn. And performing various activities repeatedly still did not always get me results. I had to continue sustained practice over time until I could see measurable results. Why is physical activity any different? We are built on a society that searches for quick fixes, diet pills, boot camps, physically altering surgeries… Why work hard when you can have a simple solution and all it will cost you is money? But those costly quick solutions are empty roads. You will not have a foundation that you would from regular physical activity. Even if you look good from a cheat solution, you are cheating yourself in every possible way. Your lack of physical activity will cause your body to prematurely wear and break down. You will not have the strong mindset that comes with scheduling, showing up, and performing regular exercise. And you will lack the fire in your belly that comes with working hard and being inspired to push through those exercises. Never, ever cheat yourself!

If you've tried an activity in the past and it really did nothing, ask yourself the real questions: Did you learn the proper way of performing the activity with a trainer and classes? Did you practice regularly? If you went a few times and got little out of it, that is your answer. If you did it on your own and did not use proper form, that is your answer. Learn the correct techniques with professionals if needed. Give yourself months—not hours, days, or weeks—to practice a particular exercise, and then you will see over time that it will do LOTS for you. No matter what physical activity you do, you will discover the benefits over time. You will get better at it and feel good about yourself. You will get fit. The results will come. Give yourself time and routine, and do not put a time constraint on your progress. The less pressure you put on yourself, the easier it will be.

* * *

Upon reflection, you will notice that for much of the above discussion, the greatest hindrance to physical activity is not your body. It is YOUR MIND.

Most, if not all of the top excuses that you are using to not exercise are based on your *mindset*. Your thoughts can drive you to greatness or they can limit your efforts. Sustainable physical activity is not possible if your mind is not into it.

If you are guilty of sabotaging your mind, then again, do not punish yourself. You are human. What you are doing is very normal and real; so many people do it. Even the greatest athletes are guilty of the limiting mind.

There is good news, though. We have a solution as part of the Chosen Commandments that will work on your mind while assisting you to develop calmness and purpose in your existence. You will learn to live in the moment and believe in yourself while wanting to grow further. That magical cure is meditation.

TEN

CHOSEN COMMANDMENT #5:
Meditation

=⟨⟨⟨⟩⟩⟩=

You have completed four of the six Chosen Commandments. You have the basics of living an amazing life down. Now you are ready for the next level. The path toward your enlightenment begins with meditation.

As you progress through the 6 Commandments of the Chosen Life, I will dare say that you may follow a similar path to mine, in the sense that your last Chosen Commandment may be meditation.

Meditation is truly the HARDEST Chosen Commandment to adopt and follow. It may be the Chosen Commandment that will give you the most trouble and aggravation as it will challenge the root of your lifestyle and being. It is also the Chosen Commandment with the greatest upside. You know what they say: no risks, no rewards!

The risk in implementing a meditation practice is that you are working on areas that are severely neglected within you that need the most amount of work. You will be challenged like you have never been challenged before. Your mind and your soul can only evolve and shift up to certain points without meditation.

In other words, to reach your highest levels, you are going to have to accept that with meditation will come discomfort and pain. In whatever form you practice meditation, you will likely not be very good at it when you first start. You may and will give up at certain points. I can essentially assure you of agony to begin with, and the future rewards coming far down the road. You will need to trust and believe in *why* you are meditating. Do not worry about what is to come or what has happened in the past. If you are ready to live in the moment, you are ready for meditation.

It is time to feed your soul. To calm your mind. You are being called to learn about yourself and to train your thoughts. Meditation will help you learn who you are and become who you want to be.

The vast majority of us on Earth live in our minds. This is a fact. The mind is not always a great place to be. Until we truly work on calming our minds, we will never break free of certain cycles, such as doubt and punishing ourselves. Symptoms like depression fall on us as we regret the past. Anxiety hits when we worry about the future. In our minds, we are either living in the past or future, but rarely in the present.

Without living in the moment, how are we possibly going to be our strongest mental selves?

Yoga and meditation go hand in hand in so many ways. For me, yoga was a gateway to meditation. Learning to lie in a śavāsana position before and after every yoga class was my introduction to meditation. I worked my way up to guided meditation classes at my yoga studio and then eventually at my Buddhist temple.

Today there are online videos, classes, and apps, many of which are free to use. Meditation is everywhere now. It is up to you to find it.

Let's start from the beginning. To uncover your meditation practice, let's begin with *the top ten excuses to NOT meditate:*

1. **It is boring.**
2. **I cannot sit or lie still.**
3. **My mind can't stop racing.**
4. **I've tried it before. It doesn't work for me.**
5. **I can't find a studio near me or a class schedule that suits me.**
6. **It is too hard to learn.**
7. **I am not Buddhist. Meditation goes against my religion.**
8. **I don't have time to meditate.**
9. **I don't like it (even though I never tried it).**
10. **I am not a natural like you, meditation does not come easily to me.**

I know you have heard the *term* "meditation." Unless you have been living under a rock, meditation is everywhere! So many experts and teachers are advocating for the use of meditation. But you, my friend, tend to be resistant. You have your excuses and are holding onto the fact that for whatever reason, meditation is not for you. That is okay. It took you a lifetime to build your wall to defend yourself against allowing meditation into your life. Now it will take us another lifetime to tear down that wall and build a foundation of openness in which meditation fits into your world. It can happen. It will happen when you accept that it is there.

Do you honestly believe in your mind that meditation is reserved for Buddhist monks and spiritual enthusiasts? What if I told you that anybody and everybody can use a form of meditation in their lives? For you, meditation may be defined as sitting still for hours in a fixed posture and holding your hands across your legs, deep breathing, and chanting. You would be technically correct. But what if I told you that you can walk and meditate? Or lie down in bed and meditate? Meditation can be anywhere and everywhere. As long as we get our basics down, meditation can be the simplest thing in the world. So do not focus on what you *think* meditation is or has to be. Learn what forms meditation can take and simply find and adapt what works for you.

Note that meditation, like the other Chosen Commandments, does not work in isolation. Insertion of meditation into your lifestyle will improve your ability to follow the other Chosen Commandments:

- If you learn to meditate, you WILL sleep better.
- Meditation will create further ease to consume more water as part of your lifestyle.
- Meditation will lead to better and more focused nutrition and eating habits.
- Meditation will result in more structured physical activity for you.
- Once you are able to meditate, your yoga practice will only grow and thrive.

Every part of your life will be better if you meditate. You have nothing to lose and everything to gain. All your life decisions and choices begin with your mind. How you think, act, and feel is connected to your mind.

If I can offer you a guaranteed solution to fix every part of your life, why would you not take it? Meditation is here. It is ready for you.

Let's create the best life for you possible. You have learned to sleep, drink water, eat well, and perform physical activity. Now it is time to bring it all together with a strong and focused mind. You are ready for meditation.

* * *

It is time to build our meditation system.

1. FIVE-MINUTE FOUNDATION SETTING

Let's start with the simplest possible meditation. Choose how you want to sit. You can sit on a chair. You can sit on the floor. You can use cushions or any props that you wish. Pick any seated posture that feels right to you. If you start by sitting on a chair, eventually move to cross-legged on the floor. But do not focus on *how* you are sitting or the props. All I want you to do is sit up straight. Set a timer for five minutes. Put your hands on your lap. Close your eyes. And breathe.

Breathe in through your nose. Breathe out through your nose. Choose whatever length of breaths you want. But make sure your eyes are closed. And try to sit still; avoid fidgeting as much as possible. I am not asking you to sit for an hour. *Just five minutes.*

During your first sessions, you will have dozens, if not hundreds of thoughts. That's okay. Keep sitting. Keep breathing. Hands stay on your lap. And keep focusing on your breath.

Anytime you go to meditate, please try to make it as early in the day as possible. All of my spiritual teachers have taught me to meditate in the morning for maximum benefits. The earlier in the day you meditate, the more open and clear your mind is. You have the opportunity to create a fresh start for your day with an open and positive mind.

While meditation has the long-term effect of calming the mind, this can take a great deal of time and patience. When you sit down as a novice to start a meditation session, you will find that many thoughts come to the surface—good and bad ones. As you are alone in silence, it is inevitable that overthinking can occur. It takes time and energy to learn to clear out thoughts in general when meditating. As you become an experienced meditation practitioner, the number of thoughts you have will begin to lessen and you will begin to feel clearer.

I can attest that late-night meditation sessions caused me to have nightmares and uneven sleepless nights. You can certainly try it out and perhaps your mind and body work differently. It doesn't hurt to meditate at different times in the day to see what works well for you and what is sustainable for your schedule. Know that if you are unsure, try to meditate as early as you can in the day.

Watch the clothing you wear during meditation. Use loose-fitting and flexible clothing that will not constrict any parts of your body. You can practice in your yoga outfit, in undergarments, or your birthday suit. Whatever is comfortable for you. Wearing too many layers that are constrictive will make it harder for you to sit comfortably and peacefully, so try different clothing options until you find the right combination. If you are hot or cold, add or remove clothing as needed.

Also, please try to schedule your meditation sessions just like you schedule all the other parts of your life. Commit a week ahead as to when you plan to meditate. I advocate having at least three sessions per week of any activity in order to make it a regular practice. Start with once a week if you need to and work your way up to three meditation sessions each week. Stick to a schedule and commit to following through. Organized planning leads to fruitful results.

No matter the number of times per week you practice, stick to five minutes per session. Your five-minute sitting meditation sessions are the scheduled ones.

Feel free to supplement your sitting meditation practice with other forms of meditation. You can always walk and meditate, sit outside with a cup of coffee or tea and meditate, or lie down in your bed and meditate. The key to meditation practice is not the form at this point in time. You do not have to close your eyes and try to turn your mind to another world. Your focus should solely be on breathing. It is about learning to breathe in and out of your nose. *Breath is life.* When you are meditating, you are breathing in new life to yourself and breathing out what you do not need. You are learning to breathe. You are learning to live and rejuvenate yourself. You are learning meditation.

2. TEN MINUTES (OR MORE) OF SITTING

Once you have achieved five minutes of a sitting meditation over a sustainable period, start to practice for ten minutes. Over time, if your body and mind allow you to go beyond ten minutes, by all means, go for it. But I do not want you to burn out.

You may feel that you are not doing it correctly and have doubts that your meditation practice is going well. Let go of those worries. This is not a competition. If you are able to sit still, with your eyes closed, breathing in and out of your nose, legs crossed, hands on your lap for ten consecutive minutes, you have won. The competition has been met. Even if you have been thinking thoughts the whole time, don't worry. Cleansing of the mind will come. For now, simply build yourself to the point that you can sit for ten minutes per session.

Once you are doing a minimum of three meditation practices at ten minutes each per week, you are there. You will never have to do more than this in your life!

When you are ready to learn further and grow your meditation practice, then we have tools for that as we go through the various components of the meditation system.

3. MEDITATION CUSHIONS

Meditation is the cheapest activity to perform on the planet. You need nothing. You come as yourself. Wear what is comfortable. Sit on the floor. You can put a pillow or blanket underneath you. You can spend zero dollars and have a meditation practice. Money is not a factor when it comes to meditation. What is needed is simply your time and allocating your availability to *sitting still and breathing.*

For more advanced practitioners, you may want to invest in meditation cushions. Look up shops in your area, or order online. I like to go into stores and try out the cushions and speak to the store reps. They are usually advanced meditation practitioners who can help you find the right cushions based on the level of your practice and body form. There is a great deal of variety when it comes to meditation cushions, including size, shape, and materials utilized to construct the inside and outside of the cushions. I would suggest not focusing on the appearance of the meditation cushions. Instead, try sitting on each one until you find the right level of firmness and comfort that you can envision utilizing during meditation practices in your future.

Meditation cushions are not a myth or a hoax. They do work! The right meditation cushion will allow for an easier time to sit still and practice meditation at your pace. Plus, owning a meditation cushion may motivate you to practice further and more steadily. I eventually purchased several cushions and placed them in ideal locations in my home and office that were most tranquil and conducive to meditation. Try it out—you have nothing to lose!

4. MEDITATION APPS

I love meditation apps on so many levels. They can be used for a myriad of purposes to achieve life goals, not only to learn meditation. I personally enjoy using meditation apps, as there are many different ones that you can find and use. Most of these apps have free versions and if you enjoy them, you can purchase the paid version. I highly encourage you to try them out at your leisure. You may be taken aback by how quickly you fall in love with your chosen app.

I mainly used meditation apps to learn how to sleep. Guided sleep meditations helped me find my comfort pattern for a consistent, great night's sleep.

Meditation is a very individual activity and one that we are often uncomfortable with learning early on in a group setting. An app allows you to receive instruction while still giving you privacy and freedom to learn at your own pace. The amount of uses for guided meditations is endless on the road to self-improvement. For example, some use meditation apps for conscious eating habits, or to build better relationships with others.

If you're unsure about which apps to consider, search the top-rated meditation apps. You can also speak to meditation practitioners you know and trust. There is a world of meditation apps out there. You may find the one that works for you.

5. MEDITATION CLASSES

Once you have mastered meditating for ten minutes at a time regularly each week, with the possible help of meditation apps, you are now ready to graduate to the next levels.

For me, like every other activity I have learned and practiced, I would have never grown without masterful teachers instructing me. I have lost count of the number of facilities I have practiced meditation in, but there have been many. Not just in quantity, but in the diversity of the settings. I have experienced meditation in small pitch-black rooms, all the way to large and beautiful temples containing sun-filled meditation spaces and breathtaking pictures on the wall.

Let's summarize some particular meditation classes and settings that you may want to consider:

YOGA STUDIOS/GYMS: You might be surprised that the facility you are a member of offers meditation as well. If you belong to any kind of club or facility that offers workouts and/or yoga, check to see if they have any meditation classes. I took my first meditation classes at my local yoga studio. Every Sunday afternoon I would join the class to learn how to sit or lie down for an extended period of time, while following the instructions for guided sessions. These are more casual settings for meditation classes and are a ton of fun. A must for beginners, in my opinion.

ORGANIZED MEDITATION CLASSES: Surprisingly, there are a lot of meetups and group-organized sessions dedicated to meditation. These are generally not affiliated with any religious group; they are simply a group of people with a passion to learn and grow their meditation practices. I have seen people outdoors in the park on nights and weekends, in condo meeting rooms, people's homes… They are everywhere! Again, search for meditation classes in your area and speak to people you know who may be familiar with such gatherings. Make sure to be safe and only go to trusted groups and areas. The more inclusive and public the gathering, the safer it will likely be. For one-on-one meditation classes, do your research on the instructor and make sure they are safe and legit.

RELIGIOUS TEMPLES: I have attended countless meditation sessions at my chosen Buddhist temple. But I have also attended Hindu temples and other religious facilities that offered meditation sessions through invites from friends. A really great way to learn about religious meditation sessions is by speaking with friends and colleagues who may have access to such facilities. Research on the internet. Find out if you have to RSVP or drop in. Double-check the cost and requirements. While religious meditation classes are often very structured and rigid, it will be up to you how prepared you come. The key is to drop any limitations and expectations that you may have. Some of the language spoken may not be your dialect and will be foreign to you. Your purpose is not to come and change your religious affiliation, but simply to learn meditation through a different set of eyes.

If you belong to a particular religious affiliation or temple, perhaps check to see if they offer meditation sessions. And if not, perhaps suggest that they do! You may open a whole new world to your temple through gathering in meditation. I understand that religion may not be your cup of tea, especially attending a religious institution that is not your own. If that is the case, please be ready to open your mind and heart. You are learning to meditate. I am thankful that I learned to grow my meditation practice through Buddhism. And in the process, I became a JewBu.

RETREATS: For next-level meditation mastery, it doesn't get better than this. While a meditation retreat will not allow for the perfection of meditation (there is NO such thing as perfect), it will certainly help foster love and excitement for your practice. I love retreats in general for any kind of learning and growing. I have done yoga retreats in the past and they are a blast. Meditation retreats are the same way. If you research Vipassana, you will find that in order to qualify for their retreats, you will need to sign up for a ten-day SILENT retreat. Imagine a world where you have no phone, computer, or television. And there is no talking for ten total days. All you do is sleep, eat, walk, and meditate. All in silence. While I have never undertaken Vipassana personally, the idea screams of heaven to me. Perhaps it seems like hell to you. But in all seriousness, it is one option, but certainly an extreme one that is not for everybody. For every person I know who has completed Vipassana, they all say the same thing, that the experience was life-changing. But if this is not the option for you, know that there are day retreats and weekend ones to start. Ask around, look online, and see if you can find one close to you. Going away to a dedicated area for the purpose of meditation is cleansing and uplifting. Once you go, you will find that your meditation practice will grow in leaps and bounds. That is a fact.

OPEN THE THIRD EYE: If there is a final frontier for meditation, it is when you learn to open the mystical third eye. It is not easy to explain it if you have never experienced it, but imagine that there is a third eye lodged in between both of your eyes. When you are meditating with your eyes closed and breathing, initially a third eye does not seem to exist or is calcified from years of non-use, for you have become so focused on your thoughts that you cannot begin to open your mind and the third eye.

For me, the third eye became a real thing once I learned to meditate in a calm state. I let go of all my worries and thoughts, the to-do lists in my mind, and I simply focused on the breath. Once my body was in a complete state of calm, my mind eventually learned to follow. When my mind was in a relaxed state, I started to see different colors in my mind. The inner lights within my mind would flicker on and off. Eventually, an opening between my eyes occurred. This is known as the third eye.

Whenever my third eye opens, I see different things. People. Shapes. Colors. I don't go looking at what is in the third eye; I let it come to me (the same thing will happen with you once you consistently practice meditation). Sometimes I see my past or my future. On occasion, I see the present. The third eye teaches me a lot about what I am feeling. It gives me clarity.

While meditation teaches me how to be present and live in the moment, the third eye taught me to see life and worlds beyond my imagination. *The third eye is a product of a successful meditation practice. It is not the goal or end game.* But it is certainly an incredible bonus which I am grateful to experience. With enough time and patience, my hope is that you get to experience the same joy through your meditation practice.

It took years of practice to learn how to open my third eye. This may or may not ever occur for you. Know that there is no pressure and if you never do open it, this does not mean that you have failed or have any less of a meditation practice. But be conscious that the third eye exists and be open to it opening for you. The more you practice and learn from experienced practitioners, the more likely it will happen for you. Always give it time, space, and patience. If it will be, it will be.

To understand the state of seeing life through your third eye is to be in a complete state of calm. When your third eye opens, it's almost like seeing into the opening of another dimension. Your soul practically leaves your body, as you travel through the vision of the third eye into the vision that is ahead of you. It's practically like watching a movie—with you often being the star. The third eye does not open to those who are closed and tense within their minds. If you are truly interested in learning more about the third eye, do not think about it early on if you are starting a meditation practice. Focus on the basics and learn how to meditate. You will not be able to find the third eye through actively seeking it. You need to let go. When the third eye is ready for you, it will let you know.

For some people, the third eye may never open. And that is not a bad thing. You can still have an amazing meditation practice without the third eye being open. But should you ever experience looking through your third eye during meditation, remember to say thank you and smile. Enjoy the ride!

* * *

I am so grateful to meditation on so many levels for the life that I live. Before I learned to meditate, I was truly a very unhappy person. I was tired and moody all the time. My anxiety was constant and out of control, and depression creeped up on me on too regular of a basis. Meditation helped me drop the guilt, worry, and hate. I learned to love through meditation. I loved myself first and foremost. I also learned how to live in my own mind and acknowledge my thoughts. Over time I learned to control my thoughts. It was no longer the case that my thoughts controlled me.

When I reflect on my meditation practice, it was constructed many years ago. I took my first meditation class in my early thirties. To say that my first experience was awful would be an understatement. I could not sit still for barely two minutes. The entire time I was fidgeting to stay seated, while also trying to stop the voices in my mind. All I could do was think about my to-do list and what would be happening for the rest of the day after the meditation practice, and then the next day. It was a beautifully set up practice with a dark room, candles, and soft music. The instructor guided us through the steps to sit and breathe. It was such a relief when the practice was over! I vowed to continue the journey and come back the following week. And I did!

Over the next few months, I continued to join the Sunday meditation classes at the yoga studio. In the interim, I also found a spirituality and meditation store and bought meditation cushions, and started to join meditation classes I found online and through friends. I can't tell you that I became a meditation expert, but I was starting to incorporate meditation more steadily into my world. I meditated on my own for ten minutes per day every morning and went to a meditation class almost every week. What I was finding most was that yoga and meditation started to work together for me. Learning to focus on the breath in meditation really helped me grow my yoga practice. And the time I spent meditating in yoga during śavāsana before and after each class proceeded to open up my meditation practice.

Yoga and meditation really started to feed off one another and help me grow and heal as a person. After each yoga and meditation practice I feel calmer, happier, and more alive. I feel energized with yoga and meditation as part of my world.

It was the out-of-body experiences during some śavāsana classes that most shook my core. I would become so relaxed during some śavāsana sessions that it felt like my spirit was literally lifting out of my body and watching over me. A complete state of nirvana! Once I was able to take that kind of control over my body and mind, I started to hit new plateaus in life. I was able to fall asleep regularly and peacefully each night, as I could calm my body and mind in an instant every time. With a still body and a calm and focused mind, I could concentrate better on breathing and eventually see through my third eye.

When my third eye opened, aside from colors, I would see two possible different images. Sometimes I would view darkness and a black hole, which indicated to me that I was not in a good place in life and needed to make changes. Or I would see the sun, an open bright canyon-like setting, with myself or others always dressed in white. That was my happy place. Knowing that I could now separate my soul from my body and open my third eye at different times, I felt peace and tranquility within myself. Each of those moments felt like the happiest times in my life.

Over time I started to experience meditation retreats over weekends and began to grow my meditation practice. Once I discovered my Buddhist temple, I came with an established meditation practice and was ready to expand my learning and understanding of meditation and spirituality.

Buddhism did not look for me; rather, I looked for Buddhism. But it had to come when I was ready; when I could open my mind and heart and take in what I would learn and experience. I wish that I could have found this peace and calmness in my life earlier. But I'm glad that it came when it did.

It was not until I was regularly practicing yoga and incorporated meditation into my life that I started to truly connect with my soul. From there, I was exploring my Jewish roots and developing a Buddhist lifestyle and mindset. As I attended the Buddhist temple more regularly to meditate and learn, I was also attending Jewish synagogues more regularly. When I was praying and worshiping at the Jewish synagogues, I was incorporating meditation into the process. I was focusing on my breathing and my mind began to open to the experience at the synagogues. My mind was no longer drowning itself out with worries and plans for what I was to do after I finished at the synagogues. I was learning to live in the moment and be present during each and every service. I was hearing the words and songs like I never had before, even though I heard so many of them hundreds of times in my life. Meditation eventually led me to Buddhism, which in turn opened and reignited my passion for Judaism. It's amazing how they all work together.

It was on that path that I became a JewBu—but that was not possible until I was fulfilling all 6 Commandments of the Chosen Life. I was looking inward and discovering myself. Meditation really brought it all together for me. Without meditation, I would not have discovered my soul and my spiritual path. Through meditation, I really learned to connect with myself. Every part of me—body, mind, and soul—learned to speak and interact through meditation.

Out of all the Chosen Commandments, meditation is one of the easiest and cheapest paths to begin, yet it is the hardest one to accept and grow over time. For the number of people I know who have tried and left yoga, I can't think of many who even tried meditation, let alone grew a meditation practice. To sit still and be alone with your thoughts and mind is one of the toughest challenges you could ever face. The easiest thing to do is give up and say that it is not for you. Do you *want* to give up? Or are you ready to really connect with yourself and build yourself up to the best version of *you* that you can be?

My hope is to inspire you to find your spiritual path and what that means for you. I know that you have a soul deep down. You know, as well. But how open is that soul? How inspired do you feel on a daily basis to learn and grow? Building up the spiritual side of your world takes time. If you are ready to begin that process, then you are ready to learn meditation.

* * *

Now that you understand the options available to you to commence meditation and the rewards that await you, let's debunk those misconceptions and excuses that you previously made about meditation:

IT IS BORING.

Is meditation boring? Or are you bored? Face it. By sitting still in meditation, you are alone with YOUR mind and YOUR thoughts. If you are bored, then don't blame meditation. Look inward. Blame yourself. You are boring yourself. A hard realization to swallow, I know. But don't be hard on yourself.

If you are bored, then you are not loving yourself. Take a new approach. See meditation as the opportunity to build and grow your relationship with yourself; to calm your mind and be at peace each and every moment that you can.

Practicing a new skill is not always exciting. It takes repetition. But once you get really good at it, you will benefit from your new-found skill. See meditation as a new skill that you are building. It is not boring. It is so exciting to grow, learn, and develop. It is a skill that will shape you for the rest of your life. Every part of you will benefit from learning it. That doesn't sound boring to me. That sounds revolutionary.

I CANNOT SIT OR LIE STILL.

Fair enough. You are not good at something. I find it humorous when people say that meditation is only for people who can sit still. Quite the opposite. Meditation is for people who *can't* sit still.

The more you *can't* do something, the more you need to practice. If you truly cannot sit still (or lie still to start) for five to ten consecutive minutes at a time, eyes closed and focused on your breathing, then you need to make a 911 call to meditation.

It's not that you can't do it. It's that you are *not* doing it. You do not naturally possess skills in every area of life; you need to learn how to do it. And you need lots of practice.

Everyone starts somewhere. Most of us start being unable to do something. That does not hold us back from trying and starting it. It simply means that we need to be more determined and practice more and more.

Next time you tell yourself that you can't sit still, turn it around and tell yourself that you WILL sit still. Adopt a positive mindset. Lead yourself to new results.

MY MIND CAN'T STOP RACING.

So let me get this straight: Your mind won't shut off, so this is why you *won't* practice meditation?

Did you consider that this is exactly why you need meditation? Don't think that everyone who comes to meditation has a calm and peaceful mind. Rather, most practitioners are in your boat. Their minds won't stop racing, so they are learning to stop it by practicing meditation. A beautiful thing.

If you enjoy an overactive mind that dominates your thoughts and feelings—while in the process affecting your mood, ability to function, and sleep—then I agree, meditation is not for you.

If you are acknowledging that your brain tends to go into overdrive, and you want to work to fix it, then give meditation a chance.

Look, for the first dozen times or more that you try it, your mind may not shut off and in fact, will race even more. That is okay. It is normal. Give it time and do not set out to accomplish particular goals in certain timelines. Learn to be and live in the present. The more you practice, the stronger you will get at calming your mind. Give yourself the benefit of the doubt and don't give up.

I'VE TRIED IT BEFORE. IT DOESN'T WORK FOR ME.

If this isn't the top excuse for most or all of the Chosen Commandments, it is certainly up there. Why should meditation be any different? Do you know what you call someone who tries something once, twice, ten times, daily—for a month, even—and quits? That's right. A quitter. Is that how you see yourself? Are you a quitter? I hope that is not how you view yourself. Here I am presenting you with the opportunity to heal every part of yourself. No drugs. No expenses. Are you really going to pass that up because you have to invest time and work at it? You are not a quitter. You are a winner. Don't let your mind defeat you. Make your mind work for you. Don't tell yourself that meditation does not work for you. Tell yourself that meditation will do the work for you. Think positively and you are already half-way there.

I CAN'T FIND A STUDIO NEAR ME OR A CLASS SCHEDULE THAT SUITS ME.

Depending on where you live, there might not be convenient organized meditation classes near you. That's okay. You have the system to learn meditation right in this chapter. The first step is to practice ON YOUR OWN! Nothing fancy. No tricks or gimmicks. Learn to sit and breathe for five minutes at a time. And slowly work your way up to ten minutes. You also have apps that can help you, and accessories you can purchase to assist you along the way.

Over time, you can start getting creative to practice group meditations. There are online videos and classes you can join, for example. Plus, you can think outside the box. You can research religious temples that hold meditation sessions and classes. Even if you do not belong to that religious sect, I'm sure they would be pleased to have you join them and bring your energy to the group.

So don't give up because you can't immediately find an organized group for meditation. By learning to meditate on your own you may in fact organize your own group meditation sessions in the future. How cool would that be?

IT IS TOO HARD TO LEARN.

We have been through this before. In learning to adopt the Chosen Commandments into your lifestyle, you are not being asked to perfect difficult tasks. You are not installing an air conditioner. Or fixing a roof on a house. You are not constructing a jet engine for an airplane. You are being asked to sit. Close your eyes. And breathe.

Three of the simplest tasks on the planet. Nothing more. You already know how to do these things. They are nothing to you. In fact, you do them every day repeatedly. For most of your life! All you have to do is put the three of them together for an extended time. Don't tell yourself that this is an impossible task to achieve. Tell yourself that this is the easiest thing to do. You know how to meditate. It is ingrained within you. Now let it out freely. Stop holding yourself back.

I AM NOT BUDDHIST.
MEDITATION GOES AGAINST MY RELIGION.

To be clear: nobody is asking you to become a Buddhist or to convert to any religion. You can follow your existing religious path, adopt one or more new ones over time, or become an atheist. That's your choice. That has NOTHING to do with meditation.

The fact that I fell in love with Buddhism is my choice. And becoming a JewBu was also my choice. Meditation led me to finding my spiritual calling, but it was not a prerequisite to become a Buddhist in order to meditate. Meditation is many things, but it is not an exclusive religious tool reserved for Buddhists. I meditated before I ever experienced Buddhism.

Many religions and cultures believe in the powers of meditation. So do medical practitioners. It is a strong tool to build mental health. The fact that it also builds spirituality and fire in one's soul is a bonus. If you have strong religious principles and values within your chosen religion, I salute you. I dare say that adopting meditation into your life will only bring you closer to your religion, as it did for me in Judaism. You are not cheating on your religion by learning meditation. You are building a strong foundation for your life and well-being. Every other part of you—including your religion and spirituality—will only benefit from it.

I DON'T HAVE TIME TO MEDITATE.

You cannot spare five to ten minutes per day, at least three days per week? At the bare minimum, I am asking you to set aside fifteen minutes PER WEEK for yourself. Do you have time to sit on the couch and watch TV? Do you have time to be on social media? Go on your smartphone and see how much time you spend there. Ten hours per day? Five hours per day? Two hours per day? If you have time for social media, you have time to meditate. It is not a lack of time. It is a lack of priorities.

By adopting the 6 Commandments of the Chosen Life, you need to allocate time every day to maintaining the six key components to improve your life, well-being, and to help form the best version of you. Don't say that you don't have time for yourself. Remember, to love yourself is the foundation on which life is built upon. Once you learn to love yourself, you will learn to make time for yourself to work and build upon all the steps that you need to take. You have time to meditate. Start immediately. Show yourself. And schedule your sessions ahead of time each week. By putting your meditation sessions on the calendar, THEY WILL HAPPEN!

I DON'T LIKE IT (EVEN THOUGH I NEVER TRIED IT).

This argument didn't work when you were three years old. And it won't work now.

For most of you who claim that you don't like meditation, let's get real. You haven't even tried it! Make the commitment to yourself. Build a steady practice for at least six months. If you really don't like it, then you need to question why you don't like it.

Look, meditation will never be the same thing as sitting on a sandy beach and sipping on a piña colada. Or maybe it can be if you make it enjoyable in your mind.

If you go into an activity and decide that you will hate it—then you will hate it. Do you go to work every day dreading every second of the day to come? Or do you go in with a positive attitude looking forward to an amazing day ahead? Think about it. Meditation is a metaphor for your whole life. Are you living it in peace and happiness? Or in sorrow and despair? If you really don't like meditation, then you need meditation. Immediately. Remember that. Meditation is not your enemy. Meditation is your ally to help and heal you.

I AM NOT A NATURAL LIKE YOU, MEDITATION DOES NOT COME EASILY TO ME.

Good news. We are all truly on the same track. I have not met one person who was a natural at meditation. In fact, the best practitioners are those who built a practice over time and found their meditation paths and routines that worked for them. Meditation is not a G-d-given gift. It is a skill acquired through practice and determination. If meditation does not come easily to you, then you need meditation. Do not fight the battle. Embrace the challenge. Keep trying. Day after day. Week after week. Month after month. It may (and likely will) take a long time. But it will come to you. And you will get better at it. Your mind, body, and soul will align much better as you become more experienced. The best things in life are rarely handed to us. They are earned. So think of meditation the same way. Don't expect someone to hand it to you. Go out there and earn it. You will enjoy the road ahead that much more because it will come from you.

* * *

Now that you have learned and adopted meditation in your lifestyle, you have five of the six Chosen Commandments down! Only one more to go: yoga.

I purposely chose for you to start with meditation before yoga. This is a much easier path than the one I took with respect to the Chosen Commandments. I adopted yoga first and learned meditation through my yoga practice. Once you have meditation regularly in your life, yoga will be a snap!

The hardest part of yoga for most practitioners is śavāsana, which is lying on your back with your arms and legs stretched out in stillness. With meditation, you have learned to breathe while sitting down for a set amount of time. Now take the same breathing and focus what you learned in meditation, and get ready to adopt it lying down and in various physical poses called *yoga*. With meditation under your belt, you are already halfway there.

You are now ready to adopt the final Chosen Commandment in our series—the original Chosen Commandment that started it all for me and helped me build the foundation for a strong and powerful life. I owe my existence and everything I have today to this wonderful practice. Get ready to experience *yoga*.

ELEVEN

CHOSEN COMMANDMENT #6:
Yoga

Congratulations! You have done it. You have made it to the sixth and final Chosen Commandment: YOGA!

I struggled for the longest time whether to label this Chosen Commandment as the top or bottom on the list. In my case, yoga was the first out of the six. It was my starting point; the conduit to help me commence and process all the other Chosen Commandments into my life. Perhaps it will be for you, as well. But chances are, it will be your last Chosen Commandment, simply because you are either following some or all of the other Chosen Commandments already. Or, it is simply easier for you to commence with smaller steps.

Do not get too focused on the labeling of the order of the Chosen Commandments. Simply know that having all six in your life is the gateway to higher living. As I indicated earlier, when you read through the 6 Commandments of the Chosen Life initially, please follow them in the order they are presented in this book. Once you create your systems for implementing each into your own life, feel free to refer to and apply the Chosen Commandments in the order that you wish.

Reflecting on my journey, I would not have been able to create my life systems of the 6 Commandments of the Chosen Life if it wasn't for yoga. Without yoga, I wouldn't have been drinking water. Sleeping. Exercising. Eating better. Or meditating. Before yoga, I was a perfect 0/6 in the arena of the Chosen Commandments. 0%.

A failing grade. Looking back, it is amazing that I even made it to the age of thirty. I was in poor health, physically and mentally. I was barely getting by. Ask yourself: do you want a life where you are simply getting by? Or are you ready to get ahead?

By making it to this stage of the book, you have an understanding and a game plan to build five out of six Chosen Commandments into your life. And I have saved the best for last in this case for you. Let's now dive deep into the gift to humanity that is termed *yoga*.

My name is Jonathan. And I love yoga.

I heard every excuse in the book over the past ten-plus years of why people choose not to practice yoga. Here are the top ten in my estimation:

1. **I am not flexible enough.**
2. **It is boring.**
3. **I cannot sit or lie still.**
4. **It is too hot.**
5. **I don't want to get injured.**
6. **I can't find a studio near me or a class schedule that suits me.**
7. **It is too expensive.**
8. **It is too hard to learn.**
9. **I don't like it (even though I never tried it).**

...And my personal favorite:

10. **I am not a natural like you. Yoga does not come easily to me.**

Having practiced yoga for over thousands of hours at dozens of different studios, I would place myself in the category of "experienced yogi." Heck, my home studio still calls me "Warrior 1."

But I do not want to rain on your parade. Confession time? I hated yoga when I first started, just as much as you likely do right now. When I first really started to practice in early 2012, I was attending the same two yoga studios approximately three times per week. And for the first six months, I hated every class. I looked forward to going to each session, but within five to ten minutes I would be miserable. I actually wore a watch to class at this point (after six months I stopped doing that and have never worn one since). Every five minutes felt like five hours. I was standing at the back of the class as well. I was barely able to keep up with the teacher. Regardless of the teacher or the type of class, I was struggling. I felt like everyone in the room was better at it than I was and that I would never get it. The people in the front of the room near the mirrors looked like elite athletes to me. I felt that I was not one of them and would never be. I wanted to give up each time I went. But I never gave up.

What would possibly drive someone who hates an activity to stick to it? If the natural inclination was to quit, why did I not do it? Because I was done running. If I sucked at yoga, then in my mind I had to try harder. I was realistic with myself. I was not a natural athlete. I spent over ten years without any real physical activity of any kind. I was never naturally flexible. I didn't feel that I had much to work with. But I didn't care. I didn't set out to become a yoga Zen master. I wanted to get healthy mentally and physically. And in my mind, yoga was the easiest route to get there.

Think about it for a moment. I went to yoga in many ways because I was lazy. To me, yoga was the easiest route possible to achieve my goals. All you need to do is bring a yoga mat, a water bottle, maybe a towel to put on your mat, and that's it. You can wear almost anything (or almost nothing) that you wish. All you have to do is show up and lie down. You can put in maybe ten percent effort if you want and half-ass the poses. It doesn't matter. All that *does* matter is that you showed up. Your entire validation is that you got yourself to the yoga studio or class, entered the room, and lay down on your mat. Everything else you do after that is gravy! *Yes please, sign me up for that,* I thought.

It's ironic that I swore off yoga after the first class I ever took, yet the thought of the class tapped into my subconscious. The image that I had in my mind from that yoga class and from general stereotypes was health. Specifically, healthy living. In my mind, yogis took care of their bodies. They drank water. They ate well. They didn't smoke cigarettes. Yogis prioritized their health and well-being. Most of all, yogis seemed really happy. I wanted that happiness. I wanted to tap into the yoga lifestyle.

Even though I thought my body was not flexible and would not allow me to ever "be good" at yoga, I figured that as long as I showed up, I would learn to adopt a healthier life routine. I did not decide to take up yoga because I naturally loved it. Yoga was purely a means to an end for me at the beginning. It was the path of least resistance. I wanted to be healthy, look better, and feel happy. If yoga was going to get me there, c'est la vie.

After marinating on it for a couple of years, I finally woke up one morning and realized that I was out of excuses. I was out of time. Changes were going to be needed as I could not go on living in the manner that I was. I bit the bullet the very same day I had my epiphany and signed up for my first of a lifetime of yoga studio memberships.

As a beginner, let's get a key point clear: the physicality of yoga is not easy. And depending on your physical makeup, health, and talents, it may take you a lifetime to achieve the poses, if you ever do. But that does not matter. The misconception of yoga is that it is taxing on your body. To me, that is a myth. With the adjustments you can do and props you can use, almost (if not everybody) can and should practice yoga. Physically, you will do what you can. Yoga is not a competition. It is not a race. There is no best or worst yogi. It's a room with a bunch of people who are practicing yoga together. That is it. Not more or less. However, it is not the physical part of yoga that is truly grueling. It is the mental component.

Did you ever feel the urge to struggle with yourself mentally? If so, then lie down in a room with no cell phone by your side or other technological distractions and be alone with your thoughts. You will find this part much more difficult than any yoga posture you will ever attempt to reach. So, while you may think that your main barrier to practicing yoga is physical, it is really mental at the end of the day.

Your self-made doubts that you will be able to lie in a room and be alone with yourself—and your thoughts—will all come to fruition.

Do not be afraid of what may come out during a yoga practice. Remember: the starting point of everything is self-love. Learn to love and appreciate what your mind has to offer you. The happier you are with your own thoughts, the easier that practicing yoga will become.

The benefits of practicing yoga in relation to practicing the additional Chosen Commandments is a given:

- If you practice yoga, you will drink more water. You will have no choice as you must stay hydrated!
- By incorporating yoga into your life, your sleep will improve. Your body, mind, and soul will be more relaxed each day and sleep will come more naturally to you.
- Yoga will lead to more nutritious eating habits. I have never finished a yoga practice and craved junk food such as fatty pizza or fried chicken, for example. My cravings and appetite started to steer to better food choices, thanks to yoga.
- My body craved more physical activity as a result of yoga. I found that yoga encouraged me to get back to the gym and lift weights. It motivated me to get into boxing. And my sex life and stamina were off the charts! To get a physical activity booster in your life, yoga is a tremendous place to start. No matter what point you are at in your life from an activity standpoint, yoga can help you get to where you need to go.
- Meditation would have likely NEVER entered my mindset and lifestyle if not for yoga. Thanks to a consistent yoga practice, I developed incredible meditation skills over time. Once you start your own meditation practice, you will find that your body, mind, and soul will all benefit as a result. It sure did for me.

* * *

The benefits of yoga are there—they are staring at you in the face. You may have thought about it seemingly forever. Now, you are finally ready to pull the trigger. Maybe you want to start practicing yoga, but you have no idea where to begin. As always in this book, not to worry. I got your back.

Let's review the system for incorporating yoga into your lifestyle:

1. PURCHASE EQUIPMENT

Good news. We don't need much here:

YOGA MAT: I would encourage you to purchase a yoga mat. You can rent one from the studio if you join a place, but it is good to have a mat that you can call your own. When you have your own mat, you can practice yoga anywhere—in your home, office, cottage, studio…wherever you like. Don't skimp on this and buy a discounted five-dollar mat. Head to a yoga shop or studio and ask them which brand they recommend. Look at material, thickness, softness, grip, durability, quick-dry function, color, price—and pick the mat that is right for you. Once your practice grows, you will want a second mat, and likely more. Please also keep your mat clean; most yoga studios have an area where you can spray your mat after class and hang them to dry.

YOGA TOWEL(S): No matter how great a yoga mat is, I like putting a yoga towel down for ease of grip and to avoid slippage during a class. Don't use a traditional towel. Find a yoga towel that is quick to dry and is made to put over yoga mats.

A little pro trick: Wet your towel lightly before you practice. It will grip your mat better than a dry towel. I like having several towels on hand (one for the number of days per week that I practice yoga). Make sure to wash them as soon as possible after classes as they get stinky!

A note on towels: A common error that I see in many yoga studios is people bringing a towel to the practice room in order to wipe down their face and/or body. Do not fall into this trap! If you find that sweat gets into your eyes, feel free to wear a headband or tie your hair with an elastic. But try to avoid wiping yourself down during yoga if you can. By wiping yourself down, you are actually heating up your body. Learn to embrace the sweat, as it is there to cool you down.

WATER BOTTLE: You do not want an open container that would spill if it fell during class. It must open and close easily and be easy to drink from. The insulated types are great for staying cold throughout the class. A good size is necessary to hold sufficient water so that you do not run out during practice. Pick one that is easy to clean. These are all important details to think of. Consider owning a backup bottle in case bottle number one is forgotten or lost.

CLOTHING: Wear what is comfortable and/or appropriate for you. Do you prefer baggy or tight clothing? Make sure your goodies/junk are covered/concealed/stay intact. Not all of us are comfortable with full exposure during a yoga class! Consider all parts of your outfit. For men, it's underwear, shorts/leggings, and a top (tank or T). For women, it's underwear and bra, leggings/shorts, tanks/Ts. Consider the color of your clothing and how it will react to sweat. Keep a good amount of your chosen outfits available between different classes each week. Do not wear the same outfit over and over as they will start to wear and tear easily. And please keep them clean, just like your yoga towel!

YOGA MAT BAG/STRAP: You need a way to carry your mat to class. I like the bag, personally. Some people prefer the strap. I use the bag to avoid getting my mat dirty or damaged in my car and during transport.

YOGA BAG: Whether you pick a backpack or a gym bag, have some sort of easy-to-carry bag that will hold all your gear between classes. Consider having some sort of plastic insert bag so that your musty clothes don't make your bag smell funky!

LOCK: Most yoga studios have lockers. Protect your valuables!

FOOD: Be sure of what you are eating before and after class. Even a simple banana and protein bar can do the trick. A handful of nuts or dates help. Make a plan and try different combinations of food that will be light in your stomach, energize your yoga practice, and saturate you after class.

HYDRATOR: Dehydration is no joke. If you plan to become a serious yogi, there are many healthy electrolyte drinks and additives you can buy to add to your water during and after class. Electrolytes will become your new best friend.

2. YOGA SPACE

Now that you have the required equipment, let's decide where you will practice yoga.

I am very partial to practicing in a yoga studio. I have SO many reasons to recommend this route. In my humble opinion, you will learn and receive the benefits of a yoga practice much better in a yoga studio than you will at home. Even taking a class at a local gym is not usually the same. It may be taught by a certified yoga instructor, but it will not have the heated room, wooden floors, and ambiance of a yoga studio. My recommendation? Research local yoga studios in your area. Speak to your friends, family, or colleagues. If you know any established yogis in your life, pick their brains. Make sure the yoga space has the hours that work for you, including a variety of class time slots and types of classes, a convenient location from home and/or work, the cost of a membership, and studio amenities. Do not be afraid to buy an intro pass (most studios offer a free class or discounted daily/weekly/monthly pass for new potential members). From there, you can always try out multiple other studios that you think may work well for you. The more studios you try, the more likely you will find the space that works best for you. Sign up for a membership package that fits your needs and budget. I am a huge fan of unlimited memberships as they give you an incentive to practice yoga as often as you can or want, guilt-free.

3. CALENDAR

Now that we have the yoga equipment and yoga space lined up, it is time to create a practice schedule.

Check your calendar next week from Monday to Sunday. Then compare calendars from several yoga studios and see how they compare to your schedule. How many days would you like to practice yoga? Make the commitment RIGHT NOW. One day? Two? Three or more days? For a new practitioner, I will let you know that ideally, I would love to see you practicing a minimum of three days of yoga per week, which is the sweet spot. It will keep you lubricated and in yoga shape without falling out of routine. Eventually you can build up to a daily yoga practice if you wish, but I would not go too hard or too fast because you run the risk of burning out early. Practicing three days a week will leave you wanting more, but still fulfilled. Commit to classes and days you know you can attend. Make sure to leave enough time to get to a yoga studio and prepare for the class, as well as complete the class, shower, get dressed, and make it to other appointments you may have. Always build in buffer time. You never want to rush in or out of yoga.

Once you put the yoga classes on your calendar, know that they are confirmed appointments, just like a doctor's appointment. Unless it is an actual emergency, you will honor your commitment and show up. Most yoga studios allow you to sign up for classes online. If you no-show for too many classes, you may get the boot!

4. PACK YOUR YOGA EQUIPMENT THE NIGHT BEFORE

Do not get left rushing to a class without your essentials. Depending on extreme heat or cold weather, you may not want to leave your yoga mat and equipment in the car. But get your mat and yoga bag together with all the equipment you need. When you are done with a class, best practice is to put away all your dirty stuff in the laundry room area at home and then pack your clean equipment so it's ready to go for the next class straight away. Good routines lead to results happening!

5. FOOD PREPARATION

Preplan what you will be eating and drinking before and after your next class. Decide if you need a cooler or ice pack, how or when you will be eating, and how (or if) you will store what you will eat and drink. I generally try to carry foods and drinks with me that don't need refrigeration and can go in my yoga bag (such as the aforementioned dates, a banana, or a protein bar). If your food and drink choices need refrigeration, you will likely have to carry a cooler. That's fine, but make sure you bring the food and drink selections with you. It sucks to start or end a yoga class hungry and weak.

6. SHOW UP

This is not hard, but it is for many. You got everything else together …and for whatever reason, you don't end up going to your class. Especially as a beginner, I only want you to set *one* goal for yourself: *show up.* That is the victory. Anything you do during the yoga class will be a bonus. Simply *get there.* Once you are there, you will be motivated to put your best foot forward during the class, but you have no pressure to be an expert yogi. Your only mission is to *show up to the class,* lay down your mat on the floor, and go into śavāsana. Let nature take its course from there.

* * *

I wish that my body, mind, and soul took instantly to yoga. But they did not. I took my first yoga class ever in 2009. I got dragged to the class by my girlfriend at the time. I hated it so much that I did not go back for *three years*—until the point in time when I was prepared to commit to my actual yoga practice.

Imagine if I had given up one of my life's biggest passions because it was hard the first time. I almost did. And so do many others.

Really think about this now. How many things are you good at and love the first time you try them? Can you instantly play the violin or another instrument? How about hitting a baseball, riding a bike, or playing other sports? Did you walk and talk instantly as a baby? No. You had to learn and practice. Most things you do in life did not come in an instant. They took time, effort, and practice. So why can't you give yoga the time and space it takes to develop in your life like everything else? If you do not like it instantly and you are not good at it right away, do not despair. It's new to you. Your job is not to instantly be good at it and to love it. Your job is to show up and practice. Let time figure everything else out.

I will always look back at my yoga streaks of 395 and 365 consecutive days between 2014–2016 as some of the greatest days of my life. They were the simplest and clearest periods for me that I can recall. Each day was very simple. No matter what I had planned otherwise, I knew that I would be practicing yoga. I knew I would feel refreshed, energized, and motivated each day. No matter what I had going on, I knew I could handle it because I had yoga in my life. It took me the course of a year (2012–2013) to adapt from three days a week to a five-day per week practice. By the time 2014 hit, I became the every day guy.

Please do not feel that you have to do what I did; you do not have to become me! You need to find a lifestyle pattern that is sustainable for *you*.

Any amount of yoga you practice is better than zero. Find a way to get regular yoga days into your schedule. For three days a week, it is a commitment of approximately six hours, including travel and preparation. Surely you can commit six hours a week to heal and refresh your body, mind, and soul. Find your schedule. Adjust the schedule as needed. What you need today may not be the same as what you require weeks or months from now. Do not make your schedule a pressure point—it is a commitment that you are making to yourself as a gift.

My yoga practice suffered during the Covid-19 pandemic. Even as I evolved to CrossFit and boxing, I was still a yoga practitioner pre-pandemic. Once the lockdowns happened and my yoga studios shut down in 2020, my yoga practice was slipping away. To get back into routine I signed up for virtual classes and kept them up for a couple of months. From there, I found online videos and instructors so I could watch classes at home at my leisure. I even rolled out my yoga mat on the dock each weekend when I was staying at the lake. But eventually, without a defined yoga studio space and classes, I let my yoga practice go. A torn groin became a convenient excuse for stopping yoga altogether for over a year. I eventually stopped feeling guilty over not going to yoga. I figured I would come back when I felt like it.

Once the restrictions were lifted in early 2022, I noticed that my home base yoga studio had reopened. I did not go back right away. I had built a busy life without yoga, so incorporating a new addition into my life would not happen overnight.

Then, one day, when my body, mind, and soul all felt good and connected, I felt inspired to return to yoga. After a year away, I was ready to rejoin the yoga world. I signed up for a class immediately, and went back to the studio the next day for another class. Since then, I have gone back nearly five days a week for the past few months.

I essentially went back to yoga at the same time that I started writing this book. After a year away, I figured that my body would be super tight and be unable to handle most of the yoga positions. I was wrong. Thanks to muscle memory, my body remembered all the postures right away and I felt like I never left the yoga studio. Some positions were a little stiffer than others, but overall it was truly like riding a bike.

Returning to yoga after my hiatus also reaffirmed for me its overall incredible benefits. While I always appreciated yoga during my days of daily practice, the effects are even more evident as compared to when yoga was not in my life. With yoga, my body is more flexible, loose, and free. My mind is clear and focused. My soul feels energized and more alive than ever. I am much happier again. I am calmer. More patient. Motivated. Ideas start flowing through me once more at a rapid pace. I am much more productive. The relationships with my friends, family, and peers have strengthened. People seem to like me more and want to be around me. With yoga, I have a vibrant energy. I have the "yoga glow." I am now more connected to myself than ever before. And it is clear to myself and the outside world that the best version of myself is back again. All thanks to yoga.

If you have ever steadily practiced yoga, then you will know what I mean when I say, "Yoga glow." When you have a great yoga practice, you leave the yoga space with a yoga glow. Your skin looks and feels energized. You radiate with positive energy. You are calm. To the outside world it looks like you have a glow to your personality and skin. It is the best feeling in the world. If you want to absolutely radiate positivity, practice yoga. You will be glad you did.

* * *

I remember reading a message several years ago at the front desk of my yoga studio: "'I regret going to yoga today,' said no one ever." Think about that. I have practiced thousands of hours of yoga alongside hundreds of different students. Never once did I sit outside of class and hear somebody say, "Damn, I wish I didn't come to yoga today." It's true. So if you know that yoga will only improve your body, mind, and soul, then you know that it is all reward and no risk.

Ask yourself: what is actually stopping you from practicing yoga? It is time to remove the final barriers. I have given you the system and benefits of incorporating yoga into your lifestyle. Now it is time to make it happen.

Still not sure if you want to incorporate a yoga practice into your lifestyle? Let's go back to the top ten excuses NOT to practice yoga. Allow me to incorporate the responses that I want you to consider if you are one of the guilty folks who has ever used one or more of these excuses:

I AM NOT FLEXIBLE ENOUGH.

I have practiced yoga for thousands of hours. Neither am I! My body is constructed in such a way that I can only dig to certain depths for many of the poses. We cannot all be fifteen-year-old gymnasts, nor do we necessarily want to have that kind of flexibility. Whatever your body can or cannot do, accept it. Your flexibility does not define your yoga practice. For any amount of time that you spend practicing yoga, I assure you that your flexibility will improve. If you are zero percent flexible today and become even ten percent flexible in a year, is that not a huge jump? Do not focus on what you aren't. Embrace who you are. Yoga is not about flexibility; yoga is about showing up.

IT IS BORING.

I'm sorry to tell you, but not everything in life is interesting. You are not going to a monster truck rally, eating ice cream on a pier, or jet-skiing. You are putting in work. You are healing and building your mental and physical state. It may seem very uninteresting for a long time, and that is okay. If you are bored, that means you need yoga. If yoga is not stimulating you, this means that you are being challenged out of your comfort zone. Do you want to grow and develop new skills? Of course you do.

A little trick I tried: Every time I went to a yoga class, my goal was to get better at *one movement*. Even if I could move a millimeter deeper or transition it more fluidly, one shift was my goal. The most boring activity can turn into an exciting one. In this case, yoga.

The degree to which it is boring or exciting is contingent on your outlook, so don't think of yoga as boring. Do not make that conclusion, especially if you have never gone or only gone a handful of times. Tell yourself every time you go how much fun you are having, and how interesting it is to learn. Repeat these mantras to yourself and I promise you that yoga will suddenly become the most interesting part of your day...and week!

I CANNOT SIT OR LIE STILL.

Now you will start to see a pattern. You cannot do something. Really? You can't or you *won't* sit or lie still? What is stopping you? The voice in your head? You don't like what it has to say? Sorry to break it to you, that voice is you.

If you really can't sit and/or lie still, then you need to practice. You have to learn. Your mind is racing and your thoughts are in overdrive. Is that how you want to live? If you can't sit or lie still in yoga, then I am going to assume you have really poor sleep, as well. If you think of sleep as an Olympic sport, are you winning a gold medal each night? Probably not. Your sleep is likely suffering because you cannot lie still. You cannot calm your mind. Practice yoga with the art of stillness, and you will be calmer. Your sleep will be better, and you will be focused on improving other aspects of your life, too.

IT IS TOO HOT.

Yoga can be hot. Yes, it is true. It is much like the way that an all-inclusive resort is when you go on vacation. If I offered you a free trip to Tahiti to lie on the beach for a week, would you take it? Or would you not go because it was too hot? That's right, I thought so. You would take it in a second. Learning to be in a hot room takes practice and skill.

Many of us are mouth breathers; that is making us tired and weak. By not breathing through your nose, the heat of a yoga room can feel overwhelming. Practicing yoga regularly will teach you how to breathe in and out of your nose. By becoming a nose breather in yoga, you will feel more alive and alert. You won't be gasping for air as much, if at all. With every class you attend, the room will start to feel less and less hot. The heat will be a welcome feeling, especially on a cold winter day. And if you have a medical condition that does not allow you to be hot in a heated yoga room, then you can always find a yoga space in a room-temperature or cold room. There are options if needed.

I DON'T WANT TO GET INJURED.

None of us want to get injured. I don't know a single person who sets out to live their daily life hoping to get injured. But unless you are in a padded room or wrapped in bubble wrap, then you always run the risk of injury. You can stumble on a loose step. You can get hit by a falling object. As long as you live life, there is always a chance of injuries happening. But I am not asking you to jump over trucks on a motorcycle or wrestle with alligators. By practicing yoga, you are increasing your chances of becoming flexible and helping your body become loose and limber, thus *decreasing* the chance of future injuries. Why do most pro athletes now incorporate yoga into their lifestyles? Because it is sexy? No. Because their trainers want them to increase their chances of avoiding injuries. And if your body does not react well to a certain yoga posture, then you can always learn a modification. Like any other sport, if an injury does happen, you will heal and become stronger after. Don't let the risk of loss ever stop you from doing something. Otherwise, you will live your life on the sidelines in regret, always dreaming of what *could* have been.

I CAN'T FIND A STUDIO NEAR ME OR A CLASS SCHEDULE THAT SUITS ME.

Unless you live in a very small town or in the Arctic, chances are there will be one or more yoga studios near you. Search online. Look them up. Again, find a location that is close to your work or your home. Once you find studio options, try them out as I indicated in the yoga system above. And if you are that rare bird who has no studios around you or classes that fit your schedule, don't despair. Does your local gym offer yoga classes? If not, you can practice on your own with online videos or in a group through virtual classes. Even if you have a studio, you may not be able to make it to classes sometimes based on travel, your work schedule, or general timing. Don't be afraid to learn and incorporate independent practices on your own. The more options you have to practice yoga, the more likely you can incorporate it into your lifestyle regularly.

IT IS TOO EXPENSIVE.

We discussed earlier in this book about budgeting your money. Make yourself a list of every dollar you spend for a week, or even up to a month. Chances are that there is some sort of excess spending that you can replace yoga with. Perhaps eat out less? You can also make your own coffee at home rather than ordering them out. It is not a question of yoga being too expensive or not affordable; in most cases, it is simply that you are not prioritizing your money to your health and well-being sufficiently. Life is all about priorities. Prioritize YOU and what your body, mind, and soul need first and foremost.

If you still find that you cannot afford a yoga membership after going through your financial budget, there is no need to worry. Many yoga studios offer energy exchange programs, where they will offer you a free or heavily discounted yoga membership if you devote a certain number of hours per week or month to assist in the studio, including cleaning and working the front desk. So again, it is about prioritization and making it happen. If you want yoga badly enough, talk to the manager at the yoga studio. They will be more than happy to help you.

IT IS TOO HARD TO LEARN.

I am not asking you to learn to perform open heart surgery or drive a forklift. Strap on a pair of shorts and a tank top, go lie down on a mat. Sip some water. And do as many stretching exercises as you can that are being taught and guided to you by a licensed teacher. You do not have to think about it or memorize the postures. Show up and try. That is not too much to ask. Practice yoga enough and you will learn the very basics, at least. And that can get you through a lifetime of classes. Remember: it is not a competition. All you need to do is practice—not just for yoga, but for your overall well-being. Do not give up on your yoga practice. Do not give up on yourself— no matter how old, inflexible, and inexperienced you may be at yoga. We are all at the same level. Don't worry about learning. Simply learn to be.

I DON'T LIKE IT (EVEN THOUGH I NEVER TRIED IT).

We have covered this before. If you don't like everything that you have never tried, how would you ever evolve? You would never see new places or try new foods. Stop limiting yourself. Stop worrying about what you think you like and don't like. Open your mind and heart to evolving. Come out of your comfort zone. Yoga has so much to offer you and asks for so little in return. You will be giving yourself the gift of life. Use this approach in all aspects of your life. Open yourself and try. And then try again and again. Always have the beginner's mind and the curiosity of a child. This is how you will evolve and grow. This is progress.

And my personal favorite...

I AM NOT A NATURAL LIKE YOU.
YOGA DOES NOT COME EASILY TO ME.

We have covered this one, as well. You are not Beethoven. You can't simply sit at a piano for the first time and start playing. You need to learn and practice.

Congratulations, you are like most of us! I am no different. I started off as a raw yoga rookie, as well.

We all have to start somewhere. Even though some of us will pick up some postures quicker and better than others, so what? Yoga is like life. It is not a competition. It is a practice. Accept your place in the universe. Be proud of who you are. Love yourself. Stop being hard on yourself. Do what you can. Don't worry about what you think you need to be. Love who you are in the moment and whoever you will evolve to over time. You are special. Because you are you. Once you have this feeling within you, then you are truly living and breathing yoga.

* * *

The greatest gift you can give yourself is self-love and from there to incorporate the 6 Commandments of the Chosen Life into your lifestyle. Do not focus on the final results, as they are always changing and evolving. Enjoy your ride and every moment of your journey as you are reborn.

Once the Chosen Commandments are a part of you, the second aspect of our path together is done. With the tools you have acquired, you are ready for the third part of *The Bible 3.0.*

It is time to work toward enlightenment.

PART III:
ENLIGHTENMENT

TWELVE

Intermission: The Road to JewBu

———∽∞∽———

Welcome to your halftime show. Consider this part of the book the "intermission of the performance." You have consumed nearly half of the chapters. You have done so much work already. The hard part, in a way, is done.

I encourage you to read through every chapter thinking about the lifestyle choices you want to make and create for yourself. Know that all the items listed in the third part of this book are next-level components. To be truly successful at them, you need to have the 6 Commandments of the Chosen Life completed and integrated within your lifestyle.

Once the 6 Chosen Commandments are part of you, you are truly ready for working toward higher enlightenment. From here on in are the next steps to reaching even greater levels of life achievements.

I felt that it was very important to take a break right now from the work you are performing on the Chosen Commandments. Please continue to marinate them in your subconscious. Now I would like to tell you the story of my life when I fully connected with all of the 6 Chosen Commandments in my lifestyle. In my case, this was when I became a JewBu.

For myself, yoga, as I discussed, was a gateway for all the other components of the Chosen Commandments. As I developed a strong yoga practice, my sleep, water, physical activity, and nutrition all strongly improved and grew. The final piece for me was the meditation practice. It was a very difficult barrier to overcome as I mentioned in the meditation chapter, but one of the most rewarding decisions I ever made once I regularly practiced it.

I remember feeling very good one afternoon. I was driving on the highway. I had a nice meal and yoga class that day. I was rested and hydrated. As I drove, I saw a sign: "Buddhist temple: next exit."

I thought to myself, *It's a sign!* Literally. I took a mental note of the name of the temple and highway exit. When I got home later that day, I did some research. I had never been to a Buddhist temple in my whole life. Growing up in the Jewish faith, I had been to synagogues hundreds of times. I had been to two Christian churches and one Hindu temple for wedding ceremonies. I was very curious to see what a Buddhist temple would be like.

I had grown up with Buddha statues in my home. My mother is fully Jewish and very devoted to the Jewish faith. She also keeps a copy of the Old Testament (AKA the Bible 1.0) at her bedside and reads from it nightly. It was a wonder to me that she would have Buddhas in our home. I asked her about it a couple of times. When I did, she always indicated to me that Buddha, for her, was not about religion and prayer. She simply liked the look of the smiling Buddha because it brought her great comfort and joy.

There are two types of Buddhas I became familiar with: The jolly, voluptuous Buddha, laughing and enjoying life. And then there is the silent, peaceful Buddha. My mother focuses on the jolly Buddha. I enjoy both.

While attending dozens of different yoga studios in my life, I inevitably saw a Buddha at most, if not all, of the studios. I would study each one and they spoke to me. I felt comfort and happiness having a Buddha around me, perhaps because it was ingrained within me from childhood. I noticed the connection between Buddha and meditation, first at my yoga studio which initially introduced me to meditation, as well as at independent meditation classes that I went to with friends held at various centers. I knew that if I was ever serious about having a deeper understanding of Buddha, I would need to grow my meditation practice. Once I saw the sign for the Buddhist temple, I decided that I was now open to giving it a try.

My first time at the Buddhist temple was to take a look. I met some of the volunteers there and got to view the temple, inside and outside. It was a beautiful, welcoming place. I felt that I had been there many times before, even though it was my first time. Compared to other Buddhist temples around me, which I researched after finding that one, I was pleased to see that they offered a variety of classes and programs in English. Because of that, once I was comfortable with the space and environment, I scheduled to attend a Thursday night guided meditation class.

Truthfully, I had some mixed feelings. It was my ego talking to me and the doubts and limitations within my own mind that were starting to come out. Even though I was excited to learn about Buddhism and meditation further, there was a part of me that felt like I was doing something wrong. How could I go to a Buddhist temple if I was Jewish? Shouldn't I only go to synagogue? Was I going to the Buddhist temple religiously as a form of prayer, or was it spirituality? I didn't have the answers.

I certainly felt the mix of excitement and nerves at the same time. My deciding factor was simple: I had made it this far on my journey. I broke through so many barriers that I set for myself. There was no reason to stop now. Going to the Buddhist temple would not change that I was Jewish. I was not a "bad Jew" by deciding to go. I was an open soul who was thirsty for knowledge and connection with myself. I would never know what I would find if I didn't go. Therefore, I committed to going. And I went!

The first Thursday night class went by in a flash. The monk sat with the group. We were in an intimate, open room. We found comfortable cushions. We all sat together. We learned how to chant and meditate. And the monk spoke of some Buddhist teachings. I walked away that night feeling energized and alive. I could not wait to return. And I did.

I went back over the course of several months to more Thursday classes. I also joined Saturday meditation and some Sunday all-day meditation retreats. During some of the sessions, the temple served yummy food, including an arrangement of spicy samosas, rice, lentils, and chick pea dishes. I was able to meet more students like myself who were there to learn and grow. The positivity was absolutely radiating from me.

I also purchased books to read on Buddhist teachings. My spirit was starting to grow and evolve in new ways. When people asked me what my background was (religious, cultural, etc.), I would answer that I was Jewish and was interested in Buddhism. I would say this to be authentic to who I was, but there was a part of me that was worried about offending or confusing people. As time went along, those worries began to vanish. The majority of people became fascinated when they heard my response and asked me to elaborate, to the point that I would start to say that I was a Jewish Buddhist. And then one day it hit me: *Hey, I'm a JewBu!*

Everyone can have their own definition and meaning for labels. When I say the word JewBu, it often has a fully religious connotation to people. For me it is a combination of religion and spirituality. Religiously, I consider myself Jewish. Spiritually, I am both Jewish and a Buddhist.

I do not pray to Buddha as a god. I appreciate having him in my life as a friend and teacher. I am a Jew who enjoys reading Buddha's words and incorporating his spirit into my lifestyle. If that is religion for you, then I am okay with that. I see labels and meanings as very subjective to the audience that receives them. I am a JewBu. Whatever that means to you can differ from my own meaning. We may end up at the same place but take different roads to get there.

It wasn't until I was authentic and truly opened my soul to find my spirituality that I really began to see meaning in my life. That is how I found my identity as a JewBu, and when I did, I fully came to appreciate how the lifestyle I was living consisted of the 6 Chosen Commandments. Once I found my Chosen Life, I was then able to elevate myself to unite my strong body and mind with a soul that was growing as well. Without accepting my new road to being a JewBu, I would have still lacked spirituality. And without fully connecting my mind, body, and soul, I could not have started to work on the further steps toward enlightenment.

Ironically, it was through my newfound Buddhist spirituality that I developed a deeper love affair with my Judaism. Even though I was quite active in synagogues at different points in my life, I started to see Judaism differently. Judaism became something that was no longer just thrust upon me at birth that I had to be a part of. Rather, I felt even more connected to Judaism because I was seeing it in a new light.

I was hearing the words and prayers differently at Jewish services. I started to meditate while spending time at synagogues. Religion started to become therapy for me. I had heard the same words and prayers hundreds of times before, yet they started to have different meanings for me. I feel the reason for my transformation was that I was learning to live in the moment each time I attended religious services. I didn't feel obligated or trapped to be there. I was there—fully, actually in place—body, mind, and soul. While I physically and mentally attended synagogue when I was younger, I was spiritually checked out. Once my soul decided to catch up, the game changed.

When following the 6 Commandments of the Chosen Life, I became a monk or a JewBu, so to speak, which brought me back to my spirit. Learning about Buddhism taught me a lot about Judaism. If I didn't connect with my Buddhist feelings, then I wouldn't be so drawn back to Judaism. I thank Buddhism for making me feel that I am a more complete Jew. And I, in turn, thank Judaism for opening my mind and heart to Buddhism. It is a cycle that feeds off one another beautifully.

It is for this reason that I want you to envision your journey through my experiences; for you to fully understand that you are made of your mind, body, and soul—and how they work together.

From there, it is my wish that you understand each of the concepts within the Chosen Commandments and to work on them. Everything has a process and a time. Before you are to work on enlightenment, you need to have the foundational systems of the Chosen Commandments down.

A gentle warning at this time: If you attempt to work toward enlightenment before incorporating the Chosen Commandments as a part of your lifestyle, you run the risk of encountering blockages. You need to have the essentials of life in place through the Chosen Commandments in order to move ahead. Otherwise, you will not be mentally and spiritually open to the concepts and notions presented as part of the path to enlightenment.

You cannot begin to travel if you can't see the road. Working through the Chosen Commandments will allow your vision of your life's road ahead to appear. Then, through enlightenment, you will learn to make the necessary decisions in your life that will help you move ahead to the destinations you ultimately seek.

At this juncture, I want you to start reflecting on who you are. How do you identify yourself? What is your religion or spirituality? Do you identify with any particular faiths? Do you feel that there is a group of people out there with whom you connect on a higher level? Do you have to chart your own path? You need to find what works for you. It may be part of one or more different options until you find the right mix. This is what worked for me.

It wasn't until I was a JewBu and accepted my own self that I felt whole. By researching the term JewBu, I saw that the concept existed, but was not really grown and accepted as mainstream. I was good with that. I feel that by identifying myself as JewBu I am allowing myself to break free from limitations and barriers that may otherwise be set for me. I allow myself to feel, think, and act in ways that are authentic to me. When I first discovered this, it was liberating, and my goal became to help others find their paths and journeys so they can also discover who they really are.

The 6 Commandments of the Chosen Life helped me form my Chosen Life. I created a lifestyle in which I started to look great, feel alive, and be open and energized. Finding my inner JewBu showed me that the lifestyle I began to live was in fact constructed from the Chosen Commandments. I became open to seeing my identity and who I really am. After putting in the work that formed my road to becoming a JewBu, I then continued the steps that formed my path toward enlightenment. It is that same journey that I hope you discover for yourself, religiously and/or spiritually, in whatever form, context, or label that works for you.

The reality is that you may need to be ready to break down your life into nothing and build it up again. And maybe you will discover new roads for yourself. The grouping that you think you are part of religiously and spiritually may shift, or it may grow deeper—that will come with time. The message here is clear: *The Bible 3.0* is about *lifestyle. Your lifestyle*—how your body, mind, and soul work in unison.

When I look at my life today, I see that I wear many hats. I am a father. Son. Brother. Uncle. Yogi. Lawyer. Boxer. Bodybuilder/fitness competitor. Podcaster. Writer. JewBu. Every role that I have ultimately fits within who I am. Every part of me—body, mind, and soul —all work together as a unit. Start to think about your roles. What hats are you wearing? And can you truthfully say that your body, mind, and soul all work together in each position that you undertake?

My story is that I followed the Chosen Commandments and from there forged my life path. But that's me. Now, when you follow the Chosen Commandments, where is it going to take you? As you deepen your understanding and passion for the Chosen Commandments, one of my goals is for you to feel new energy in your soul that you have possibly never felt before—a passion and zest for life that will drive you to absolute new heights. Imagine having a fit body, powerful mind, and an engaged soul that are all functioning at maximum speed. You will be unstoppable!

To benefit from the learning and work that is to come in Part III of this book, your soul must become activated. You will engage in concepts such as minimalism, manifestation, setting goals, living with purpose, living in the moment, letting go, and so many more deep and diverse paths to come. These are powerful concepts that you will need to be truly open to in order to understand and adopt them into your new lifestyle. A closed and uninterested soul will not serve you on these roads.

I can tell you for certain that the pre-JewBu me would not have been interested in much of what we discuss in the enlightenment section. Not that I would not have been curious, but for the reason that I was not open in the full spiritual sense to comprehend them and allow these ideas to flow within me. Thus, I am eternally grateful for my journey, and for yoga to help me master, adopt, and establish the 6 Commandments of the Chosen Life. From there I was finally able to see myself as the JewBu that I am. I wished not to be complacent with a balanced lifestyle, but to seek even more enlightenment and reach even higher levels of being.

As Yogi Berra said in baseball, "It ain't over 'til it's over." I cannot tell you with certainty if there is an afterlife and what is to come after we pass. But I can tell you, with the work that I have put into myself for the past ten-plus years, that as long as there is breath in my body, I only want to learn more. I want to climb greater heights and be open to what will come into my life which will allow me to evolve into being the best me possible.

When a friend of mine went to Israel a few years ago, they offered to take a piece of paper that I could write on and put into the Wailing Wall in Jerusalem—my message to G-d. I wrote, *"May you show me the open roads and may I use my best judgment to select the right ones."* I could not see the open roads in the past because my heart and soul were closed off. As I grew as a JewBu, so did my vision and understanding. And then I didn't sit still. I worked on more elements as I saw them, and crept closer and closer each day to where I wanted to be.

As I formed a JewBu lifestyle and mindset, the key to my journey became enlightenment: the search for the guiding light. When you consider enlightenment, do not think of it as a final destination. Chances are that you are not Buddha, so the idea of enlightenment might seem far-fetched. In reality, we are always growing and developing new levels of awareness on the spectrum of a place called "enlightenment." That is why technically, there is no actual place to reach. Nor do you need to, or necessarily want to. For me, enlightenment was an awakening. A rebirth. A realization that I was uncomfortable in my own skin and did not have purpose in my life.

When I started to understand myself, the people around me, and my environment better, I was starting to become enlightened. When

I looked for deeper meaning and understanding of my purpose in life, I was enlightened. The questions that I began to ask myself, which led to the systems called the Chosen Commandments, were my path toward enlightenment.

I understand the need for quick fixes and solutions. That is how we are generally programmed. If we pay enough money, someone will either tell us the answers or do the work for us in order to save us time and aggravation. If you are truly ready to search for enlightenment within your universe, then I cannot do the work for you. I cannot give you the answers. Nobody can. I will give you, though, the greatest gift I can give you at this stage: the tools for you to discover the roads toward your own enlightenment.

There are three essential elements that will help you work toward enlightenment and ascend to a higher consciousness: your body, mind, and soul.

To be ready for an enlightened state to enter your world, firstly, your mind must feel calmness. Clear. No worried or unhappy thoughts. All the clutter in your mind must be let go. Your mind needs to be free. You cannot possibly begin to manifest the life you seek if you cannot see what you want.

Not to worry; you are about to be reminded of this natural process step by step—how to empty your life and mind of clutter, and then how to stop using your mind as a storage space of unwanted junk. Instead, your mind will comprise of a beautiful, programmable, and inspirational source of short- and long-term goals and achievements.

Your mind will begin to work FOR you instead of AGAINST you. Your mind is like the CPU in a computer; you need time and tools to delete old files and reprogram your mind to begin working in new directions. You are about to receive those tools. Learn them, remember them, and use them wisely.

From there, your soul needs to be ignited. You need a fire in your belly; inspiration to search out answers and solutions. With your mind in check and functioning at a higher capacity, you will then have the space and time to let your soul breathe and come out.

Understanding that your mind is the CPU of your body, you remember that your soul is the compass. If I left you in the middle of a field without a compass, you may never be able to get out. Think of your life. Without YOUR life compass, you are going in circles and never breaking free. Unlocking your soul is the same as finding your compass and finding your direction.

With your soul free to discover your passion and needs in life, you will live a purposeful life. You will see a light—a direction that you want to head in. The destination may be a great one or a negative one—it won't matter. You will enjoy the journey learning, growing, and feeling a passion for life. Whatever your destination, it will be a life lesson. All experiences are teachers for us. Appreciate them and utilize them for the next paths that appear. You are working toward something. You are living life. You are experiencing life. By feeling this way, you have already allowed enlightenment to enter your world.

While enlightenment is based on the interaction between your mind and soul, please remember that you need your body to get there. Your body is a vessel that carries you through your existence. If the vessel is broken or injured, it will be very difficult for you to focus and progress on your path. To work toward enlightenment, your body, mind, and soul must all work strongly as a team. When that happens, you will be ready to move forward on all levels.

Think of your life as a series of roads. You take the roads, hoping to reach certain destinations. Sometimes you end up at a dead end. Sometimes you reach the wrong destinations by accident. Occasionally, you reach the final stop, but it is not what you expected. It is time to shift your focus and perspective. Life is not about the destination. It is about enjoying each moment as you travel your path, allowing yourself the opportunity to learn and grow.

When you are in a good mindset, your body feels great and your soul is inspired. Over time you will find the "right" roads for yourself; paths that will feel good as you cross them. You will begin to evolve. You will feel happier. You will enjoy life more. That is called the road to enlightenment. It is as if you found a solid road for yourself to travel on, and you are enjoying each moment. You will never get "there" per se, as each road leads to new roads. As you are alive, the journey never ends.

You choose the roads to travel on in life. My hope for you is that at some point, that light will go up in the far distance; the metaphorical light of inspiration signaling that you are doing the correct things because you feel good within yourself, and you want to continue living in this happy, productive state. Follow that light you see within your mind and work toward the state of enlightenment within yourself.

Get ready to learn and explore more about yourself as we dig deep into Part III. While not all the concepts will work for you at first, please stay open to them. If any portions of the enlightenment section do not speak to you, do not get upset or give up. Ask yourself why you are not responding to them. If I was to bet, I would say any roadblocks you encounter on your path will constantly come back to blockages within your soul. This is an issue relating to the motivation that you are feeling to evolve and progress.

Are you ready to rip out portions of yourself that do not serve you and rebuild yourself in a stronger and more open way? In many ways, the work is not over after adopting the 6 Chosen Commandments. Rather, the real work is yet to come.

As long as there is breath in your body, may there be the hope, drive, and spirit to grow and evolve yourself. Get ready for the next stages of your being as you read and process the various states of enlightenment. Think about your own religious and/or spiritual values, and how they align with the topics in Part III. If there is a disconnect, do not be afraid to ask yourself why.

How can you open your religious and/or spiritual values to allow yourself to evolve to new, heightened states? I found it for myself through being a JewBu. As you do the work, I look forward to hearing about where you find your soul—and how you channel it for the greatest power and motivation you ever felt. Your soul is the key to enlightenment. Embrace it, listen to it, and let's get it working for you.

THIRTEEN

Meet Minimal You

———❦❦❦———

Congratulations! You have covered the first twelve chapters. I am SO proud of you. The fact that you have made the commitment to do the work and discover the best you is a great decision. And you have accomplished so much up to this point.

In Part II we covered the 6 Commandments of the Chosen Life, where I shared with you the six key activities that you must incorporate into your life routine to become the best and happiest version of you.

The Chosen Commandments work in unison; they feed off one another to help you develop and grow. If you are working at your best capacity, then the Chosen Commandments are part of your daily life. Period. I know it is not easy and that it may take you a great deal of time, planning, and effort to make it happen. The small changes that you're slowly incorporating into your life will become huge shifts for you over time. Savor the person you are today and get excited about your continued evolution. Make the commitment to yourself to continue on the path and do not give up.

Sometimes you will feel like you are wandering the desert. We all do. You are not alone. If you ever feel that you are deviating from your lifestyle or failing at keeping systems in place, do not despair. It is not a competition as we discussed earlier; it is practice, practice, practice. Every day brings a new chance for you to better incorporate the Chosen Commandments as a lifestyle for yourself.

If you feel that any areas are slipping, I encourage you to skip back to any chapter that you feel needs reaffirmation. Maybe your water intake is getting too low, or you haven't meditated in some time. Don't beat yourself up about it. YOU ARE NOT A FAILURE! YOU ARE HUMAN! By being human, we are never perfect. You can always set the bar high for yourself. Be proud of yourself as to what you do accomplish—do not be upset over any areas that need improvement. You have the main tools to thrive through the Chosen Commandments. You are doing the work—and will continue to do so each and every day.

Remember: you are not here for a quick fix. There are none. True success is built upon small incremental daily work that will lead to huge future accomplishments.

Now I have even better news for you: Our work will not end at the 6 Commandments of the Chosen Life. Heck no, we are just getting started.

At this point you understand the foundation of your existence—being *love* in body, mind, and soul. You are developing your systems to incorporate the Chosen Commandments into your life. I have provided you with the tools to commence your own work toward discovering your moments of enlightenment, where you are truly at peace with yourself, the people around you, and the world. But like everything else, we need routines and systems to get there. *The Bible 3.0* is your guidebook on this journey. Let's begin Part III of your evolution…and it begins with discovering and meeting the new minimal you.

* * *

You have too much stuff.

Think about it now. Examine every nook and cranny in your life. Your home: Check every room, closet, dresser drawer, garage, storage area—everywhere. Check your car—back seat and trunk. Go to your office (at home and on-site, if you have an external office) and take a look at your desktop, drawers, cabinets—all around you. Chances are that you will find too many things around you. Stuff/things are cluttering your physical space and your mind! To build the systems for your new lifestyle, we need a fresh canvas.

It is time to declutter your life and spaces. This will clear your mind and open new pathways for thought and productivity.

To have everything you need, you need to start with nothing. Bring it down to basics. All the stuff you are carrying, whether in your mind or in physical goods, is weighing you down.

Now that you know and understand the Chosen Commandments, it is time to live them by starting with what is around you. Start by taking away everything you can. From there, you can focus on acquiring what you truly need and value.

Perhaps you can't imagine how much stuff you have. Clothes, electronics, kitchen items, knick-knacks—it never ever ends! If you are a collector, you are choosing to bring excess stuff into your life. In addition to living with a family of hoarders, I learned the art of collecting things from a young age, as well. Even though I was quite good at keeping spaces clean, my kryptonite was collecting. It started with sports cards, then athlete autographs, G.I. Joe™® soldier figurines and vehicles, then baseball figurines, and so forth. Collecting can be an illness unto itself. It gets masked under the guise of values/profit/hobbies, but it is hoarding at its very core.

To find my minimal self, I needed to break away from collections. I sold off any and all collections that I had with no actual purpose. I dropped the sentimentality and artificial attachments to my collections and made minimal living a lifestyle for myself that I fully embraced. I told myself that if I was to have any collections going forward, the items would need to have a useful purpose. Otherwise, I would not be interested. It came down to sneakers and watches for me. I need shoes to walk. Watches to tell time. Those were the only collections I allowed myself to retain. Otherwise, I was done with the days of owning stuff for the simple purpose of accumulation.

My personal choice to become the minimal me was made after I had fully incorporated the Chosen Commandments. To focus on creating and maintaining life systems, I felt that I had to let go of other attachments that were not serving me. When we own too many things that we don't use, we clutter our lives, which clutters our minds. We cannot focus on tasks and make productive long-term goals if we are drowning in a sea of excess.

When I first heard about the concept of minimalism, I instantly fell in love. I realized that cleaning my room at home and desk at school were minimalistic approaches. Keeping things/stuff around simply because they are nice or cost money, but do not serve us, is weighing us down. Minimalism at its core is about owning less stuff and enjoying better items. Good quality things may cost more on the surface, but they will last longer; they will not need to be replaced as often. For example, I would rather have one good pair of pants than five pairs that will rip easily and I do not fully like. To become minimal you, you need to break out of the mold of needing excess and more and more stuff all the time. Focus your brain on life systems—not constantly accumulating and maintaining stuff. Plus, it's better for our planet.

My hat is off to Marie Kondo. She has created her systems for decluttering and has become a world phenomenon as a result. If you struggle with decluttering physical spaces, by all means, check out Marie or other organization consultants to see different points of view on how to get organized. Systems like Marie's may not work for you. Like every other system you build, there is no "right" way of doing things. Marie is very specific in her Japanese style of organization. When I think of Marie Kondo, I am so grateful that she is bringing the idea of decluttering, minimalism, and organization to the masses. My thoughts are, as long as you get there, it doesn't matter what you did to produce it. The key is to focus on the end result you want, and then find the systems that work for you.

With all due respect to Marie Kondo, I was practicing decluttering before she was born! I remember two key activities that I used to practice from the time I was approximately six or seven years old (if you are curious, I am eight years older than Marie). These organizational routines involved my two spaces: home and school.

HOME: Twice a year, I would empty EVERYTHING from my room. I would leave my bed, desk, and dresser (all big furniture) in the space. But I would take everything else out and put it in the hallway. At a young age (and before the internet, eBay, and Kijiji), there were only two places my stuff would go: I would return all the things in my room that I felt I had to keep or wanted to have. I would put those back slowly and have some sort of order/reason for where I put them. Once I was done, I threw out everything else that was excessive or served no practical purpose.

SCHOOL: I had my desk—and later, a locker—that I would empty once a month. I would grab some cleaner from the janitor and wipe down the spaces completely. I would then return what I had to, or wanted, to keep. As for all the junk or excess, I threw that out.

Simple, you would think, right? If I had written books back then, maybe I would have been seen as a trailblazer for Marie Kondo earlier in life. Who knows? Was I branded as a hero back then? A pioneer? Nope, quite the contrary. My family and teachers cast me as some sort of villain for my decluttering ways. I was doing things that were unheard of at those times. Hoarding was much more common than you can imagine back in the day, and it followed people throughout every part and space of their lives. It still does for many. Hoarding is a disease, the need to keep things to make us happy. I foresaw the effects of this illness from a young age, fought back, and rejected it. But it can follow you, especially when it comes to the workplace.

I will never forget my experiences as a young lawyer, fighting the system in the hopes of creating a paperless world in law one day. I always kept the top of my desk completely clear, only putting out the active files and books that I was currently working on. As for the rest of my files, I liked to put them on open racks on top of credenzas. I also tried to never use drawers or cabinets, and I was never a fan of closed storage spaces—I only used them when I had to. I felt that closed spaces were where items would go to die; they would be out of sight and out of mind. Closed spaces are breeding grounds for clutter. So are tables and desktops! So I tried to keep my work spaces always clear. A clear space leads to a clear mind and more productivity. But few professionals saw that approach as productive for many years. I got a lot of grief for it.

I remember a senior partner walking into my office one day. I will never forget that conversation. He asked me what I was working on. I told him the different files that were currently on my active list. He looked at my desk and commented that I must not be very busy from the looks of things. I asked him why he thought that. He commented that a full desktop of files and papers shows that you have a lot going on and that an empty desk is a sign of a lack of activity. Therefore, according to his logic, by having an empty desktop I was giving the appearance of not being a very busy lawyer. I told him that this was far from the case. I relayed to him a story from my articling term as a student lawyer that stuck with me:

For one of my first files in law, I was summoned to a partner's office. I was working at a downtown Bay Street law firm with over one hundred lawyers. I was young, green, excited, and nervous. I walked into the partner's office and was stunned; I asked him if there was a break-in, as there were open books, files, and papers everywhere. It looked like someone had ripped open files and thrown papers all over the office. He told me no, that was the way he "organized" his office. He had systems and knew where every piece of paper was placed. The more we talked, I realized that this lawyer's systems extended to all parts of his life. His hair was disheveled, likely not cut in weeks. He spoke with a constantly stressed and urgent tone. His clothes were mismatched and dirty. This was a person who did not have their stuff together; the exact opposite of who I wanted to be. I said to myself back then that this was the old way of functioning as a lawyer. It was outdated—and I would evolve myself and my profession out of this mess. Clutter and chaos do not make for a good lawyer. It would hold me back and I wanted no part of it.

As my current employer listened to me, he shook his head and began to walk away. I walked with him to his office next to me and we discussed time management and how to keep busy. When he heard my schedule and active file list, he was surprised. One of the things he told me was that keeping an empty desk was "career suicide." He could not fathom how an associate lawyer could be so busy yet have so few papers, files, and books on their desk. As we kept the conversation going, I made note of his desk. It was packed to the rafters! Every possible file that he was working on was on his desk, all intertwined. I wondered to myself how he kept himself organized, considering how papers from one file could get lost in the shuffle of another file so easily. I made a mental note of some key books and files that he had on his desk and the exact positioning of them as I left the conversation.

Approximately a month after that conversation, I returned to that same senior partner's office. I had a big grin on my face as I looked at him. He asked why I was smiling. I told him the simple answer: the same piles of clutter that were on his desk a month ago were still there! The same order of files and books were in the same place. I even walked toward them and showed him the buildup of dust. He was not using his desk to work, I told him—but rather, as storage. How did he expect to have a clear mind to work on his files when he was, in fact, not even actively using what was on his desk? He was in shock. He was frozen. This was a powerful senior partner in a law firm that commands respect, and he looked like my Shih Tzu when she has an accident in the house. Then there was the bowing of the head in shame. He wanted to crawl under his desk. I thanked him for proving my point, and we never spoke about the subject again as long as I worked with him.

* * *

As I got older, my systems began to evolve. I had more spaces to keep organized and had different needs.

I kept my home cleaning process similar to my office cleaning routine. Twice per year, I emptied out each space entirely. But I evolved to putting all my things in four piles: keep, throw out, donate, and sell.

When I lost more than forty pounds in yoga, none of my clothes fit me anymore. I took all my clothes out of my closet and dresser and tried them on one by one. When essentially nothing fit, I had no choice but to get a new wardrobe. I kept maybe two T-shirts and sweatpants and decided to donate everything else. Clothes are hard to sell, and it is such a shame to throw out clothes when they can go to someone who can use them. So, unless an item has extreme value and is relatively easy to sell, my first reaction is to always donate or give it to somebody I know who will use or cherish it, including clothes. Paying it forward is the best way. The last resort is to throw things out.

The hardest part of minimalism is knowing what to keep. For me, that has shifted over the years.

I do not have a set system or a timeline of when something has to go. Some people say that if you do not use it or wear it within six months or one year, get rid of it. Some say that you cannot put something new in your house unless you take one thing out. If that works for you, awesome; go for it! I can tell you that taking everything out of each room twice a year and making my four piles has worked great for me. Maybe you want to do something similar only once a year and use only three piles; don't get fixated too much on having the perfect system. Anything you do to clean today is better than what you did yesterday. Anything you sell, donate, or toss has freed up space in your home. Fantastic! Start with baby steps.

Try my method of home cleaning once. See if you like it. Then, pick a date when you will do it again. Put this task on your to-do list and/or calendar. Assign a due date, and then do it again. Over time, develop your systems. Feel free to write them down; I encourage you to make a checklist. Seeing things in writing will hold you accountable to the process, and then you will actually make it happen. Decide if your organizational process will be once a week, once a month, every season, or once a year. Pick a timeline and stick to it.

Move on to your other spaces after you have cleared your home. If you have a car, organize that. Take everything out of your car. Give it a good vacuum or cleaning, then put only the things you really need and want back in your car. Everything else, you decide—sell, donate, or toss. *Boom!* Just like that. You will probably be appalled by how much garbage and wrappers we can keep in our cars. That is gross! A clean car will lead to a clean mind. You will feel free, happy, and on top of your game. Let's get it done!

Your workplace is next. Whether you have an office, cubicle, or desk—it doesn't matter. Make sure to set aside the time to go through it. Carefully empty the space as much as you can. Put everything but the big furniture into a hallway or the corner of the room if needed. Go ahead and make four work piles: keep, sell/donate, return to the company, and toss. Only put the keep items back into your workspace. The rest of the items will go away based on the piles you have created. Once complete, look at how much better your space looks in the office. Your workmates will either think that you are a genius or quite mad, but I guarantee you this: Having a clear workspace will make you far happier at work. You will feel clearer and less stressed. You will not feel like you are missing something. So, get yourself into the habit of keeping your tabletop as clear as you can. A decluttered workspace means a decluttered mind. Think it, accept it, and live it!

If you want to reach the Mt. Everest of minimalism, it's paperless; a world where you do not have paper everywhere, such as stickies and unorganized documents. Paperless has been a passion of mine for years. When you reach the point of being paperless in your life, personally and professionally, you will feel free and liberated. Keeping paper, searching for paper, and losing paper is a time-wasting exercise and is very stressful. We have technology in place to avoid this nonsense. It is time for you to utilize it if you have not already done so.

I could write a book or a series of books on how to become paperless (and maybe I will one day). But for the purpose of *The Bible 3.0*, I want you to be open to the concept of paperless. Start it in your personal life—see how you can utilize apps and programs to keep track of notes instead of using stickies. Scan and save documents and receipts and keep electronic folders. Shred all the paper from there. Develop paperless habits so that anything you would write on paper, you do electronically. Encourage your workplace to do the same. You will help save the Earth and trees, plus look like a superstar. Paperless is not a fad or flavor of the month—it is the present and future. The quicker you become paperless, the easier that life will become.

The 6 Commandments of the Chosen Life are all built on having systems. To have those systems work, you need to look at your life in its entirety. Your brain and life can only handle so much information at a time. The more distractions and complications we have, the harder it will be to create and maintain the systems needed. Maintaining your daily lifestyle must be your top priority. To make this happen, anything that takes away from the process needs to be discarded. Creating a minimal lifestyle will make the Chosen Commandments that much easier to follow. A cluttered physical life leads to a cluttered mind. A cluttered mind cannot focus and produce. Do not hold yourself back! Free yourself from unnecessary excess and open your mind in the process.

To figure out what you want in life, the first step is letting go of what does not serve you. Get rid of the clutter and those things that hold you back. They are blocking your life and mind. I want you to feel free; to bring your life down to the bare necessities, so to speak.

With a free and open mind, you are going to learn to finally live—not in the past of regret or the worry of the future—you are going to live in the moment. The present day, each and every moment, will be savored like fine wine. You are going to create the minimal you. And now it is time to teach that new version of yourself how to truly live in each and every moment.

FOURTEEN

Live in the Moment

—◊◊◊—

I sleepwalked through more than thirty years of my life.

For me that was a very harsh and deep realization. It hit me during yoga and meditation as I began to uncover who I really was. I had lived during those years—I woke up, I did things, went back to sleep and repeated—but for most of my life, I was on autopilot. And the sad thing was, I never even realized it.

At various times, depressive points hit me when I became aware of this. I was sad and angry, mostly at myself for having wasted so many years. Then I beat myself up on the inside for not seeing this sooner.

I had lived to survive and do whatever I was told or felt that I had to do, but I wasn't living for myself. I was living out of obligation, not out of enjoyment. By going through the motions each day, I almost tuned out my soul. My mind was focused on worries and regrets. With such a cluttered mind, I did not have the means to activate my soul whatsoever. I did not feel true happiness.

For me it was not about the achievements during that time; it was that I did not really experience the ride. If life is made up of a series of moments, then I did not have a true life. The moments were there, but I did not feel them. I did not live *within* them. I was always looking for the next task or worrying about what was not being done. I wasn't living in my present. I was in the past or future only.

There is a cliché expression about "stopping to smell the roses." As I learned to practice meditation, I adopted something called "mindful meditation," which I used often on walks. This involved not being on the phone or listening to music. Instead, I would walk and only focus on walking. I learned to enjoy the steps and each experience. I would breathe in my environment. By experiencing mindful meditation on those walks, I was teaching myself mindful living. I began to learn to live in the moment.

It may sound like the most obvious thing to "live in the moment." But how many of us can actually say that we do it? The mind and soul have a feeding cycle between them. The mind sets the tone and mood for life. When the mind is on autopilot and filled with worry, it becomes hard to think and function. A cluttered mind leads to a closed soul.

With a full mind, there is no zest for life or enjoyment and inspiration for what is going on around you. I know that is how I lived most of my life. And I have known many people around me over the years in a similar state. I learned to break out of my cycle—now I want to help others do the same.

With the Chosen Commandments, you now possess many of the tools and actions needed to set up your life. But if you are in a rush or forget, turn back to mindful living and make the commitment to live in the moment.

Focus on the breath. In and out.

Living mindfully will get you out of any worries and issues you are having in that moment. Your breath will bring you back to the present. With focus now, you will be a different person, happier, and more productive.

Take an assessment of your life. Take your time. If you need time to ponder it, feel free to come back to this chapter several times, or as many times as you need. But be honest and truthful with yourself. Do not sugarcoat it. Over the course of your life, up to the present day, are you actually present for each moment? Are you living *in* each moment, or are you there but not really there? Think about that. I will give you some examples.

Think about when you are driving. Walking. Practicing physical activities. Showering. Brushing your teeth. Eating. Going to sleep.

Any daily function that you do. Are you present in each of those moments, or is your mind racing?

While driving, you could breathe. Relax. Feel inspired. Enjoy the open road. Breathe in and out. Feel clear. Feel happy. Look at the signage. Hear the voices around you. Look at foliage and take in all the sights around you. Or, you could worry about being late. Or not making it to your destination. You could be worrying about the rest of your day and what you have to get done. What sounds better to you?

When you eat, you can choose to savor your food. Take in each bite. Again, focus on your breathing. You can feel a nice, clear breath and have a clear mind. Really enjoy your food. Chew slowly and with purpose. Taste all the different tastes and enjoy the smell of your meal. Eat and digest slowly. Feel really good during this meal. Or shovel the food into your mouth as quickly as possible and have your mind racing to where you need to be next. You could be thinking about chores and to-dos to get done as soon as you finish this meal. Or worse yet, take that food as you move to your next destination to save time and eat while driving, so as to not focus on your eating *or* your driving. Is that how you want to live? Do you want your meals to be enjoyed or be nuisances?

Still unconvinced? What about sleeping? Do you get into bed, nice and showered, teeth brushed, ready for a good night's sleep? Are you lying in bed, eyes closed, smiling, deep breathing, and falling asleep peacefully with not a care in the world except for enjoying the sleep that is to come? Or are you racing into bed tired and exhausted? Or maybe you fell asleep on the couch, in your street clothes with the lights on? Perhaps you are up for hours in bed, your mind filled with worries and doubts that are blocking your ability to sleep?

Again, what life and existence do you want for yourself?

Living in the moment is not a secret. We've all heard of it. We know it is there. But for some reason, we choose to ignore it as though it is a made-up fable that sounds really great but does not work in reality. That is wrong. Dead wrong.

Living in the moment is a tool that you can use all day, every day. It will carry you throughout each of your days. It does not happen by accident; it is a *committed choice* to create a mindful lifestyle and mindset for yourself. By learning to live in the moment, you will see life differently. Life will no longer be a chore or a burden—it will be exciting and fun. You will get to live new moments, each and every day, and experience things you never thought possible. You will learn to have a better relationship with yourself and others.

Think about the conversations you have with others. Whether in person, over the phone, video, or messaging. In how many of those conversations are you actually present? Or are you multitasking and shifting your mind from the conversation to other things?

When it comes to in-person conversations, we have no choice. We physically have to be there. It is rude to be on a call or looking at our phones when speaking with someone else. But even with the most immediate distractions being removed, how likely is it that we are mentally present in the conversation? Or is our mind elsewhere? You know the conversations. When someone speaks for five minutes and then tells you that you haven't heard a word that they said! You say, "No, no, I heard everything." Then when they ask you to repeat what they said, you can't! When that is the case, that means that you were not living in the moment. You were not present mentally for the conversation. Your body was there, but your mind was in a million other places, zoned out, and focused on worries and to-dos. You were not present or listening to the person you were conversing with. You did not give that person the time to be focused on and take in what they were saying to you.

Think of how many conversations you missed with people because you were mentally checked out while they were speaking. It's a lot, I bet.

Similarly, when we are on the telephone speaking with someone or on a video call, we have the option to multitask. But by checking out during a conversation, we are not giving the person on the other end the time and space they require. It is a fairly easy process to see how distracted we become when conversing with others. This is becoming the norm, not the exception.

Finally, messaging is the least personally intimate form of communication possible. For most people, it has eliminated the need for many in-person interactions or even telephone and video calls, because we can message when we want. We can respond when we want. We have to give little time, attention, or focus to our interactions with people. It is very similar to telephone and video calls; while you think that you are talking intimately to another person, they are very likely checking emails, cooking, or doing hundreds of other activities at the same time. You may be speaking, but you are both not fully THERE in the moment. You are missing out on interactions with other people and the opportunity to learn from their words and experiences. It is a shame.

Next time you are with a group of people, whether it's a dinner, gala, or presentation, look at the number of people who are on their phones. I have been to dinners where people were wrapped up in their phones the majority of the time. They did not give energy to others nor receive energy back. They might as well have been anywhere else rather than the gatherings. They were there physically, but mentally they were millions of miles away. It is not even insulting anymore to act in this manner around others. It has become the societal norm. The rise of the internet, smartphones and devices has led to our attention and focus being shifted away for many of our waking hours. It is hard to be present and live in the moment when we are surrounded by distractions.

We have a choice, though. We can either continue the pattern or break away and find a deeper and more meaningful way to live. The choice is ours, each and every day. We can make the commitment to break out of our comfort zones and move ahead.

So, what about our time with ourselves? Think about how much time we spend on our own. If we are not present in those moments either, we are losing time for self-growth and reflection. It is mind-blowing how much more we can enjoy each and every day if we are dialed into the present. If we are consistently distracted and ignore the present moment, life will simply pass us by and we run the risk of missing the entire show.

Think of your life as a trip. Imagine every morning that you wake up and plan your destination for the day. But rather than take in each site that you visit, take pictures, and savor the experience, you choose to be distracted and miss each encounter. You would consider that a wasted or failed trip! Think of your daily life in the same way. If you do not live in the moment each and every day, you will not get the time to experience wonderful impressions and truly enjoy life.

You will run the risk of stagnating through a wasted or failed life!

It is time for you to immediately stop allowing life to pass you by. It is time to truly live—not in yesterday or tomorrow, but in the present day; in the *right now*. In each and every moment.

* * *

It is going to take several steps to help you learn to live in the moment. This is a skill that comes with time and patience. You are learning to reprogram yourself and think differently. It is a new life approach, so do not expect a major shift to happen overnight (hint: it won't).

Let's begin by simply pausing here for a moment. Take a couple of minutes to observe your present state of mind. It may be difficult, but you need to push through the clutter and negativity and come to a point of calmness. Stillness. Once you are ready and feel that you are mentally in the present moment, please say the following phrase out loud:

"I acknowledge that my life needs a change."

By swallowing your pride and being truthful to yourself, you have evolved your existence in a positive direction. You have made the decision that you want to learn to live in the present moment. By doing this, you are already victorious. You have shifted your mindset.

If you say that your life is great and that "living in the moment is not for you"—then nobody can help you. Certainly nobody externally, because you do not want to help yourself. Truthfully recognizing that you need and want a shift is already the biggest breakthrough. I'm proud of you. That choice has already started your road to mindful living.

The biggest tool I am going to pull out of the toolbox is *breathing*. Breathe. Learning to breathe and process breath is the best friend of mindfulness. If you are ready to open and connect with your soul, the magical key is *breath*. Nothing else.

It is alarming how often we hold our breath or ignore our breath. By learning to breathe in and out of our noses consciously, we are opening our soul and igniting the spirituality within us. Breath is the lifeline of yoga and meditation. Without breath, these activities are not possible. Do not focus on your worries or regrets. Learn to focus on your breathing, and you will connect with everyone and everything.

I was, for much of my life, a mouth breather. I had deep sinus and allergy issues. I could not and did not want to breathe through my nose. I was constantly holding my breath. Little did I know that holding my breath was closing my mind and soul. I could not breathe, which meant that I could not live. I could not think clearly or see clearly. It was difficult for me to live in the present because I did not know how to bring myself there. My mind liked to live in the past or future, but never in the present. Without being able to breathe, I could not feel or react in the present. I was closing myself off. Thank goodness I recognized that and made the decision to change it. Those changes always revolved around the breath.

Once you have made your commitment to work toward mindful living, think back to the breath process we discussed as part of the meditation system. Utilize that breath for all parts of your life. When you are walking, utilize the breath. When you are trying to fall asleep, utilize the breath. When you are speaking to others, utilize the breath. In everything you do, always bring it back to the breath. It is that simple: breathe in and out of your nose. Focus on that breath. Think about the breath. Recognize the breath. Your mind will begin to clear, and your soul will begin to open. Such a simple tool with such a powerful result. Discover and utilize your breath. It is that easy!

Let's take that breath and now work it into practice. The next time you are conversing with someone on any medium—only listen to that person. Speak as needed and required in the flow of the conversation. *Do nothing else other than focus on the conversation.* When you feel the need to do something else—such as looking at your social media, or your mind starts drifting to other thoughts and distractions—return to your breath. Breathe in and out of your nose, and focus on your current conversation. Be in that moment with the person you are speaking to. Give them your full, undivided attention. If you drift, keep breathing in and out of your nose. Consciously keep going back to that breath. It will do wonders for you.

Once you pass that test, keep that momentum going in other conversations and interactions. Whenever you feel yourself drifting from the moment at hand when speaking or messaging with others, *remember your breath.* It is a powerful tool that is readily available at your fingertips.

Think of how you spend your time every day. Consider how many simple processes you complete in autopilot mode. You would think that even the simplest tasks have little value and must be completed as soon as possible, but now it is time to shift your mind and learn to be mindful even during those moments. You will make better use of your time, achieve higher results, and feel rejuvenated.

* * *

Let's take an example of an exercise that you can practice tonight. Let's incorporate breathing into two of your nighttime routines.

Tonight, before you go to bed, the first thing you will do is brush and floss your teeth. Remind yourself to not let your mind drift into hundreds of different places at this time. Focus on the state of brushing and flossing. As you perform these activities, keep centering your mind to the present. If you find that you are mentally drifting away, come back to the breath. Refocus your mind through your breath, and you will brush and floss your teeth in the most conscious manner possible. Your teeth will feel cleaner and fresher because you actively engaged in completing these tasks. You also used this time to clear your mind and prepare yourself for sleep. Well done!

From there, you will go to bed and get ready to sleep. If you get stressed and thoughts begin to race, reach back to the breath. Breathe in and out. Be in the moment. The only place you need to be is in your bed and ready to sleep. There is nothing else to do. Just close your eyes and breathe in and out. You will be amazed at how quickly you go to sleep and sleep restfully.

Remember that learning to live in the moment is therapy and healing for your mind. It is a wonderful feeling when your mind gets to relax and not race in overdrive. A mind that is working nonstop is a tiring instrument.

* * *

Now that you understand and have incorporated mindfulness into your life routine, you are ready for the next step on the journey toward living in the moment. Focusing on the mind and learning to calm your thinking is only half of the process. Do not forget about the most neglected part of your being: your soul.

Do you have a relationship with your soul? What are your spiritual and religious values? Living in the moment will not necessarily answer them, but it will certainly jumpstart the process. As your mind clears, over time you will feel your soul open! Take a look inside. Don't be afraid. See what is within you!

Many questions may come to you over time as your soul opens and develops, including: What is my purpose on Earth? Why am I here? What did I achieve? What do I want from my life? There can be many interesting but scary questions to ponder and answer. Although the questions will appear, the answers may not, and that is the worst part for many. However, don't be deterred. If these thoughts are appearing, it means you are on the right track. You don't have to give or receive any answers at this stage. Simply by asking the questions, you should congratulate yourself because it means you are seeing life as more than a simple, meaningless process. It means you are no longer drifting and you are searching for more because you are living in the present and your soul is opening up to bigger levels.

Please take the time to look within yourself. What energy and life forces motivate you? It is time to find your spiritual and religious connections. You have a soul that is burning to shine bright and drive you toward your chosen existence. With an energized soul combined with mindfulness, you will be unstoppable.

All you need to do is breathe. Continue to live in the moment. Shift back to the present. Consider what mediums you want to use in order to live life in the present day. If you have a religious background, think about attending services at your temple. If you want to meditate, then find meditation with a group or on your own. You can also go to yoga; attend a class and flush it out.

There are so many ways for you to live in the NOW. All these mediums are not about finding you immediate answers; it is about creating outlets for you to live life in the present and truly enjoy each and every moment.

You will no longer be missing out on conversations, sights, and sounds. You will be present for all of it. You will learn more than you ever have before by truly taking things in as they come and the answers you seek will arrive to you slowly, over time when your mind and soul are ready for them. Don't go looking for answers. The answers are already here, ready for you when you are ready to receive them.

I can speak from personal experience that without living in the moment, I would not have found my road to becoming a JewBu. Mindful living led me to Buddhism, and Buddhism ignited a new passion for Judaism. It was amazing how Buddhism and Judaism had a symbiotic relationship in strengthening the love I had for each religion. Discovering the connection with my soul allowed me to embrace and deepen my spiritual and religious sides. But ultimately, it was not about the outlets. It was about how I was thinking and feeling. If it took becoming a JewBu for me to find my road to enlightenment, I was going to take it.

I was fortunate that I was able to find my path along this life journey. The 6 Chosen Commandments led me to a life of living in the moment. And mindfulness allowed me to connect to my soul and unleash my inner passions which continue to serve me to this day.

I have never felt better. More alive. I stopped beating myself up for past mistakes. I stopped doubting myself and holding myself back because I told myself that I wasn't good enough. I love myself. I believe in myself. I tell myself that I can accomplish anything that I want to. The past is no longer an issue and the future is not a worry.

I am no longer living outside of the present. I am fully dialed into the present moment. I am enjoying the ride, knowing that I am doing my best and being the best me that I can be. If things don't work out, I learn from them and do better next time.

I am learning and growing, and no longer punishing myself. I freed my mind from my self-imposed prison. My mind became clear. My soul opened and pushed me in new directions. This is the best feeling in the world. And now I want you to find your experiences and grow in the directions that you seek.

No matter what stage you are at in life, know that it is never too late. You can change and evolve. The 6 Commandments of the Chosen Life are there to help you revolutionize yourself, but there will come a point in time when this work is not enough. You will look good and feel good, but you will seek more out of life. You will want more. When those feelings hit, remember the breath. Always turn back to the present moment.

Make the commitment to yourself to focus on the here and now. The answers of the future lie in living today. The more time you spend living in the now and not worrying about what will come, the more certain that answers will reach you one day. Worrying about the future will not solve anything for you. Living in the present will.

Recognizing that you have past trauma that is holding you back is powerful. That recognition will serve you well. To move ahead, you need to heal yourself first. There will not be a magical surgery or pill that will immediately do this. The healing begins right now. At this moment. And every moment to follow. Enjoy each and every moment you are living. Every day is another opportunity to practice living a great life.

There is no competition, it is only practice. No more pressure on yourself. Let go of those shackles and demands you put on your existence. Focus on the breath and decide that you are going to allow yourself to live in the now, unburdened. Give your soul the opportunity to breathe and open.

Now that you are living in the moment, it is time to move ahead and evolve. To do that fully, you must get ready to release the empty baggage you are carrying with you.

FIFTEEN

Let Go to Move Ahead

So many of us as humans are born with a flaw. Most, if not all of us, have an issue. We have a hard time letting go. We like to carry things, physically and mentally. Those things unfortunately start to weigh on us and make it harder for us to move forward.

To look ahead, it is much better to pack light. Letting go does not come naturally to most of us. It is a skill that is learned and needs to be practiced repeatedly for a lifetime.

We covered minimalism in a previous chapter. When it comes to physical things, life becomes much simpler when we have less stuff in our lives. To practice letting go, the easiest starting point is to get rid of a physical possession.

It is very different to physically get rid of an object as opposed to mentally letting go of it. For instance, you can decide that you don't need your boat and sell it. That is a great minimal decision if you feel the need to own less. However, if you keep *thinking* about your boat after it is gone and you long for it, you haven't let go of it. The object is gone in the physical sense but remains in your life mentally. To really let go of the boat in this case, you need to detach from it. You must say goodbye and allow your mind to process that it is really gone. Once you free your mind of the attachment and need for the boat, you can open your mind to new thoughts and feelings.

Think of your mind as a filing cabinet. When you have thoughts, feelings, doubts, worries, regrets, anxieties, and a mixture of all the above, you are carrying each of these mental components and filling up your filing cabinet excessively.

You tell yourself that you want to be happy. You convince yourself that you are setting out to be happy. But all you can think about when having free time are missed opportunities. Failed relationships. Lost jobs. Missed investments. Arguments with family members. Worries about the future. The list goes on and on. The mental baggage you are carrying is cluttering your mind. How can you possibly live in the present moment if all you are doing is living in the past? You can't. It will not happen. *If we are going to get you to be present today, then we have to clear up the past slowly.* It is time to learn how to let go.

We carry pain. We carry anger. We carry grudges. We carry defeats. It is time to let go of all of it. To move ahead, we need a clean slate. A fresh start.

I want you to think of someone you aren't speaking to right now. It could be anyone—a family member, a friend, or even a colleague . Did you get into a fight with them? What was it about? Are you not speaking to them so you can *show* them you are right? Did they bruise your ego in some way? Here is the problem with your current approach. Your bickering is taking up valuable real estate in your mind. Every time you see that person or think about them, your mind goes back to the reason that you are not speaking. All sorts of emotions and feelings start to go through you, likely including anger, hurt, and resentment. This state of mind is draining your valuable energy. You do not need this in your life. You said you want to be happy. You are committed to feeling happy and living in the present. How are you going to achieve this? You guessed it. By letting go.

You have options when it comes to a struggle such as our example above. The best and most mature approach would be to resolve the conflict. It is all too common during conflicts to hold on to the ego. Holding on can include not speaking to the other person and waiting for them to step up and come to you to apologize and/or resolve the conflict. As time continues to go by, the need to prove we are "right" continues to overtake more and more of the requirement to end the conflict. Do you really want to carry the burden of being in a conflict so you can gain an artificial win? Or are you better off foregoing the ego and focusing on your desired end result: keep the relationship and find a resolution?

Do not worry for a moment about appearing weak by initiating communication with your supposed adversary. You are, in fact, being the strong one by coming forward and making the effort to find the resolution. To make arguments disappear, you should always focus on the result you want and do not give in to worries or doubts about what could happen during communications with the other side.

In times of conflict, it is easy to lose sight of the big picture. Our anger goes into hyper mode and we can become closed and narrow in our thinking. When you feel this coming on, talk to yourself. Remind yourself about the value of the relationship that you are risking through fighting. You cannot control what somebody else thinks and does. But you are the master of your communication. Take responsibility for the person you are and who you want to be. Consider the alternative: A lengthy impasse with a person close to you could lead to months, if not years of lost time together. Is that what you really want? Consider all possible outcomes resulting from the communication that you choose before fighting against someone you care about. Holding onto anger is a burden that your mental wallet simply cannot afford.

When you encounter this type of scenario, make the conscious choice to not wait for the other person to come to you. Let go of the conflict as soon as possible. You can make the choice to be the bigger person. You should choose to speak to the other person. Do NOT blame them for wronging you. Let them know how their actions made you feel and be accountable for the part that you played in the interaction. *Lose the ego and the need to be victorious in this fight.* Focus on the resolution and moving ahead. Communicate to the other person that you wish to function on better terms going forward. Then, regardless of how they react, whether positively or negatively, you have done all you could do. That is the important part.

A conflict will feel terrible in the actual moment. But remember that conflict can be our best teacher. Through conflict we can learn how to value our life and what is important to us. When negativity and anger rise to the surface, we can choose to give in to bad impulses or keep an eye on the bigger picture.

Do not see an argument as a battle against another individual. It is, in fact, a battle within yourself. As long as you function as the best person you can be, whatever the other side does is irrelevant. You need to be able to face *yourself* in the mirror; to admit to yourself if you were strong enough to weather the storm and act as the peacemaker and work toward a resolution. If the answer to that is yes and you can face yourself in the mirror, then you will usually find that the end result will be a positive one. By doing all that you can to make peace with the other person, you more than likely will be able to resolve the situation. Positivity can be contagious. If you put out the good vibes, then more often than not, they will come back to you. Remember that!

Sometimes, though, even the best plans for resolution do not always go our way. While we could approach a conflict with an open mind and heart, the other side may not feel that way. That is okay. Whether your adversary wants to make up and be close again or not, you can be at peace with your own actions. If your attempt at peace is rebuffed, do not allow the retraction to lead to further anger. Instead, rely on communication. Be open to giving the other party time and space; they may need that to find their bigger picture. Accept that. As long as you know what footing you stand on with this person, then you can let go of the negativity that occupies your mind. You will be free to look ahead positively and feel good in the present. What the other person chooses to do and think is their choice. You are in control of your mind, thoughts, and outlook. Keep that perspective, as you consider that how you perceive YOUR existence can alter your reality.

Missed opportunities are another big load that we love to carry. Overthinking our perceived losses is not helpful at all. We can certainly remember past actions when future circumstances arise so we can make better decisions in the future. But we cannot go back in a time machine and redo past choices.

Imagine that person who sold their Apple stock, which is worth a thousand times more today. Or that person who blew the interview for what they felt was their dream job. Those losses are gone. It's over. Recognize it, appreciate what happened, and then move forward.

Businesses have the ability to write off bad debt. Let's say, for example, one of your customers went bankrupt and cannot pay you the money they owe you. As a business, you would write off that debt at the end of the year, take the financial hit, and move forward the following year with a clean set of accounting books. Why can't you do the same in your personal life? Seriously. If you are thinking of something that went wrong, whether a day ago or years before, think of it as a bad debt. Write it off in your mind. Accept the loss. And start your mind on a fresh page going forward. Strengthen your mental fortitude. Let it go. Yes, it can be that easy.

I wish the wake-up call had come earlier for me, or so I told myself at the beginning. Realizing in my early thirties that I had lived the majority of my life with past hurt and regret in my mind was a troubling realization. I'll be honest; early on, I thought often about giving up. Not on life, but rather, on trying to change the course. Since I had drifted, I told myself, why bother trying to fix things? This is where I am so grateful for yoga and meditation. It took me hundreds of hours of practice, but over time I started to open up my heart and soul.

I realized, as time went by, that I was focusing on absolutely the wrong things. Yes, in a perfect world I would have had my moment of enlightenment ten years prior to that. But that didn't happen. And nothing will change that.

But how lucky was I to awaken out of my sleep now rather than ten years from now? Or never? I shifted my mindset. I learned to become grateful for the opportunities ahead of me rather than the ones I missed. Previous mistakes were starting to be seen as learning tools rather than life sentences.

A deep realization hit me at one point: I was in prison. I had put myself in there from a young age and allowed the people around me to keep me there. Nobody else was going to free me. Only I could liberate myself.

I could not change the past nor worry about the future. Those things were not in my control. I saw the light. I wanted to live in the present. I wanted to enjoy each moment that was available to me—that is what really mattered. It did not come easily, but when the realization connected within me, I decided that I did not want to live the life that I thought I was forced to live. *I was ready to live the life I wanted*—one where I would only do what made me happy—a much gentler and more peaceful way to live.

When we are taught bad habits, we have one of two choices: to follow them or do the exact opposite. For me, I had to see what I did *not* want to do in order to eventually find the road that would serve me. From a young age, I knew that I did not want to be a hoarder. The idea of cleansing myself of non-essential physical items and having a more minimalistic approach always excited me. That's where I was shocked and dismayed to learn in my thirties that I was what I despised—I was a hoarder. Not of physical goods, but mental thoughts.

I did not want to admit it to myself for a long time after that hit me. Yet, that's the funny thing about yoga and meditation—you have nowhere to run from your thoughts. And as I sat in silence for all those hundreds of hours, I could not escape my reality. If I was truly committed to a minimalistic lifestyle and *not* hoarding, then I needed to learn to let go of the past.

I had to let go of the thoughts, mistakes, and regrets that didn't serve me. Over time, I needed to learn to forgive myself. Images of past situations arose. Failed relationships, missed business opportunities, and other life blunders would rise to the surface. I would need to acknowledge them, learn from them, and slowly say goodbye and purge them.

Don't think for a moment that I was able to accomplish this feat quickly. Letting go is a skill that I have to utilize daily. When I am at my weakest points, mentally and/or physically, the easiest thing to do is shift into a negative mindset and punish myself. I have to consciously remind myself to let go; to shift to the present. The best way I know how to shift quickly is to:

- **Recognize**
- **Take action**
- **Remain conscious throughout**

The good news? The more I practiced, the better I got at it. It takes work and determination to let go. But feeling happy and peaceful makes it worth it.

You have learned the tools to clear and declutter physical objects from your life. Focus on your mind now in the same manner. When your phone or computer hard drives become full, you delete old files and empty the trash. You free up storage space. Do the same for your mind.

* * *

When a thought or feeling pops up that is associated with something negative from the past, recognize it. Ask yourself if what you are pondering right now is serving you. Will this help you productively in any way, or are you simply making yourself feel bad? If the answer is that you are recycling useless thoughts in your mind, tell yourself that. Say it out loud if you have to. Tell your thoughts that they are not helping you; that they are only bringing you down and draining your energy. You are breaking up with those thoughts. Make that commitment. They can leave now and not come back.

If you must make the feeling that much more impactful, then by all means, hold a funeral for your departed negativity. Tell yourself that the past is dead. It is buried in the ground or cremated. We cannot bring back the dead, so there is no use in trying. Say goodbye to past hurt and negativity. Mourn it. And then begin life fresh without it. You will feel lighter, freer, and so much happier.

Practice your new skill right now. Tomorrow. Every day more burdens of negativity arise, free your mind. Let it go.

I love the expression that our mind is the most valuable real estate we have, and the rent is too expensive for people to live there. This is often found in past relationships. Think about "the one who got away." Your high school sweetheart. A broken engagement. Divorce. The person who cheated on you. Whatever it is, so many of us have that one person stuck in our minds. This person is given full-time space to live in our minds RENT FREE! They have likely moved on themselves and barely give us a second thought. Yet here we are, allowing this person to live in our minds. Not only is this unhealthy for our own mindset and self-worth, but think how much this is holding us back. How could you give your full love and attention to a current or future relationship if you are stuck in the past? You cannot. The solution? Give that person the eviction notice. Boot them out of your mind. Free up the space so that you can rent it to someone who has earned the space and will enjoy it. Plus, you will love having that new person in your mind!

Family. Lord knows we love them. But they don't always teach us the best habits. If a person has parents and/or siblings who have a very difficult time letting go of things, then it is very easy to learn and repeat the pattern. Do not fall into this trap. Even if your loved ones tend to be unforgiving or carry grudges, you don't have to as well. Be your own person. Live the life that you *want*—not how somebody else wants you to.

If you are one of the lucky people who has excellent role models around you who are able to let go of past negative feelings and emotions, congratulations. Embrace those people and discover what makes them tick. This will help you find the life patterns that will work for you.

If you are in the camp where you have people around you who have not learned to let go, recognize that, as well. See what they are doing that is holding them back. Your job is not to fix them; rather, you need to see what NOT to do so you can find your own positive mindset. The focus is within. Do not let outside distractions sway or clutter you.

You made the commitment to be happy and enjoy your life. So don't worry about what the other people around you are doing. Find your peace and tranquility. You will never be able to control how other people think or react. And you don't have to! Worry only about yourself. You are in control of your mind. Nobody else is. You don't owe anybody anything. Your primary obligation is to YOU. To love yourself. To find your happiness.

It always begins and ends with love. But love cannot flow through you if you are stuck. A clogged mind cannot send and receive love through the heart. Free your mind of images, thoughts, scenarios, restrictions, and any other blockages that you identify with. Allow yourself to be free to feel and give love. It is the best feeling once you start on the road to get there.

Love comes from within your soul. The clutter is in your mind. So you are essentially using your soul to heal your mind. Remember that you are made up of your body, mind, and soul. When one part of you suffers, you have reinforcements to help. In this case, when your mind is overloaded and holding you back, your soul is there to assist. By recognizing and acknowledging the spiritual side of your existence, you are better equipped to assist your mind when it is overloaded.

There is no better medicine for a mind that needs healing than love. That love is best produced from within. Communicate with your soul. Tell it that it's time for self-love. Do not expect to be "cured" overnight. The past that you carry in your mind has likely been there for a long time—possibly months and even years. The cleanup will take time.

You need to have patience with yourself. At any point that you are consciously working toward letting go of the past, do not set a time limit or target for yourself. Embrace the notion that you are working toward letting go in your mind. That reinforcement will trigger the love from your soul that you so desperately need.

As you commit to the process and work, I promise you that it will get easier. Day by day. It's a journey. You are practicing. There is no pressure. Every bit of work that you are putting in is more than you did before. Do not focus on what you failed to do before today. Be happy that you are working on yourself today. From there, it will only get easier and easier.

If only letting go were so easy, then everyone would be doing it. Conceptually, it sounds like the simplest thing to achieve. But the reverse is the case. What should be so easy is, in reality, one of the most difficult mental hurdles to overcome. The fact that you are working on it is a huge step in the right direction. Recognize, however, that it is but a singular point in your timeline. You will need to do constant work to help yourself achieve and maintain a more focused and positive mindset—one that is not filled with negatives of the past.

For one thing, I can't tell you how often a person can be ruminating on a negative point in their past and NOT even see it! If you can't even recognize what you are doing, then you cannot even begin to fix it. Thus, part of your journey in achieving mindfulness and learning to live in the moment is about being conscious when negativity from the past enters your mind. It is that "a-ha!" moment where you feel your energy draining from your body and notice the thoughts in your mind that are creating that result.

You are halfway there if you can spot and notice negative thoughts. Once you have them firmly in your sight, then you need to perform the work to let them go. Banish them from your mind. Invoke that action. From there, keep regular maintenance going. If the thoughts reappear, remind them firmly that they are to be gone. And keep doing this, over and over. It may seem silly or childish at first, but what you are doing is allowing yourself to heal.

When the negative thoughts are gone from your mind, they will likely leave a cut and a scar. This needs to be healed. Like a bandage and ointment would fix a physical wound, love will heal your mental wound. Love is the most powerful tool available to you. It is readily available anytime you need it. Don't be afraid to apply as much love as needed to any mental wounds you have. While scars may remain, you will be stronger and better for it. Always think positively when looking ahead, and be grateful for the feeling of how you feel in the present.

If you had a physical wound, you would probably not pour acid on it and make it worse. So why are you doing that to your mental wounds? Rather than applying love, I always see people beating themselves up mentally. They blame themselves for the past. They punish themselves for regrets. Their minds transform from a place of happiness and peace to an actual man-made prison.

If you're choosing to punish yourself for what happened in the past, you cannot possibly move forward. You remain stuck in the past because that is what you feel you deserve. Nothing saddens me more than when somebody says they deserve to punish themselves; that the past defines their present and future. I don't believe this and won't accept it. If you feel that you are incarcerated in your mind for past actions, then call the governor and ask for a pardon. You served your time with good behavior. It is time now to be released.

Erase your perceived past wrongs from your mind. Move ahead as a free person. Especially do not put yourself back into that mental prison in the future. If mistakes happen in the future, then own up to them. Learn from them. Forgive yourself. You will do better next time. Do not punish yourself again; love yourself even more. You will need it at this time more than ever. This will allow the wounds to heal and for you to move forward.

* * *

Think of how great it would be to plan ahead, to have dreams and aspirations, and to set goals and targets for the life you want to live. This is possible, very much so. You can achieve the life that you want. But it will take time. Everything has a process and order to it. To look ahead, you must be present in this moment; you need a clear and open mind. To live in the present, you need to resolve the past.

If you think that letting go is simply about resolving the past, you are only part of the way there. Yes, it is tremendous when you feel that negativity from the past is no longer with you, but letting go of the past is just as much about creating your present and future. Your past, present, and future are all connected. They have an intimate and close relationship. They are, essentially, the same moment. If one is blocked, the others suffer, and the past is usually the main culprit. Thus, the need and want to let go needs to be ignited within you.

Keep an eye on the big picture, always. This is why you do not want to focus on the past. It is dealt with and gone. You can look forward to the future. Feel excited about it, but do not live in it. *You will live in the present moment. All else will take care of itself from here.*

Since the future does not yet exist, it cannot contain baggage that you are holding onto for an indefinite period of time. When it comes to your future, I want you to view your outlook in a different manner.

As much as you know to let go of the past, you must also not focus too much on outcomes. If we worry too much about the future and what will happen, that holds us back, as well. For worries about your future that have not come to fruition, you are not going to necessarily let them go. Rather, for your future, you need to evolve your mode of thinking.

It is time to focus on learning how to set goals, both short and long term, so you can move ahead. In other words, you are not letting go of the future itself or planning; rather, you will learn to let go of the worries. Focused work on planning your future is much different than debilitating worrying.

Once you are actively living in the moment, future worries should fall by the wayside. By shifting your mental approach to how you look ahead as a source of optimism while maintaining your focus in the present, the future no longer becomes a source of struggle. The future is an opportunity for growth that you are not dependent upon but instead look forward to as it develops in this and every moment.

We will learn going forward how to plan ahead while living a life with purpose. Setting goals is wonderful, but they do not define us. If we live in the present, then outcomes don't matter.

If we do not achieve the results we seek, we can try again. We can change plans, evolve our style, or set different targets. We can look ahead and think of what we want to achieve and where we want to be. We may get there, but not how we pictured it; the *results* may be there, but maybe not exactly as we thought they would be.

And that is all fine, because life is not a competition or a race. It is a journey that you get to practice over and over again.

I hope this moment of enlightenment has or will hit you one day as it hit me. My entire focus and view of life—and my existence— changed once the pressure was off. This certainly made it much easier to let go of the past which was gone and could no longer serve me, as well as the fear of not achieving the future that I demanded for myself. The more I let things be instead of pushing hard, the more naturally the universe provided me with mental images of my dream life over time.

As I learned to let go, I started to move toward a life including manifestation. Once I committed to the art of manifestation, everything began to open as I had never seen or expected before.

Likewise, consider what you envision as your own dreams and what your Chosen Life looks like. Imagine that you can see it and one day live it. If you are ready to let go of what doesn't serve you and to learn how to create your ideal reality, then you, too, are ready to invoke manifestation into your world.

SIXTEEN

The Art of Manifestation

—⟊⟋⟊—

You have done it. You are on the road to clearing out your life.

Purging your excess physical possessions through minimalism and freeing your mind of unneeded thoughts and worries by letting go will allow you to feel free and alive. Living in the moment will give space for you to function in the *present day*. How excited are you right now? You should be over the moon! The world is completely open to you.

I spent many of my early years comparing my existence to others. We are all guilty of this at some point or another; we think that we will be able to figure out our lives by modeling ourselves after others. I know that I've caught myself seeing people who are seemingly happy-go-lucky who appear to not have a care in the world. As I have gotten older and met more and more people over the course of my lifetime, I have learned that this is not usually the case. We can think that we see one thing on the surface, while it can be very different as we search deep within.

Remember, you don't live in anyone else's mind. You cannot possibly know what other people think about throughout their days. Don't even bother trying to guess. The only mind that you can CONTROL is your own.

We are all going through the same trials and tribulations. So don't worry about how your mind is doing compared to someone else's. Focus only on yourself. It is the best road traveled.

Now comes the time to learn how to utilize your newfound openness to create your own self. That's right. You are going to become the creator of your life and existence. You are going to take control of your destiny through the power of your mind.

Imagine being able to envision the life you want to live—and then making it a reality. Rather than relying on "outside forces" to decide your future, you can take control of yourself and your existence to make your dreams and wishes come true.

This is not mental voodoo or having delusional thoughts. Rather, by opening and focusing your mind, you will be able to create concrete and feasible intentions that you will make happen. The power of mentally creating changes to your life is called manifestation. The only tool that you will need to focus on is your mind as we start the process now.

Learning the art of manifestation should both excite and scare you at the same time. The good news is that there is no pressure in the steps you will undertake. You must let your mind be open and free. And then your journey of manifestation begins.

We are going to walk through how to steer and create your future through manifestation. Each step along the way, make sure you keep asking yourself the same question:

"WHAT DOES THE LIFE I WANT TO LIVE LOOK LIKE?"

To follow the course of manifestation, our process again returns to the power of your mind and how you use it.

As strong as my mind is, it took me so many years to learn how to focus my thoughts and energy. To look ahead, we have to keep in mind our patterns of thinking of the past. *Manifestation cannot work unless we have a clear mind that is open to fresh thoughts and the creation of positive ideas.* That is the hardest part of manifestation; it is not about the creation of ideas into reality, but rather, starting with a clear mind. This simplest step was always my struggle. Think about your own mind and how it works as I explain the evolution of my own mindset.

Speaking personally, I always felt a level of guilt if my mind wasn't being actively used for a purpose. As soon as I had a break from the action, my mind would always race to new directions. I could never enjoy the present moment I was in. I constantly felt the need to think. I would always use my mind. I would ponder what I had done wrong in the past and overanalyze each aspect by trying to dissect each moment in the instance. Or, my mind would race to the future and try to think of what could happen in different scenarios of my life and how I would prepare and deal with each.

Essentially, my mind was always living in the past or in the future. I was never truly in the present. It was no wonder why I got sick throughout my childhood and early adult years so often; I had bad sinuses and allergies, plus a very sensitive stomach. When I felt under constant pressure all the time, it took a toll on my mental health and from there my physical well-being.

I choose not to blame others for my state during these moments because ultimately, the buck stops with me. No matter what circumstances were presented to me or what people said, I CHOSE how I reacted. I couldn't let anything go. I felt the need to prove myself and convince others that I was correct. That is a ton of pressure.

I don't miss that state of mind at all. I learned to let it all go. I healed my mind over time. The scars may be there, but the hurts and pain are healing. And they continue to heal every day as I make the conscious decision to live in the NOW. Free and open.

If you are reading this in bewilderment, that's okay. Learning to free my mind did not happen overnight. It took months and years of work. At the time of this writing, I have been actively working on it for over fifteen years and it's still a daily process. *I had to put in the work to learn to think about nothing.* Shouldn't that be the easiest thing to do?

This is not meant to cause you physical or mental pain. Rather, you are going to have to accept that in order for you to put in the work, then you need to get off your butt and actually do it. Reading my words and conceptually thinking about what you will do is one thing. Invoking action is a very different thing.

My road to manifestation would have never happened if not for yoga and meditation: Chosen Commandments #5 and #6. For you to make the commitment to build and walk your path toward enlightenment, you need to start the journey on a fresh slate.

I can tell you that the practice of yoga and meditation worked with me to clear my mind of regret and worry. I could not see the life that I wanted until I accepted and learned the life that I did *not* want. My initial hours spent in yoga and meditation taught me that the paths I walked for my early years were not serving me. To the outside world, I looked like I had my shit together. I had education, work experience, and a family life. But people could not see the person within; the person who was unhappy on a daily basis, constantly worrying about the future and regretting the past. I was faking it and people were buying it. But through yoga and meditation, I saw that the person I was really lying to was myself. It was time to come clean with myself. I made the commitment to stop living the lifestyle I was living and to be open to what could be. The turning point of letting go was my road toward the power of manifestation.

I followed a pattern for my first thirty or so years. I existed. I was functioning. I worked toward goals that I thought I HAD to achieve. I was living the life I thought was expected of me. I didn't know better as I simply thought that I was doing what I had to do. The possibility of being alone with my thoughts terrified me. Thus, I resisted even attempting yoga and meditation when they were first introduced to me. I gave the same excuses that most who shrug them off do. Being alone with my thoughts and taking inventory of myself was a path that did not come easily to me. Being accountable to myself and listening to my thoughts was a skill that I was never taught.

Everyone's path and timeline are different. If I met you and we conversed for hours or days, I still could not tell you where your life is headed. Only you can ultimately decide that. But then you have to make a philosophical decision. Do you believe that you control your own destiny or that all the actions you take won't matter for your life? It's a big switch and one that you should not decide lightly. From a higher level, we can debate how much the universe has predetermined our lives for us. I believe that, but you may not. That's okay. But even if we can agree that there is a higher power that has a plan for us, we still have to remember that we ultimately can control our path.

Think about it for a moment. If you choose right now to walk into traffic in front of a car, will someone stop you? If you are in a relationship, work or personal, you can go right now—end it and walk out. You can sell your home. Move to a different country. YOU get to decide that. YOU control that. You have a lot of power over yourself and your life.

So, while there may be a higher power that has created the framework for your existence, YOU are the one living your life. This may scare you, but it should not. It should empower you. Motivate you. No matter the life that you have lived up until now, it is not too late. It is never too late until you pass. You can evolve. You can work to achieve and live the life you seek. The secret? Figuring out what the heck you want from this existence!

I have experienced way too many conversations where I asked someone what their goals were and what they wanted out of life and a common answer that I received was, "I don't know." So let me get this straight. You are waking up every morning. You are working. You come home. You go back to bed. Repeat. Are you going through the motions or are you working toward something tangible? How can we possibly live the life we want if we don't even know what that looks like? Now that is scary in my opinion.

To create the visualizations of what you want, it is vital to keep things simple and in perspective. It's not what we see externally, it's the mental ideas of what we create in our minds and the feelings associated with them. You may not consider yourself a visual person by nature. That is okay. Whether or not you can see the outside world or create images in your mind, we all have the capacity to close our eyes and create the feelings of what we want within ourselves. It may take time, but the more you practice, the easier the experiences will come to you. Those mental ideas and feelings are the keys to learning the art of manifestation.

Once you appreciate that you have the power to redirect your life through manifestation, you are firmly standing on the path toward creating the best you possible. Amazing! With a twinkle in your eyes and fire in your belly, it is time to understand the formula of successfully creating and fulfilling a manifestation. I will outline for you the key steps and provide a real-life example of how you are able to manifest in your life. Throughout the discussion, consider your commitment to following the steps of manifestation. Do not simply go through the motions. Be prepared to truly engrain them into your life. This is no easy task. But the greatest rewards come from the work that you put into your existence. Now it is time to really test your commitment and zest for taking your life to new levels. I know you can do this. And deep down, you know that, too!

Manifestation is best exercised by following this simple recipe:

Step 1: Learn to clear your mind.
Step 2: Receive sensory input of the life you want to live with an open and inspired heart, then feel it in your body.
Step 3: Make your intentions (focused thoughts) a reality.
Step 4: There is no timeline.

Four simple steps, seemingly. But they are impossible to happen unless you are committed to starting with Step 1. Throughout your manifestation journey, always start and come back to Step 1. Manifestation can only happen if you are able to clear your mind.

You want to be able to bring manifestation into your life. That desire will only flow if you provide your thoughts with a clear roadway.

STEP 1: **LEARN TO CLEAR YOUR MIND**

Do you control your mind? Or does your mind control you?

Focus on starting your manifestation journey with a clear mind. Easier said than done, given how the mind functions.

The urge will come to immediately start exploring and filling your mind with all sorts of thoughts and plans. After all, you just freed your mind of so much clutter. Shouldn't your mind now be open for maximum use? In theory, yes. That comes with time. But for now, I only want you to focus on one thing: NOTHING.

Nothing, you say? That's right. *Nothing*.

That may make no sense at first glance. I get it. We are so used to doing things. Planning. Worrying. Re-planning. Thinking. Over-thinking. Isn't it time to take a break? When we get physically injured, we rest and heal. We take time off from our workouts. Picture your mind as being injured or wounded from overuse. Let's give our minds the same love that we would give our bodies. Let's do nothing. Let's rest your mind and let it heal. Learn and embrace calmness. What a novel concept!

Once you empty your mind, you will focus on nothing indefinitely. Yes, you will go about your daily life and continue to function as you always would. But when thoughts come that involve the past or future, especially negative ones, you will steer your mind to nothing.

The time for regret and worry is done. Now the mind can relax, heal, and feel nurtured. Simply allow yourself to be. The commitment is there to allow your mind to connect with your spirit and energy. Your mind slowly becomes a blank canvas.

An example of this practice in my life comes back to yoga and meditation. To utilize the power of yoga and meditation, I initially needed to unblock my mind. This was a lengthy process, as I had never known the concepts of being and living in the moment. I started to feel that my mind began to open and clear during the first three years of my yoga and meditation practices. As I continued to open mentally, I questioned what the next steps for me were. I wanted answers. I demanded to see my goals and how I could get there.

The more I pushed, the more blocked mentally I became again. And then it hit me one day: the answers are within me. They are sitting right there. I am simply not open enough to see them. *The more I push, the more I block myself.* If I can let it go and allow myself to enjoy the present moment, the answers will come when I am ready for them.

So, let's enjoy the ride now and not worry about what is to come.

I began to let go. The more I let go, the more answers I received. I started to allow manifestation into my world.

I originally utilized yoga and meditation to simply clear my mind. As my mind slowly cleared and opened over time, it was the same yoga and meditation practices where mental images of my future life began to hit me. My clear mind was not enough if I did not have the setting in which to allow ideas and images to be created. If my mind was the blank canvas, yoga and meditation were my art studios where I was able to paint beautiful and positive images of the life that I wanted to live. While I could paint images anywhere in the world that I was, I found that I was always most inspired during yoga and meditation. Why? Because those are settings that are distraction-free.

Without having outside influences penetrating my thoughts, I was able to be alone with my thoughts while at yoga and meditation. All of my greatest life changes and evolutions hit me during those practices. When my mind was most clear, I could see the direction of where I wanted my life to go. I learned how to manifest. That is the amazing power of yoga and meditation. They can help heal and calm. But they can also inspire new, amazing directions in life.

To calm your mind, the key will be to find any sort of activity that relaxes you. If you cannot practice yoga or meditation, for example, perhaps take a walk. Do something active if possible. Lie down and close your eyes. Cook. Paint. Read a book. Watch television. There are no right or wrong answers here. Whatever activity you find that allows your mind to relax and not worry or stress about issues that you think you have in your life, then you are on the right track.

Once your chosen activity calms your mind, it will help show you the roads in life that you could take. It will be up to you to see those roads and choose them.

Whatever methods you use to clear your mind, embrace and utilize them to their capacity. Only when you are truly able to clear your mind will you be ready for Step 2 in manifestation.

STEP 2: **RECEIVE SENSORY INPUT OF THE LIFE YOU WANT TO LIVE WITH AN OPEN AND INSPIRED HEART, THEN FEEL IT IN YOUR BODY**

It is time to receive sensory input and feelings about the life you seek. These are the roads in life you'll want to take that will best serve you.

Eventually, once your mind is clear, sensory input will come to you—such as images, smells, or other sensations—that will, appear, so to speak, on the blank canvas of your mind which will inspire and motivate you to direct your life to new heights. Once you receive that input, you need to feel in your body as though your future life is happening now, in the present moment. *The reception of those sensory inputs and feeling as though that reality is happening now is manifestation: the art of sensing and feeling what you want your life to be like and working toward achieving it.*

Welcome to a new frontier for you. *You can create the life you seek.*

As with anything, the work needs to be put in. There are no shortcuts or deadlines. Consciously put in the work to make it happen and things will unfold as you never would have believed before.

As described earlier, I personally learned to receive sensory input about my future life through mental images. I am a visual person, so I learn visually. Then the feelings of those experiences came about in real time in my body through consistent yoga and meditation practices. In short, once I was able to regularly clear my mind, I was able to view images and feel experiences of the life I wanted to live. Having my mind as a blank canvas, I could "draw" almost any image I wanted, which came with a particular feeling associated with each one. The images and feelings came best when I let them come to me naturally, rather than forcing them (hence receiving sensory input).

Note that you are not limited to receiving information about your life through yoga and meditation. *You can receive them at any time, or in any state of activity or inactivity.* While I personally find that visualization for manifestation is best created during yoga and meditation, thus being the reason why I use my experiences as an example here, I want you to remain open to receiving what your life will be like *anytime and anywhere.* In essence, do what serves you best for this exercise.

To fully understand manifestation, an important reality hit me as I tried to reason why I needed to *visualize* and *feel* what I wanted in life. *I needed to create an intention of what I wanted before visions could come to me.* I could not possibly achieve the life that I wanted if I didn't know what that was! How was I going to find my path? Simple. *By thinking nothing and simply being.* The answers would come if I was open to ideas and open enough to receive them.

I thank yoga and meditation for opening my mind to who I could be and what I could experience in life. Yoga and meditation opened my senses and being, which allowed me to build and rebuild myself. When I am practicing these two arts, I feel that the universe is showing me a mirror. When my mind is most clear and inspired, I can envision the best me in that mirror. When I can see that vision clearly, then I know that I can make it happen. You can do the same, regardless of how you receive information through your own unique sensory input.

After clearing the mind, manifestation always begins with sensing the end result in your mind, and then feeling what that is like in your body. On some levels, it can be something you want or need. Whatever the reasoning is behind it, the key is to see the end of the road in however way you sense that. It can be something material, such as a car or a house, a job, a relationship, a travel destination—anything your heart desires.

When sensing the end result and feeling the experience in your body as if it is happening now, again, you don't need to pick the end goal consciously. The sensory input will naturally come to you. When you feel happy, clear, and open with a clear mind is when the experience of what you seek will appear to your senses. Once you grasp it, you will smile. You will not know at this point *how* the experience will be achieved, when, and what it will look like exactly. But you will know that you can make it happen.

When you sense your end result, however way this comes to you, tell yourself out loud and internally that you will make it happen. Sometimes you will need to take an actual physical picture of what you seek and look at it daily, or write it in your to-do list and review it repeatedly. Whatever you feel reasonably needs to get you there, do it. But again, manifestation is not when we simply consciously go to seek a final goal. It works best when the sense of the result enters our being organically and from there we wait as we achieve it practically over time.

The experience that shows up for you should fuel a passion within your soul. It will not become a reality unless you are determined to make it happen. It is your will that will allow your mind to become clear, to become a canvas for what your life can be. Nothing will happen or go anywhere unless you are passionate about it and want to make the shifts in your life for them to happen. Don't give up. Don't stress about it. Simply enjoy what appears and believe it to be true. By believing in your future life that you want to manifest, you are believing in yourself. Don't give up quickly or easily, otherwise you will be giving up on yourself!

It is an exciting breakthrough when what appears to you can ignite the fire within your soul. As you have already learned, the mind cannot do everything on its own. Otherwise, it burns out. True and continued success will come when the mind, body, and soul work together. In this case, your mind will receive the sensory input. Your body will feel the feelings. And the soul will fuel the desire to make them a reality.

This is the power that I want you to feel for yourself—to take control of your existence and make your positive creations a reality. You have the power to create your Chosen Life through manifestation. As long as you are ready to put in the work and understand that it is a foundation being built over time, with a clear mind, you are able to create the life you want to live.

STEP 3: **MAKE YOUR INTENTIONS (FOCUSED THOUGHTS) A REALITY**

The transition from sensory input and feelings to reality is the third step of manifestation.

In my experience, creation will happen through your concentrated energy and efforts. By putting *intentions*—concentrated thoughts—out to the universe based on what you received as sensory inputs in Step 2, the reality of your thoughts will come to be.

Consciously putting your intentions "out there" is the purest form of manifestation. It feels like the universe hears your thoughts and over time, your thoughts come into existence. But you need to put those thoughts into form. You need to speak those thoughts daily to yourself in order for them to become real. Perceive your life and what it would be like with your intentions (focused thought) happening in reality. Never waver. Do not be afraid to tell people about your thoughts and what you see happening in your life. Be very strong and firm with yourself. If you put it out there, then it will happen. You have the power to set the course of your life.

Doubt and negativity have no place in manifestation. If you plant the seeds of doubt, your garden will not bear fruit. It's that simple. If what you wish to happen is to actually manifest itself, you must put out there with 100 percent certainty at all times that it's achievable. With doubt and negativity, you will consciously work harder as a result, and your unconscious will work just as hard, if not more. We are unaware of how dangerous it is when we allow our subconscious to sabotage us.

Our minds are powerful tools. They work best when they are fed positive fuel called love. The functioning of the soul connecting to your mind and body is real. Once you spiritually love yourself and allow your mind to be free to explore and evolve, there are no limits.

You may think you are not good enough. Not deserving. Too old. All of that is crap. That kind of thinking is a closed soul, one that does not feed love to the body and mind. If you cannot love yourself, then you close your mind from operating at its best capacity. Never limit yourself in that way. Ever.

Please note that there are many different techniques available to you in transforming your intentions (focused thought) into reality. Some common ones that I can recommend are:

1. **Writing things out in a journal and putting them in a binder.**
2. **A sign or a vision board in an area that you frequent often, such as an office or a kitchen.**
3. **Add due dates to your calendar in setting timelines for actions you wish to take.**
4. **Create a checklist that lists what events need to take place for your reality to become true.**

The key here is that you do not want your intentions to become and remain daydreams. They must not feel like unrealistic hopes that will not come to fruition. To turn your thoughts into reality, you must make yourself accountable by putting in the effort required to make the dream happen.

In making Step 3 occur, note that you continue to live your life as you were previously. Your daily life and routines do not necessarily change right away. The only difference now is that you have the conceptualization of your Chosen Life and you are ready, willing, and able to make it happen. By speaking and thinking about your intention daily, take comfort in knowing that it will happen.

But *when will it happen*, you ask? Not by setting a deadline. To achieve the vision of your life, you must not have a timeline. Be open to when it happens.

STEP 4: **THERE IS NO TIMELINE**

As a big proponent of manifestation, I often get asked for an exact timeline to create and achieve it. I laugh each time I'm asked, for manifestation does not work that way.

Firstly, timing in itself is bigger than us. We do not know what else is happening everywhere else in the world and in the universe and beyond which contributes to timing.

Second, everyone's timing is different. It will come down to when your mind and heart will open. That is when ideas and visions will come to you.

Yes, we are back to the heart! Dear heart, we did not forget you. As we discussed, the opening of the mind allows it to receive love from within your soul. And then your soul and mind are able to function and flow in sync. How lovely is that?

To be able to successfully manifest, you need your heart to open and feed your mind and body with love. In a happy and loving state, you will be free and open to achieving any life that you seek. What you are manifesting can only become reality when you feed it with the belief that it *will* happen. Belief in your visions of your future life comes from the love that you give yourself on a daily basis. Belief and love go hand in hand. If you are committed to manifesting your future, never forget to love yourself in the present.

As I will mention again and again because I am so thankful for it, I can truly attribute yoga and meditation as the primary gateways that allowed me to live the life I currently live. It came to me over time, not all at once. My feeling is that my subconscious was relaxed and able to process smoother. From there, notions of what my life would look like would seemingly hit me out of the blue. I achieved my dream career, got into the best shape of my life, deepened my connection with friends and family, and learned to love myself unconditionally. Meaning again, that the life possibilities were within me, I simply had to be open enough to see them. The same ability is within you.

For the steps of manifestation to come to fruition, you cannot give yourself an expectation of when, how, and even what the result will look like in its completed form. You need to trust in the process. Trust in the universe. And trust that your energy will create positive results for you. If you do not consistently believe in yourself and the life you envision, manifestation will simply not work for you.

At some point, you may ask yourself, "Why isn't my reality happening?!" When you are truly manifesting, keep reflecting on the four steps of manifestation. Having the four steps in your back pocket will help keep you on track. Don't get discouraged. Manifestation is not about meeting or beating timelines. It is about you believing it will happen. From there, simply allow your reality to unfold when it is ready. Let go of the time expectation. But never your belief!

A timeline that you set as part of manifestation is, at best, a guideline. It is more to keep you on track so that you do not drift or give up. Setting a timeline goal also means that you may need to adjust your due dates, as often and for as long as may be required, until what you seek becomes reality. If you are able to use calendars and timelines in this manner, they can help rather than hinder you. But again, *do not hold on to any timelines as your focal point.* Continue to BELIEVE in your manifestation.

How will you know that you have achieved a manifestation result? No magical bell will ring all of a sudden. You must consistently put in the work. Clear your mind. See your vision that you are manifesting. Put in the work to make your thoughts a reality. And always be willing to let go of the timeline. Together, with the work that you have put in to learn to live in the moment and by following the 6 Chosen Commandments, the manifestation will come to fruition. Just not necessarily when you expect it or in the form that you think it will be.

* * *

Now that you have the tools of the four steps for manifestation down, it's time to consider how you can create a practice of manifestation that will help shape your path and future. You are now ready to take the tools you have learned and make your vision a reality.

Let's take a common example of a manifestation that you can create and fulfill. Perhaps you have considered a career plan for yourself if you are currently in school, or you have thought of a career change later in life. I'm sure that this thought has hit your mind at one time, whatever your age, income, education, and life experiences. Take the first step to clear your mind. Close your eyes. Think about yourself today. Consider that at some point in your life, you were destined to enter a particular profession and achieve a certain career position. Focus your thoughts and think about it. Feel it in your body. Write it down for yourself when you are ready. Review what you have written.

If you tell yourself that making this career choice is impossible, then it will never happen. You will create a self-fulfilling prophecy. Your intended career will be built on a weak foundation of doubt. Thus, it can only crumble. If you do not believe that something will happen, then everyone around you will think the same thing. Nobody will do it for you. If you want your dreams to happen, then it starts and ends with you. For it is you that must put love into your intentions. Believe in yourself no matter what. If you limit your dream by saying it will not happen, then it has a 100 percent chance to fail.

But what if the reverse happened? You had that same intention and said to yourself, "YES! I can have the career I seek!" From there, every day you tell yourself that you WILL achieve your desired job. Every time you tell yourself this, you smile. You can find a picture of people on the internet working in your chosen profession and put it as your phone wallpaper. Tell everyone you meet and know that you will achieve your dream job one day. You put the energy out there! When you meet people in real life who work in your dream profession, you ask them how they got started in their careers. You start gathering information. You do all sorts of online searches yourself. You contact schools related to the career you want. Come hell or high water, you *will* fulfill your intended career. It is written in your mind. And you will manifest it into existence.

Through long-term manifestation, if you consistently maintain the belief of your career goal, you will make it happen. You will apply to schools or for an apprenticeship depending on the job that you seek. You will see the roads and options of how to make your dream career a reality. By having the belief solidified in your mind consistently, the odds are so much higher that you will actually accomplish the goal. Never lose hope but trust that your vision will manifest into your reality.

Manifesting does not come from a place of doubt or fear. There is no pressure to make your manifestation happen. Your manifestation is fueled by love, excitement, and determination. When you set your sights on the prize and put all your energy into it, you have increased your odds of achievement by a thousand percent!

If you want to see the most powerful example of my own ability to manifest, then keep reading. The proof is right before your eyes. *The Bible 3.0* would not have come into existence if not for the power of manifestation.

I always loved the idea of writing a book. It was an important idea to me that I intended to achieve while on Earth. I started and stopped writing a book several times in my life. Nothing ever took. I never felt IT. Or the timing never felt right. Whatever the reason, a book from beginning to end never flowed from my fingertips. I have always loved to write and have written hundreds of articles and blogs. Would a book ever come from me? I told myself during my younger years that I wanted that to happen. I needed it to happen. Then my dream became a pressure point. I no longer enjoyed the notion of writing a book. I practically felt obligated to write one. So I gave up. The belief fell away.

I decided in my mind that writing a book was likely not going to happen. So I let it go. Then I stopped writing for over ten years. I didn't think about it. Deep down, I didn't miss it. I was living my life and taking things as they came. Writing was not in the cards back then and I was fine with that. Along the way, while I was relaxed and open, I had a vision of *The Bible 3.0*; it hit me out of the blue one day. I could see in my mind the book in its entirety. I held onto this image and allowed it to marinate in my subconscious.

From there, one day, I felt the urge to write again. Having the vision of *The Bible 3.0*, I realized I was manifesting it into existence. Whether it was written or not, in my mind it was a done deal. It was happening. I didn't have to hang my hat on hope or fear that doubts would creep in. I let nothing else come into my mind except for the fact that the book was going to be written. So I began to write. And write. And write. Before I knew it, there was no more writer's block. I learned to love writing again. And I willed a book into creation practically overnight.

* * *

Please keep in mind that manifestation is on a different level than goal setting. To compare them, manifestation is actually goal setting on steroids. It is about formulating life-changing occurrences that come together with your mind, body, and soul working in unison. Goal setting alone is just from the mind. And above all else, remember: if you can believe it, then it will happen!

One of the beautiful components of manifestation is that various seeds can be planted within you over time, and you never know for certain which seed ends up blooming. As long as you plant enough seeds and give yourself the time needed to blossom, they will come to be. Time is the least known variable of the equation; never force time upon manifestation. Simply be, and let it come when it's ready for you.

As you strengthen your ability to manifest your Chosen Life, you will be well equipped to achieve goals for yourself of all sizes, which can be short term and long term. Goals are most readily executed when you create the platform for them to be achievable. Therefore, it is no coincidence that a person who is strong in their manifestation skills will conquer many goals throughout their lifetime. Let's learn now how you can set and achieve all sorts of goals in your world.

SEVENTEEN
Set Your Chosen Goals

━◦◯◦━

Do you want to feel like you're trapped in quicksand? Imagine a life five years from now, yet you've made zero progress. You lived day to day, just to get by.

A stagnant present translates to a bleak future. An evolving present translates to success and self-worth. What do you want for your future? Get ready to ask yourself this question on a daily basis, as you are now ready to learn the art of setting and accomplishing goals in life.

If you want to truly have your best life, it starts with short-term and long-term goals. You need to have a roadmap in your mind. What do you want to accomplish today, tomorrow, next week, next month, next year, and in the next five years? The trick will be to focus on the end results and what you want to accomplish. From there you will create a list of the baby steps you need to implement in order to make them happen. By following this process, you will end up achieving more than you ever thought possible. This will also happen in less than no time simply because you didn't just dream and give up. You broke through your limitations and transformed your goals into reality.

Goals are a good thing. In fact, they are crucial to establish and execute plans for success. Do not get intimidated by the thought that setting goals is a chore. You want to live the best life and you want to evolve into the greatest form of yourself possible—so if you are committed to living the Chosen Life, then goals are your friends. They will work with you to get you to where you want to go.

It is one thing to manifest an idea of what your life could be like, which is a key initial step. However, to practically implement the manifestations and end results, goal setting is an absolute must. As you approach this goal-setting material, you will be able to apply it not just from your mind only, but from your mind, body, and soul working together after having incorporated the previous work.

Goals can be any shape and size. No goal is too small. The starting point is knowing the end result you want and then learning to work your way backward to figure out the steps to get there. We will do this together in this chapter.

It may seem very contradictory: how does one live in the present, yet set future goals at the same time? A very fair question, but one that is easy to answer...

When you are establishing your goals, note that you do NOT live in the future. *You are not dependent on the achievement of various goals.* Your mindset always remains in the present. Your *focus* is always on the present.

In other words, do not drift to a future world and try to live there. This will not help your goals be achieved any faster. In fact, an unfocused mind in the future will hinder the process.

As you consider future goals that you wish to establish, do not depend on them. Instead, always focus your mind on the present. *In the now.*

In framing your mindset, remember to always be hopeful of the future and remain positive. You must have the belief that the end result (or goal) will happen. Positive thinking breeds positive results. Your mind, though, should always be redirected to the present. You will then be able to consistently be in a state of mindfulness, which will be the key to having a clearer mind to see the goals up ahead.

Another key point to consider when setting goals is the magnitude of what you plan to achieve.

Goals can be both short and long term. You can set smaller immediate goals and bigger long-term goals. The process will be the same to organize, plan and execute them. The main differences between the two are simply the number of steps and timelines. Otherwise, your outline to achieve goals will be the same, short or long.

In preparing to set and achieve goals, here is a five-point checklist that I recommend using as your guide:

1. **Establish the end result.** What is the tangible goal that you want to achieve?
2. **Deadline:** When do you want the goal to be achieved?
3. **Prepare steps:** What do you need to do in order to achieve the goal?
4. **Assign due dates and timelines for each step.**
5. **Starting point:** Understand where you need to begin your steps.

From my perspective, goals come to me when I don't push for them. As you have learned throughout our journey together, there are so many tools available to clear your mind. When you learn to utilize mindfulness and live in the present moment, your mind will be in its most clear state and ready for full utilization. You will not have to push to think of ideas; rather, the ideas will come to you. When you are not distracted or in a state of negativity, you will be astonished at how many goals you will set that will help resolve the needs and wants in your life.

At this stage, you do not have to worry about *how* you will get there or what the process will be. Simply focus first and foremost on figuring out the goals you wish to achieve. The rest will come as you follow our simple checklist.

Now, let's run through each of those steps in greater detail to understand how to successfully utilize the goal checklist to work for you. It is a simple formula that can be replicated time and time again. By following the checklist, you will be able to establish more goals than ever imaginable and see tangible results. Your present will always feel calmer and happier because you will be working on and achieving results on a consistent basis.

1. ESTABLISH THE END RESULT

The goal checklist may seem backward to you. After all, shouldn't you begin at the starting point and work your way to the end? On the contrary, goals are not created for the start, they are created for the end.

It is a fallacy to think that you can start at the beginning in order to establish and successfully implement a goal. You cannot reach a destination if you do not know where you are going.

I have asked many unhappy people I know what they would wish to achieve if they could have their dream lives. Many have answered me with, "I don't know." Not knowing what you want in life means you are traveling without a map. You are wandering aimlessly, hoping to reach an unknown destination. That does not sound like a recipe for success to me. It is a warning sign for failure. If you want to succeed and get ahead, you need to keep your eye on the prize.

Through manifestation, you have already learned that clearing your mind and living in the present moment can lead to visions of the life you want to live. In goal setting, manifestation can be a key starting point to establishing your desired end result. If it is a tangible goal that you want to make happen, then you will need to follow the rest of the steps in the goal-setting checklist to do that. But know that manifestation at the very least can help you create the idea or inspiration of your end goal: the absolute starting point to goal setting.

Visions through a clear mind firmly entrenched in the present have been the starting point for achieving all my greatest goals. Personally, I find that when I am angry, hurt, or sad—any mix of negative emotions—it is difficult, if not impossible, to set goals for myself. When I am not in a positive mindset, I defer goal setting for when I am happy and feel open.

I also do not go *searching* for goals and feel any pressure or desperation when thinking about them. I focus on the positives in my life and tell myself that achieving more goals will not make or fix me. Achieving goals is a bonus, but being in the present is what really counts. I have discovered that the less pressure I put on myself to think of goals to achieve, the easier it is to identify them.

Goals are all around us, waiting for us to find and achieve them. But our own unique goals are embedded within us. It is up to us to be open and see them!

A warning sign as you start your list of goals: Recognize the difference between *wants* and *needs*. As humans, we have desires that fuel us for survival. We find areas of our life that require improvement or fixing. Those I identify as *needs*. We also have the areas of life where we desire more than the necessities to live. Those are *wants*.

Examples? To get to work, you require a car. That is a need. Buying a basic car to get you from A to B fulfills that need. Purchasing a car that is far beyond your budget but has lots of bells and whistles—that is a want. *Make sure not to confuse the two.* Needs are required to survive. We can live without wants, but if we work hard and plan for them, we can still make them happen.

When you inventory your list of needs and wants, please make sure to *prioritize the needs*.

Do not focus on a frill item over a life requirement. Wants can and should be attained, but only when needs are met first.

The commitment from your end is to take the time to envision the results you want in life. There are so many ways to do this. You can use an electronic and/or paper checklist to write down a goal as it comes to you. Sitting down and conscientiously brainstorming goals is another option.

As I was lying in śavāsana during yoga, a thought hit my mind: *I really want to create a website.* This website would be very important for my business. It would help focus my energies and resources toward a productive project. It is something I want to do, yes, but it certainly fits into my list of needs, first and foremost.

So, for our example of a goal, we would write down in the electronic to-do list: *create a website.* Congratulations! We have now set our first goal.

See how easy that is? I am not concerned about labeling this goal as a short- or long-term goal as of yet. Depending on the process, it might be achieved quickly or take time. That is okay. We will figure that part out. For now, your mind can be happy. A goal is set.

As you read through this chapter, feel free to join in on the fun. If you have become inspired to achieve any particular goals at this moment, please write down your goal now. If not, once you are ready in the future to set your short- and long-term goals, then flip back to this section. Follow the checklist, as well. Once you have come back to this section, please write down the goal that you wish to achieve in your to-do list. Look at it. Smile. Let it sink in. You are living in the present and looking to further yourself in the future.

There is no pressure to achieve your goals. Do not look far ahead. Know that you are already a champion simply by creating a goal for yourself. Whether it comes to fruition or not is irrelevant.

Setting goals for yourself is such a key step for evolving into the best you possible. Creating the steps and then executing them is a skill you will learn and practice over and over again.

You don't have to think that much ahead. We have a goal and let's savor it. For myself, I am going to create a website. You have your own goal in mind. Now let's create a deadline to achieve our respective goals.

2. SET A DEADLINE

The deadline. The boogieman of goal achievement. When most of us hear the word "deadline," we think of pressure. Because time is limited in life, we tend to worry as soon as we hear the word. We instantly think, *How am I going to get everything done by that time and date? What do I have to do? I have so many other things to get done! I am feeling so much pressure!* If this is how you view deadlines, then it is time to shift your focus. Deadlines do not need to be your enemy. They can be your friend.

When a deadline is assigned to achieve a goal, I feel SO much relief. Why is that? Simple. I know that I do not have to work until the end of time on my task at hand. I have a finite ending. I don't have to worry about *how* I am going to get there because that is living in the future and bringing negativity into my mind. I am living in the present. I will figure out the steps to achieving my goal in the present. For now, I know that there is a rainbow at the end of the road.

The deadline gives me relief. It's like going on an airplane, flying to another country, and knowing my estimated date and time of arrival. Think of your goal as a journey to a destination and the deadline as the timing of when you will get there. Set the deadline with positivity and feel good.

To help alleviate the pressure of a deadline, note as well that it is a *tentative* deadline at best. Life circumstances arise. Things change, and you may need to be flexible to change your deadline. That is okay!

What is *not* okay is to set a deadline for a goal, fail to create the other steps in the checklist, and simply let the deadline pass with inaction. If you are following the other steps in the checklist (which you must do if you are serious about achieving a goal), then it is perfectly reasonable to go back to your to-do list and change the deadline. Who knows, sometimes you may even move it up!

Recognize overall that the deadline can be fluid and not set in stone. *But the stronger you feel about wanting to achieve your goal, the more seriously you should take your deadline.* Work on all the other steps in the checklist, knowing and recognizing that the deadline is there. Do not see this as a pressure point, but rather as an exciting destination to reach.

In addition, be very realistic when setting your deadline. Recognize that there may be several steps necessary to achieve the goal. The reason why you are setting a deadline is that it gives you a measure of when you should complete your steps so you can accomplish the goal. The deadline provides you a framework to work with. Think positively and realistically and put down even a range of time that you think it will take to complete the goal. Once you establish the *deadline range*, if you want to feel less pressure, go with the longer deadline.

There is no harm in taking more time if it means you will be happier and less stressed while working on completing each step properly.

When I imagine establishing my website, of course I want it right now. But I know that is unrealistic. There will be so many things I need to do to get it up and running. In my mind, when I envision my website, I see a three-to-six-month window until completion. Then I am free to choose six months as my initial deadline, which feels like an abundant amount of time to have the website created and implemented. I feel good about this. I need a website. Recognizing that I am going to create a website feels exciting to me. I have a target and focus. I think of nothing else regarding this goal other than the fact that it is set, and I know when I plan to have it completed. It feels good. Forty percent of the way there!

Now let's turn to the goal that you set. What is the deadline you want to achieve? Depending on the size of your goal and the number of steps, it could take anywhere from one day to one or more years. Only *you* know based on the goal that you set for yourself.

Do not put too much time and strain into this step. Simply give yourself a realistic deadline and write it down on your to-do list next to your goal. If nothing else, you now have your starting point.

As we go down the checklist, it will be much easier to create the steps and timeline for each if we know our overall deadline perimeter. Take a second and third look at your goal and deadline. I am very comfortable planning on completing a website in six months. Do you feel the same about your goal and deadline? Once you do, it's time to tackle the list of steps needed to achieve your goal.

3. PREPARE THE STEPS

In the process of goal creation and achievement, I would say that this third step is the trickiest part of the process. The reason why many goals are never achieved is because they are set for failure. You read that correctly.

Imagine a basketball team taking the floor of an NBA game. The game is about to start, and the players stare blankly at their head coach. In the locker room, the coach told his/her players that they want to win the game. A goal was set. But the coach failed to mention what steps the players would take during the game.

Without a game plan and plays to run, the players wander aimlessly and without purpose throughout the game. Their chances of success are very low. The team on the other end of the court sat with their coach ahead of time and were given the steps to take in order to win. Each player knew their assignment and what they would be doing throughout. The team that knows and understands the steps they need to take will win. The team without steps (and in essence, a plan) is doomed to lose.

If you want to be on the winning team, you will create the steps for yourself.

It is always better to write more steps rather than less when creating your plan. You can take bigger steps and break them down into smaller ones. You can rearrange them as needed, plus you can add or delete some along the way. Do not get too fixated on having to get all the right steps down in an instant. Every step you write down creates more certainty for yourself as to what needs to get done. Value your steps. Thinking of one step will help you envision more steps as you go along.

Fear and anxiety come from the unknown. If I left you in the middle of an ocean in a rowboat without a paddle or a map, you would have extreme anxiety about how to survive and where you are going. On the other hand, if I put you on a cruise ship with a captain and crew, GPS, and an itinerary, you would be calm and happy knowing that there is a plan and steps as to where you are going and how you will get there. So, let's find your captain, crew, GPS, and itinerary. Your goal will come closer to fruition each day if you recognize and work on the steps needed for achievement.

The steps are your closest allies. Goals move from unachievable and unrealistic targets to possible through the creation and implementation of steps.

More good news? *You do not need to do this alone!* You can turn to the internet and watch videos or read articles on the topic of your goal. If you have close friends or colleagues, you can sit down with them to pick their brains. You do not have to reinvent the wheel!

Research the steps needed to achieve your given goal and write yourself notes as you go along so that you don't forget any items. There is also nothing wrong with asking for help. In fact, it can expedite the process and give you more certainty.

If your goal is in an area that you are unfamiliar with, ask people that are in the know. Delegation and receiving consultation are a sign of strength, not weakness. Remember how teachers and trainers can assist as part of the 6 Commandments of the Chosen Life? Utilizing experts in nutrition, physical training, yoga, and meditation, I was able to advance my goals of learning and growing in those areas much quicker and more successfully than if I tried to go at it alone. If you have a goal and deadline, but do not know what steps you need to take to get there, DO NOT GIVE UP! Research and get help. It's not how you get there, as long as you do get there.

In creating my website, my initial steps are simple. I know that I have no training in creating a website. I created a basic website many years ago, but I do not have the time, energy, or abilities to create a modern-day powerful site, so I know that I am better off not to create the website myself. I speak to colleagues I know who have amazing websites and ask for the contact information of their website creators. I look up websites on the internet that look appealing to me. I find the contact information for those site creators. I narrow my list to three to five website creators. I reach out to the top three on my list and put together a request message. I let them know what kind of website I want. I ask each creator to create a proposal which includes the cost range of the site, the timeline that it will take to create it, and the steps needed to get there.

Since I have no idea how much it costs to create a website, having various quotes will allow me to create a budget: a key step early on in goal setting. If the budget cannot be met, then I have to revamp all of the other steps in order to realistically achieve my goal. Money is a scarce resource for many of us and goal achievement must fit your budget.

Therefore, decide early on in the process how much you plan to spend and if it is doable. Taking money pressures off the table helps goals come to fruition much easier.

From there, hearing the expected deadline to complete a goal from a professional lets me know if my deadline is realistic, as well. If different professionals have different deadlines in my mind, I question them on how they came up with their deadlines. Once I hear their explanations, I know whether to keep or change my overall deadline. Lastly, from my research and conversations, I find out the steps required to complete the goal. I ask for a full list, or I write it down myself. Without much or any experience in the field, it is unrealistic that I would know and be able to list all the steps needed to achieve the goal—no matter how much time and energy I put into it.

So don't limit yourself or feel uncertain. Take the time to let others show you the steps needed to complete your goal. Once you see those steps on your to-do list, a huge sense of relief should encompass you. By having your listed steps written down, you are SO much closer to completing your goal. Then you simply need to create timelines to complete them and get started!

Remember Step 4 in the manifestation chapter: *there is no timeline*. When creating a practical timeline for goal setting, it is still possible that your end result may not fully come to fruition or may look differently than you originally envisioned. However, there are certain goals you *can* achieve—ones that are practical and tangible—and that is what we are referring to here. At the end of the day, you can only control and manage yourself. The rest is up to the free will of others and the universe.

In interviewing the website creators and researching videos and articles, I now have a clear sense of the steps I need to take. Here is the example of the steps to take in my goal:

- Set budget and payment schedule with developer for website hosting, creation, and monthly maintenance
- Confirm platform for website and hosting
- Hire web developer
- Create name for website and register domain (myself or developer)
- Launch a "coming soon" on the domain page

- Create list of pages on the website and send to developer
- Create content for each page and send to developer
- Developer to send questions/additional content needed for site
- Answer developer questions, finalize content for site
- Developer to develop draft website, then send to me
- Make revisions/meet with developer to revise draft website
- Developer to revise site and send updated copy to me
- Finalize site with developer and plan launch date

What a feeling! My goal of creating a website is now broken down into thirteen easy steps. And the good news is that there is very little that I have to do! Much of the heavy lifting falls on the website developer whom I need to retain.

Knowing the steps that I need to implement to complete my goal, I feel so much better about the process. There is certainty and a game plan. I know now that my website will happen.

Follow the steps and success will follow—much like the NBA team that comes onto the court with a game plan, or the captain on the cruise ship with the crew, GPS, and itinerary. My steps are my GPS and itinerary. A completed goal will soon be around the corner, as well.

Using the basis of the steps that I prepared for my goal of creating a website, list the steps to help achieve your chosen goal. Take the time to make sure you have at least the basis. Whether you did it fully on your own through research or with the assistance of a professional to advise you, at this point your goal should move from a broad, long-range vision to a list of concrete and manageable steps to implement and achieve.

Make sure your steps are written down and check on your steps often, daily if you can, but at least weekly. Get ready to revise the steps if you have to add or delete any parts of the process. *Do not rely on your mind to retain to-dos.* As you think of the revisions to the steps, write them down. By having a written plan, your mind is allowed to be clear, focused, and happy. A calm mind is a productive mind.

Now that you have your steps, you are sixty percent of the way there! Now it is time to assign due dates and timelines to each step. This is the ONLY way to ensure that they will actually get done and in a timely manner.

4.   **ASSIGN DUE DATES AND TIMELINES**

I absolutely love this part of my goals. When I get to the point where I have the goal written down, a deadline to achieve, and the steps to get me there, I really feel like I am rocking. This is the part of the trip where either momentum goes full steam ahead and the goal is well on its way to being completed, or I fall flat on my face.

Many people think that goals cannot be achieved simply because the steps to achieve them are unknown. I would counter this by saying that even if you have your list of steps written down, without assigning them due dates and timelines, they will sit in limbo indefinitely!

The assignment of due dates and timelines is the glue that will keep you focused and on track. Knowing when tasks will be done will create a high probability of actual achievement.

I've been there before, many times: I've created my goal, with a deadline for completion. I made the list of steps to complete my goal. But then I do not assign due dates and timelines for completion. You know what happens? Time goes by and my to-do list stays stagnant. Nothing gets done.

By not actively working on my steps, I have no chance of completing and achieving my goal. Steps by themselves are guidelines. By assigning due dates and timelines to them, they become active and achievable targets.

Before you begin to actively get to work, make sure you create the due dates and timelines for each step. By doing this, you will make the goal a reality.

Let's say that I decided on January 1 that my goal was to create a website. Let's take a look at my list of steps and assign timelines and due dates.

Take note that you will only set timelines for work that is within your control. When relying on third parties, they will establish timelines on their schedule. We can't micromanage every single little detail. The key is to make sure that everyone agrees on the deadline for each required step for the goal to be completed on time.

- Set budget and payment schedule with developer for website hosting, creation, and monthly maintenance: **Timeline: work one hour every Saturday in January. Deadline: complete February 1.**
- Confirm platform for website and hosting: **Deadline: complete February 1.**
- Hire web developer: **Timeline: work daily until completion. Deadline: January 15.**
- Create name for website and register domain (myself or developer): **Timeline: work daily as needed February 1–14. Deadline: complete February 15.**
- Launch a "coming soon" on the domain page: **Deadline: complete March 1.**
- Create list of pages on the website and send to developer: **Timeline: work every Tuesday and Thursday February 1-February 28. Deadline: March 1.**
- Create content for each page and send to developer: **Timeline: work every Saturday and Sunday February 1-March 29. Deadline: April 1.**
- Developer to send questions/additional content needed for site: **Deadline: May 1.**
- Answer developer questions, finalize content for site. **Timeline: work daily May 1-May 14. Deadline: May 15.**
- Developer to develop draft website, then send to me: **Deadline: June 1.**
- Make revisions/meet with developer to revise draft website: **Timeline: daily as needed June 1–14. Deadline: June 15.**

- Developer to revise site and send updated copy to me: **Deadline: June 25.**
- Finalize site with developer and plan launch date: **Deadline: July 1.**

Do not get fixated on the style and form of the list of steps, timelines, and due dates. Plug the steps, due dates, and timelines in your to-do list and calendar as needed and that will WORK for you. Knowing that you have steps to accomplish, assigned timelines and due dates, and a system to keep track of them, then you are already ahead of the game!

Watching my goal of creating a website being planned, take the time now to look at your goal and steps, then make sure to assign the due dates and timelines for each of your steps. Once you see them in writing, you should feel a huge sense of relief. It means that the goal is coming together. It will happen. Now you need to put your thoughts into action.

Some steps may be done simultaneously, while others are staggered and fit into a pattern to begin once others are finished. That is where you should not be afraid to rearrange your steps to fit the order that you feel will work best for you. Create your destiny. Once you know what you need to do and the timelines and due dates, you can focus on the steps—one at a time, or together. You decide what you think you can accomplish and in what order. Having a detailed plan gives you control and certainty. Your mind does not need to focus on the unknown. It is all in front of you. When you complete Step 4, then you are ready to begin.

5. FIND THE STARTING POINT

The last step in the checklist should be the easiest to achieve. I mean, you have done all the hard parts already! Imagine coming this far and not knowing how to begin! It doesn't make sense conceptually, but mental blocks and the fear of failure can really hold us back. In setting your goal and starting your journey to complete it, know that the result is irrelevant. You need to try your best and come up with the best plan possible that you feel will work for you.

Once you have the game plan in front of you, get excited instead of scared. You have the opportunity to try something new. Looking at the list of steps, the starting point is staring right at you. Grab a hold of it and let's go!

If you don't know where to begin (which is VERY normal and affects us all), start by taking a look at your list of steps. Consider which is the easiest step to begin with and/or the most effective step to jumpstart all the other steps in the process. For some people, starting with a perceived difficult and time-consuming step will hold them back. For them, having a quick and easy step would be best. For others, they want to tackle a very difficult step in order to feel that they have accomplished a lot. Know your personality type and choose the step that gravitates best to who YOU are. It doesn't matter where you begin if you get all the steps done. Simply start somewhere; you can't finish if you don't start!

In getting started on my goal of creating a website, there could be several starting points in my estimation. I could have started with selecting the domain name, which I find is a fun and light process. I also could have started with making a budget and deciding my costs. For someone who enjoys finances, that could be a great opening step, but for those that find money and calculations intimidating, this step could be a non-starter and delay the start of the process.

My starting point is hiring the web developer. As I decided not to create the website on my own, I know I'll need to hire a professional to make my goal happen. If I started other steps, I could be spinning my wheels and wasting time by trying to put energy into an area that is not a strength for me. Taking the time and choosing the right developer starts my project on a strong footing. In many ways, I am more than halfway there if I have my trusted hired professional working closely with me. That professional can help guide me through the other steps, including creating the budget and domain name, rather than doing that on my own. If I tried to start, for instance, with a budget and got nowhere, then I could change course at any point and look to hire the developer instead as my starter.

The great thing about creating a goal is that it is up to me how far I reach and the energy and resources that I want to devote to completing the goal. With a strong starting point underway, the checklist will be completed in no time!

As we are working together, look at your list of steps to achieve your designated goal. Considering all the factors we have discussed, where do your mind and soul gravitate toward to begin your journey? How does your body feel about it? If you have a step that appeals to you as a starting point, great. Write it down. Consider the timeline you will need for it and set a due date. By writing down this information, you are establishing that you are taking your goal seriously. It will happen, and you are under no pressure.

* * *

Now that you have completed the five-point checklist, you may be asking one more key question: How do I complete all my steps and achieve my goal?

It is simple. Keep working actively on your checklist and get ready to refine any parts of the checklist until the goals are achieved. For the checklist to be successful, it must remain fluid at all times.

As you find the starting point to complete your goal, keep an eye on all five points and keep asking yourself:

POINT 1: Am I happy with the goal that I set? Does it remain realistic and a target I want to reach? If the answer is yes, then maintain the goal as you set it. If needed, you can change the goal or even delete it if it is not plausible. But do not act in haste. Only amend this section if you have exhausted the other points and change at this time is the actual solution as you see it.

POINT 2: Based on the steps that I need to take, is the deadline that I set realistic? Do I need to extend my deadline of completion, or can I even finish sooner? You can be very lenient at this stage, but remain focused. Do not give too much time so that you will procrastinate. But you also don't want to give too short of a timeline and feel pressured to complete it. Think this through and look honestly at your due dates and timelines in Step 4. This should clear the thinking as to what your overall deadline should be.

POINT 3: View how your steps are going. If you need to take additional steps, take them. If you have completed certain steps or some are unnecessary, delete them. *But do not remove any steps that are required but that you simply do not want to do!* If a step is required for completion, then it must remain. So remain open-minded and positive. Be mindful of what steps need to be done so the job can be accomplished.

POINT 4: In accomplishing your goal, the assessment and reassessment of this stage is key. When you assign due dates and timelines to your steps to complete, make sure that they are reviewed on a consistent basis and revised as needed. If you are procrastinating certain steps, that is fine. But make sure to ask yourself why they are not being completed. If steps are not completed, then the goal will not be attained. It's that simple! No matter what though, focus attention on your timelines and due dates. Otherwise, you will stay stagnant and not move ahead.

POINT 5: As you complete steps toward achieving your goal, you can track the progress that you are making. At each stage of the process, think of where you are—and where you need to be—to stay on track. If your goal is not coming together, ask yourself where you need to start or restart to get the ball rolling. From there, take yourself to the starting point yet again or move the starting point to a new position.

Ultimately, achieving goals is about getting ahead. It all comes down to living the Chosen Life that you envision for yourself and becoming the best you that you can be! The universe can show you the roads to success, and you have to learn to take them.

Some of the best goals that I set for myself were not even successful at all. I have abandoned some goals along the way as they did not serve me at that time. Other goals were not accomplished because I could not make them happen. It's ironic that some of the goals I thought would be easiest to achieve did not get done, while some pipe-dream goals that seemed like an impossibility did, in fact, come true.

If you complete a planned goal successfully, you will feel a great deal of pride and gratitude in being able to plan, execute, and complete this goal. If you do not succeed, see it as an opportunity—either to change course and try different options, or reverse course and look to setting different goals instead. No matter the results, it is the work and planning that will serve you in the future. Through experience you will acquire knowledge. You will get to practice and be more determined every time a new goal is set.

Regardless of the result and how far I came along each path toward completing a goal, there were life lessons along the way. It did not seem like it at the time, but as I got older and my mind and soul opened, I started to appreciate what I learned. Life lessons are the best teachers that we can ask for. Let's get ready to explore the meaning of life lessons and how to utilize them on the road to enlightenment.

EIGHTEEN

Life Lessons

—◦◦◦—

We have many teachers who come into our lives, good and bad. It is their lessons that we need to most understand. And once their purpose is done, those teachers will be gone.

It is automatic that when we hear the term "teacher," our minds will turn to school—or sports, music, and any other extra-curricular activity that we possibly participated in. Of course, designated teachers or coaches, by profession, are obvious. But believe it or not, EVERYONE who comes into your life is or can be a teacher to you.

Family members. Friends. Co-workers. Your ex-spouse. Enemies. Even your pet can be a teacher. We often get caught up seeing a person in a defined role and pigeonhole our interactions based on a perceived relationship. Take the friend and enemy scenarios. We look to our friends to spend time and communicate with. We have mostly positive interactions with our friends (hopefully) and consider these key relationships.

On the other hand, a person we consider an enemy is seen as negative. We view an enemy as someone who has or can hurt us, and we avoid them as much as possible. While we tend to speak positively of a friend, we will communicate negatively when it comes to an enemy. Isn't it ironic then that the same person could be our friend one day, an enemy the next, and back to a friend in the future? The point is that we need to move away from the mental compartmentalization of putting labels on people and consider the bigger picture. Certain people come into our lives for a reason.

Let's look past our feelings about people within our universe and scope out our interactions with them. Focus on your experiences rather than the emotions.

Take note that people who come into our lives become our teachers. As a result, our experiences with these people become life lessons. Take the time to process this information. Feed your mind and soul with this knowledge. As you consider the shift in your perception, the positivity from interactions with all people should become clear, even the ones you labeled as negative.

We have discussed already that to live in the present, we must process and accept the past—and then get past it. When it comes to human interactions, negative relationships and experiences have a habit of lingering with us. In addition, we have covered the notion of letting go in order to move ahead. The benefits are endless when we live in the present, and this comes with zero downside. Imagine a life with more happiness, energy, confidence, awareness, better decision-making, and overall success. Negativity from our past will only hold us back in achieving a better life. Letting go of the past must become a lifestyle for a person who wants to take control of their life. It is a conscious daily choice to live in the present.

Most, if not all of us struggle with our body image. We hold on to the image of what our bodies used to be like, or what we think our body should be like. Punishing yourself or having negative self-worth or self-image because of how you look does not work. This will not help you. If you truly want to take care of your body and look your best, start by letting go of what was and what you think should be. Bring your mind to living in the present. You are here today. Embrace the person you are and how you look right now. You have the tools available to you to work on your body image and improve yourself over time. That will come when you are at your strongest mentally and present in the moment.

Your mind is your strongest ally. Negative thoughts and images hold your mind back from working with your body. Thus, you need to let them go. Nobody will transform overnight, physically or mentally, and gains can be had over a prolonged period when you maintain a strong focus. You won't move ahead physically if you are held back mentally. If you want to live in the now, then you must let go of what was and will not serve you.

In the process of letting go, consider that interactions with people who have come into your life all serve a purpose. As teachers, they have taught you life lessons. Once you learned your lesson, it will be far easier to let go of any pain you carry from those relationships. You will then be able to live in the present much clearer and more focused. You will also be equipped to handle future interactions with people and you will have the education you received from them. Experience leads to knowledge which leads to better future decisions.

As much as negative experiences are life lessons, so are positive ones. When our minds tend to dwell on negative experiences, we can gloss over the positive interactions with others. Why is that? Perhaps because we enjoy positive results the moment they happen. But do we truly learn from them? Positive experiences are just as strong life lessons, after all. Please allow yourself to take in ALL experiences when interacting with others and learn from them equally. While you can certainly enjoy the moments when you experience positivity, NEVER forget the life lessons that are attached to them. You are constructed in your body, mind, and soul to always be learning and growing. So, let's train ourselves to do that and learn well!

Let's now consider scenarios of positive and negative experiences with other people, as both serve us.

We have so many opportunities for life lessons when we interact with others, but it is easy to miss them if we do not look out for them. Every possible interaction you have with others can bring forth education that can assist us for a lifetime. So if we are aware that these experiences exist, we can better appreciate and understand our interactions with others, even if they appear to be negative. Consider these scenarios when you think back to previous conversations you have had with people in the past and continue to understand the growth that can come from future conversations. It is never too late to learn our life lessons, once we are ready to take them in.

A positive experience could be a co-worker who always compliments your outfits at work and provides you with feedback as to why they like them. That is very nice of them to take the time to give you that positive feedback. Of course, it made you feel happy in the moment. But while you enjoyed the pat on the back, consider the pointer that this co-worker is giving you. Take in the feedback as to why they like your chosen outfits. Perhaps in the future, you can even request deeper feedback when you receive positive messages. This information can be considered in future outfits that you purchase and wear. While you should ultimately love your appearance and dress for your own happiness, sometimes we are not the best judges of ourselves. Having a third party that is assisting us can help us consider how to take in and use their information for future decisions. Positive interaction with a third party is the best life lesson since you enjoy the experience in the moment while learning at the same time. As with all third-party interactions, we don't want to forget the notions we learn among the feelings we experience in the moment of the interaction.

On the flip side, think back to a negative experience that you may have had growing up. Perhaps a classmate insulted you during recess when you were playing a sport. They might have made fun of you and embarrassed you in front of others. Maybe you even cried at the time as a result. These negative experiences with others, especially in our younger and developing years, are really difficult to process. A negative experience, such as the one I highlighted now, can be carried with you for many years, perhaps a lifetime. The hurt and resentment this person caused you is trauma that can damage your mind and soul if left to linger and fester within you. We have already gone through the process and importance of letting go of this negative energy and baggage.

The more severe the trauma, though, the more time it will take to let go. The longer you hold onto trauma, the chances are the longer you will need to fully let go of the trauma. There is always the possibility of never fully letting go, which is okay. It does not need to be an all-or-nothing proposition. Imagine, for example, a traumatic experience that you have carried in your mind for several years. If, every day, you consciously turn your mind to living in the moment and letting go of the trauma a little at a time, you will be that much better off. If it is something that you think about all the time, imagine you learn slowly to not think about it for a prolonged time. As you build your ability to focus your mind on the present rather than the past trauma, your mind will learn this new skill and expand on it as time goes along. Some negativity can be let go in an instant and others will take time. Focus on the present as often as you can, and your mind will be that much better at letting go of negativity.

Before you truly say goodbye to a negative experience, consider that there was a life lesson to learn there. Perhaps even more than one. When that other person insulted you as a youngster, they tried to hurt you. Perhaps they were suffering from hurt themselves. We don't know what their home life was like. Sometimes people in pain lash out at others to defend themselves. They build a wall, so to speak, or they are simply not nice people. But when you were insulted, what was happening was that you were being toughened. You were better than that and you still are today. Looking back at such an interaction, it is time to reshape your thinking. Think how positive it is that you did not attempt to hurt someone in the same way you were hurt. Thinking of this person's actions, they taught you how *not* to treat others, that you can and should be confident in yourself, to stand up to bullies, and believe in who you are and your abilities. Looking back, do not be angry at what this person said and did to you. Thank them. They taught you valuable life lessons. You are better for having learned this information. You can now let the person and experience go from your mind and soul. But the life lessons stay with you going forward.

Have you ever been in a situation where you ended a negative relationship, only to jump into another one right away with a person who mirrored the previous partner? Even some of the worst interactions that I had with people in the past made me question why I ever met them. This is common in failed relationships. The instinct is to say that I wish I never met them in the first place. I came to realize, however, that focusing my mind in anger on past interactions was not allowing me to live in the present moment, which resulted in my soul being plugged up and my motivation being drained. I could not feel inspired and hopeful in the present and future if I was living in the past. So letting go was not going to be enough, for if I did not learn from my past experiences, I was doomed to repeat them. Most, if not all of us, have been there at some point. Why would we do this to ourselves? Because we did not learn our life lessons, which can occur from a negative relationship or life scenario.

I remember being in a situation where I was dating someone for approximately six months. I thought that things were going great and that we were in a loving and serious relationship. Little did I know that my supposed girlfriend at the time was still in a relationship with her previous boyfriend (she told me she had broken up with him before we got together). Which meant that I was not a boyfriend, I was the "other guy." How did I piece together that conclusion? I followed the clues. When things don't add up, then the simple answer is usually the logical one. She disappeared at times unannounced. She would claim that she was tired and had gone to bed early. This happened especially during the holidays, including Christmas and New Year. The final straw? When I saw that she had a set of condo keys on her keychain, yet she did not live in a condo. It didn't take me long to figure out that they were "his" condo keys and that she was still going to his condo while we were dating the WHOLE time. She gave a weak excuse and sadly, I took her back at that point. But the lying and feeling that I was nothing more than an escape rather than a focal point in her life was too much to bear. So she had to leave my life. I summoned up the courage one day and told her that she had lost the privilege of being my girlfriend and that she was dismissed. We saw each other a couple of times after that and messaged for a while, but she eventually disappeared. Now she is married and has a child with the original boyfriend.

I wish them both well. No ill will whatsoever. Saying that out loud feels amazing. But it took me over three years to process the pain and hurt that I experienced from that relationship. Even though I was the one who broke it off, I could not get over the fact that we were not truly together. I had allowed my mind to believe that this was a long-term and positive relationship. I loved her with all my heart, and I thought that she loved me back. While I healed over the negative feelings and hurt that I had, it took longer to process the overwhelming emotion of guilt that I felt from that relationship.

As an empathetic person, I was the perfect target for her allure. When we started off together, she knew how to make me feel like the king of the world. But then she would disappear and she knew how to gaslight me to the point that I blamed myself. She was a master at it. So when the relationship was done, she was gone and with her original boyfriend publicly again, even though they were together the whole time. I was left holding the bag and picking up the pieces. I asked myself all the time what I could have done differently. In some perverse way, I believe I held out hope that we would be together again one day. I forgave her long ago. My issue was that I didn't forgive myself.

Looking back at that relationship, there was such a strong part of me that wished that we had never been together. I wished I had never experienced the hurt and guilt that came along with that failed interaction. Today though, I see things differently. She came into my life for a reason. She was a teacher. The relationship taught me life lessons. If not for those lessons, I may not be where I am today. I learned to love myself first and foremost, to forgive myself, and not be so hard on myself.

When I blamed myself for losing the relationship, I broke the most important rule of life: I stopped loving myself. I was punishing myself and putting my mind in a self-contained prison. By being so hurt and angry with myself, I was closing off my soul completely for all that time.

I am not broken. I was damaged, but I am repaired. I learned to let go of the relationship, but only once I learned the lessons that needed to be learned from her as the teacher and the relationship as the classroom.

Perhaps she wanted to hurt me on some level. Or my feelings were irrelevant as she simply wanted to enjoy her life in the moment. Whatever the reasons, it doesn't matter. I do not live in her mind and cannot determine for her why she did the things she did. I can only control what I think and feel. I refuse to look at the relationship as a negative experience. It happened for a reason.

I do not have the power to change my past, nor do I need to. But if I let go of that relationship without learning the lessons from it, I would be doomed to possibly repeat this pattern in future relationships. That will not happen. I will not allow it, because I am in control of my mind. Living in the present with this knowledge and feeling clear, my soul opens further, and I am inspired as I look ahead to my future. From negativity came a vital education.

I also learned from that experience what I did and did not want from a future partner. I thought of how I got together with her and perhaps I could have done more due diligence as to her status before jumping into a committed relationship. She also taught me how I wanted to act as a partner in a future relationship. By digging and processing how I had acted during my time with her, I envisioned how I could best communicate and interact with my future partner.

From such a negative low point in my life came a new energy into my being. As I got stronger mentally and forgave MYSELF for what happened, my soul began to open and expand. I became inspired to learn and study boxing as well as CrossFit. I competed in a bodybuilding and fitness show. Those lessons paid off as I became a more well-rounded person and one who focused on myself to become the best me possible. While I spent a lot of time after that relationship single with the occasional date, I mostly spent the time developing and growing. I needed that on all levels and that was more growth that I experienced from a negative episode.

Consider now the positive and negative interactions that YOU have had with people throughout your life. Feel free to write them down. It could be a person who came into your life for one moment, or perhaps they have been there for many years. Consider who they are in your sphere of life and why the interactions were either positive or negative. From there, really think about the life lessons you learned from those experiences. Either direct lessons that the other person consciously taught you, or the internal lessons that you can see and understand through reflection with an open mind and soul. Sometimes we have to dig hard for the lessons, but with clarity they will be found. Once you try this exercise and spot the lessons, you will feel gratitude for having experienced the interactions with the other people. Even if the other person is considered an enemy to you, that label and the hurt attached to it can be let go. You don't need to carry that pain and anger with you. Establish the life lessons and carry that knowledge into your life going forward. The past interaction you can let go of, but keep the knowledge as you carry forward into today and the future.

Another key point to consider is that every experience is a domino effect in your life. Imagine that some of the negative experiences that you previously had never existed. As a result, your future could have been much different. In a worse way! You can never know for certain if by avoiding certain past interactions you could have changed the course of your present and future. For all you know, some alternative interactions could have been positive or perhaps negative. You can play that game all day long, but you will only spin your wheels in circles.

You do not live in the past and cannot change what previously happened to you experience-wise. But what you can do is learn and grow from the past, so that you can make better decisions for yourself in the present and future. You can spend your life theoretically regretting missed opportunities from your past, but even if those opportunities had been taken, worse results could have transpired. Your life, in many ways, is like a domino-toppling game. Insert or remove one piece and the whole slot of dominoes can tumble in an instant. Living in regret is again a negative emotion that clouds your mind and stalls your soul. This serves no purpose for you. Live clearly in the moment and be excited for a future that you are equipped to handle because you have learned your lessons.

The good news is that the teachers have a lifetime to teach us. Think about a sports coach you have worked with for years, or that best friend you have known for most of your life. These people have been in your life for all this time for a reason. They have lessons to teach you and the longer they stay, the more lessons you learn.

We often take the people closest to us for granted and simply expect that they will be there. By identifying and acknowledging the life lessons that they teach us, we learn better. It also brings us closer to these people. By not showing these teachers the respect they deserve, we may fail to learn the lessons that they teach us. By not ingraining the education received in our life within us, we risk missing out on precious knowledge through our experiences, which can hold us back in the present and future. Consider the people that most closely surround you. Understand why they are there and what they have to offer you. Your life will be better for it.

For all the precious few lifelong teachers we have during the course of our lives, we will also come across teachers who will come and go. You will find many people came to you in an instant and were gone just as quickly, sometimes by their choice and sometimes by yours. These people may have impacted your psyche, positively or negatively. It is time to stop thinking about the past feelings you had during your interactions. Consider again the lessons these time-limited teachers provided you with. The person who may have found your wallet and returned it to you, another person who hit your car in an intersection, the delivery person who told you stories once during a delivery stop at your home, or that jerk who bumped into you at the mall and gave you a dirty look—all of these people came into your life for a reason. Once their purpose was done, these people were gone. The question you have to ask yourself is what impact did these teachers have in your life? Once you understand what you learned from these teachers, the interactions will make more sense, and you will be better equipped to handle similar interactions in the future, provided that you learned from your past.

I want you now to think about the greatest teachers that you have had in your life—the people who were or are currently part of your world who taught you the best life lessons. Write down as many of these teachers as you can. How many did you come up with? Perhaps five? Ten? Twenty? The number does not matter. What we are searching for here is your TOP teacher. Taking a look at your list—who came out as number one? Was it a parent? Sibling? Best friend? Coach? I'm curious who you came up with. Yes, this is a trick question. There must be only one person who should come on top as your best teacher of all time. Are YOU on that list? If anyone other than yourself is your most important teacher, then it is time to rethink your life lessons. While other people may be fantastic teachers, the best teacher of all time can only be you.

I bet you didn't see that one coming. That's okay. Life and learning along the way are tricky things. Some of our best lessons don't come out as formal teachings. In fact, most of them don't. Experiences won't come straight out at you and say, "Hey, look at me, I'm a lesson!" It is up to you to identify these experiences.

But imagine that you are your own best teacher. Consider how many experiences in life you brought onto yourself without anyone else around. Even if there were people in the picture, you bring about and choose many of your own experiences. Most of our life lessons are not taught to us while we are sitting and listening in a classroom; they are out there in the world through actions. By choosing to put yourself in certain situations throughout your life, you have had many diverse experiences. Some went well and others may have failed. The emphasis again is not to linger on the feelings from those experiences, good or bad. The key is to understand what we take away from the experiences we have selected for ourselves.

Imagine a life where you can control the most important experiences that you have and the lessons that you learn. Get ready to savor the power that is within you.

When we take accountability for our life choices, we become our own greatest teacher. Once we see ourselves as our greatest teacher, life becomes much clearer. For most of our lives, we have felt that other people control the direction of our future. Our feelings and experiences were shaped mainly by what other people did. The key to these third-party interactions are the things you learned from them. After all, it is unavoidable that people will come and go. But the knowledge we gain from them should always remain. Everything else can be let go of.

Carrying the past with you, as we learned, is a heavy burden. *You cannot live in the now if your mind is stuck in the past.* Life lessons don't linger within our minds as setbacks. They help show us pathways in our present and future to choose the best roads possible. And you know who ultimately chooses those roads for you? Yes. It's you.

* * *

Imagine this scenario: Everyone who has ever come into your life is standing in a line. If you could walk up to each person one by one, what would you say to them? If you could only say two words to each of them, it should be this: *"Thank you."* Every single person who has ever interacted with you has provided you valuable information. They have given you the power to make the choices to steer your own life. You always have the ability to take advice and guidance from others as background information. But remember that you are always the one to consciously chart your own path.

You will never be able to guide your own waters if you are stuck in a world that others built for you. You have to recognize that. Once you do, it should become obvious that there is only one voice that will truly guide you and serve as your best teacher. It was your own voice the whole time.

While you may have never thought of yourself as a teacher, now it is time to rethink the whole life hierarchy system. You have been your best and most prominent teacher this entire time. But have you truly learned the life lessons that you have taught yourself?

Understanding that the past must be let go, you will now serve, going forward, as your own guide through the present and future of your life. Your mind should feel clear and not weighed down by past experiences. You have learned your life lessons and now feel the power of the knowledge that these lessons were meant to teach you. They were not meant to hurt you or hold you back at all. With this newfound power, it is time to truly start living and building the Chosen Life for yourself.

As you are now fully committed to living the best life you can, it's time for you to prepare to download more tools so that you can learn to teach yourself how to live your Chosen Life with purpose.

NINETEEN

Living Life with Purpose

As you continue building and evolving your best life, it's time to ask yourself a simple question: What kind of life do you want to live?

There are people trapped in a life with negativity, anger, sadness, hurt, and many conflicting emotions. None of us are perfect and we all go through ups and downs. But when setbacks become the norm, we need to step back and really question ourselves. Do we want a life that is moving downward and backward? Or are we ready to live in the moment?

It was a deep realization when I admitted to myself that I drifted through most of my life until my awakening. My mind was either stuck in past regrets or focused on the uncertainty of the future. I was alive...but I was not living life. Life always seemed more like a chore than a joy to me. It was exhausting and I was holding back for so many years because I was limiting my ability to "be." However, because I was always strong at setting goals, short and long term, for an outsider I appeared to be "successful" because I was getting things done. But without the big picture and purpose, I was doomed to drift and ultimately fail.

It was a huge mental shift to manifest the life that I wanted to live. Once I was able to do that, I learned that I could not just live for the sake of living. My life needed meaning. I was ready to explore the purpose of my existence.

In discovering my spirituality as a JewBu, I meditated for thousands of hours on the proposition that I came into the world for a reason. I questioned the meaning behind all the actions that I took and all the choices I made. When I stopped putting pressure on myself to discover answers, then strong images came into my mind. I realized that I was failing to truly appreciate and understand the BIG picture behind everything I was doing.

In all aspects of my life, personal and professional, I lacked real focus and drive. It came down to my soul being closed. I was unnecessarily exhausting my mind because it did not have my soul to work with to get my life to the next level.

Eventually, mindfulness and a clear mind led to manifestation and an inspired soul, and I started to discover my life purposes.

It was an invigorating and rewarding feeling to learn that one of my clear purposes was to help and inspire others. I am here to share my experiences, trials and tribulations, and assist as many people as I can to evolve their lives to the best possible directions. But I cannot help others if I could not help myself first. I needed to put in the work myself before I could even imagine that I would be able to branch out in so many directions to assist others.

By sharing my stories, I want to help you open your mind and really assess your life. What is the purpose of your life and all that you do? Keep this thought in mind as you explore how you are living and whether it is done intentionally and with purpose.

To keep it simple, recognize that in everything you do, small or big, do it with meaning. Do not live simply to get by, with every action feeling like a chore. Your life should mean much more than that. You are special. Embrace who you are.

Consider your purpose as a life compass. It will show you where you need to go and what you need to do. Do not wander aimlessly through life without your compass. Find the direction of where you need to go and start planning to get there!

It is time to be honest with yourself. Come clean. How much of your life has been spent drifting? Can you truly tell yourself that you have been living your life with purpose, or simply to get by?

Think about the feeling of living paycheck to paycheck. It is a difficult scenario to be unsure if you will be able to pay your bills every two weeks. It then becomes almost impossible to save up money and ever get ahead. It seems like no matter how hard you work, you find that you are either in the same place or constantly falling behind. It's a debilitating feeling—one that I am sure you do not enjoy or wish to continue feeling. But without a roadmap and purpose with your finances, for example, the pattern of drifting through life financially is an unfortunate reality.

The only way to begin the process of ending the cycle is to awaken. It's time to find your direction so that you are working toward your higher purpose. Take the time to consider this and how you can begin to make the changes within your life.

To live with purpose, you first need to accept that negativity has no part in your life anymore. Purpose comes with positivity, not negativity. If you allow negativity to steer your life, then you are moving aimlessly through your existence. Negativity forces your mind to overwork and drains both your mind and body of much-needed energy. In addition, you lack the passion for life that your soul can bring through a positive mindset.

Picture negativity essentially blurring or breaking your life compass. You have no focus or direction when you are in a negative mindset. When you feel negativity coming on, remind yourself that your life has meaning and that you want to live with purpose. Keeping your eye on the prize, so to speak, will remind you that there is always a bigger picture. It sounds very cliché, but sweating the small stuff is really not a good path to go down. It detracts from the bigger-picture lifestyle.

When I started my yoga practice, I openly admit that I hated it. I loved the idea of going to yoga and tried to pump myself up each time I went to the studio. But every time I got there, I would feel negatively about the classes the majority of the time. My mind was pushing me into negative spheres. The easiest solution would have been to give up. I had so many reasons to call it quits. I was not very good at yoga. I was not picking it up easily or quickly. My mind felt bored or overwhelmed at times. There were no immediate gains to be had. There was only present pain—in my body and mind. So why did I keep going, you ask? Because I didn't focus on my mind's attempts to steer into negativity. I kept my eye on the higher purpose.

I told myself that I was practicing yoga for my health and life. I knew that I needed to go to yoga to get into shape, both physically and mentally. Deep down, I was ready to build something special. To truly live and evolve, I needed to put time and energy into my yoga practice.

By focusing on my purpose in yoga, over time I was able to block out or eliminate many of the negative thoughts that came into my mind during classes. By doing so, I was also able to awaken my soul and build a passion for yoga that drove me to be further inspired and get ahead in my practice.

In my case, it took over six months of attending classes every week to develop a yoga practice that worked for me on all levels. But it did happen and continues into the present day. It worked because I had PURPOSE in what I was doing and was practicing my craft consistently.

Living life with purpose can begin with the simple goal of incorporating the 6 Chosen Commandments into your life. You have learned about the benefits they bring. Having a life that includes sleep, water, nutrition, physical activity, meditation, and yoga will only bring you to higher levels of existence. A little trick to help make these Chosen Commandments a part of your regular lifestyle is to always pay attention to your mindset when you are incorporating and utilizing them. Remember that situations will be what they will be. Life will be there in its present-day form, regardless of how you feel or think. The ONLY thing that will shift is how YOU see things. Do you want to see them positively or negatively?

You have so much control over your present-day life and future. It starts with your mind and your thinking. If you tell yourself that you need the Chosen Commandments and will follow them, then it will happen.

On the other hand, if you tell yourself that the Chosen Commandments are impossible for you to utilize, then you have created a self-fulfilling prophecy.

Nothing else has changed in the universe. Only your mindset. Make sure to pay attention to where it swings and always bring it back to the center.

The next time you think that something is impossible and you are ready to write it off, think again. Why are you choosing to limit yourself unnecessarily? Even if nobody else believes in you, why aren't you advocating for yourself?

Remember, it all begins with self-love. If you are not loving yourself, then you are pushing yourself down. Combat negative thoughts with love. Always love yourself. Believe in yourself. Tell yourself that there are no limits for you. So win or lose, you should always be able to sleep at night knowing that you tried your best. The effort begins with love and a positive mindset. From there, you find your internal compass and the purpose that will steer your life in the highest and best possible directions.

* * *

The equation for creating life purpose is key. Please note this and remember it throughout your existence:

STEP 1: **CREATE AN OPEN MIND**

This is the part in your control. I have given you many tools to make this happen. It always starts with the 6 Commandments of the Chosen Life—especially meditation and yoga—which function to help steer your mind to be open and clear. Then, as you work toward enlightenment, you utilize the skills of living in the moment, letting go, and manifestation. These all come with time. Your job is to show your mind lots of love, to take away the pressures and pain of the past and future and always steer your mind to the present.

Once you are conscious of the present-day mind and work toward living in the moment, remember a key reason for why you are doing this, which is to allow Step 2 to take place...

STEP 2: **OPEN AND IGNITE YOUR SOUL**

With your body, mind, and soul working together, you will be almost unstoppable. You cannot work toward or reach your purpose without your soul.

With a distracted and unfocused mind, you are losing out on a third of your being—your soul. Without having your soul work for you, there is no fire and passion for your existence. Instead, you are relying on your body and mind to do all the work for you. The result is working harder, being less focused, burning out, and not getting further ahead.

When your mind is clear and you live in the present, your mind will identify your purpose. Once your mind fires up your soul, you will be inspired and passionate to work toward your purpose.

You cannot control when your soul is awakened. Your soul will awaken when it is ready. You cannot put pressure on it to happen; the soul opens when it is ready to make itself known.

Focus on what is in your control. You can control your mind through your thoughts. Center your mind and allow your thoughts to be open and present in each and every moment. All you need to do is be mindful and stay in the NOW. Not yesterday or tomorrow. Live each moment, and your purpose will come.

* * *

I have personally tried so many avenues to find my life purpose. In terms of methods and locations, I followed every route possible to work on my self-discovery. None of that would have been possible unless I awoke and realized that I had no purpose. After all, you can't find what you are not looking for.

For much of my first thirty years of life, I never even realized that I was lacking my life's purpose. Much in the way a gambler or heavy drinker who can't admit they have an issue, I didn't see a problem with my life. I didn't realize that my life needed to evolve. Spending a lifetime with negative thoughts was not going to be fixed overnight or quickly, especially when I did not see there was an issue. I was forced to take care of myself due to health issues. So the reason I began my journey and eventually discovered the road to enlightenment was not to uncover my purpose; it was because my doctor gave me no choice for my physical ailments and I chose yoga because it was seemingly the easiest option for me to lose weight, get physically healthier, and hopefully de-stress as much as possible. Little did I know that attending yoga studios for years would build the foundation for my life's purpose.

The way I used to dread getting through a yoga class when I started my practice was the same way I used to dislike sitting through a religious synagogue service. I overcame my mental block in accepting yoga by practicing it consistently. I learned not to overthink it. I didn't worry about how bad I was when I started, and I certainly didn't stress if I would ever get better at yoga in the future. I learned to be mindful and enjoy each class by being open and present in each moment. The same mindset was then used to develop my meditation practice. I learned through yoga—and later, meditation—to be present and mindful in all activities that I was performing, including synagogue services.

I can't even begin to tell you how many times I have attended religious services at Jewish synagogues. Hundreds of times, for sure. Unfortunately, before I awakened, I did not get to enjoy the experiences during most of those services due to my mental state. I saw going to religious services as a chore or obligation, rather than as a relief or comforting mental outlet. So I would hear the words, songs, and prayers, even participate, but they went *through* me rather than into me. I was not learning what I could from those services, simply because my mind was closed to them. I didn't even realize this until I accepted and embraced myself as a JewBu and then attended

Jewish synagogue services. These services were very similar in words, songs, and prayers. The only thing that shifted was my mental outlook—I was no longer checked out.

Utilizing mindfulness and living in the moment allowed me to open the possibilities that could come into my life. This invigorated my mind and soul to uncover and work toward a deeper life purpose. I needed to put in the work, certainly. But regardless of activity and location, the shift only came when my mind awoke and became clear.

Consider now, in your life and being, if you are working toward your own life purpose. Do you see a bigger picture for yourself and your existence? If you cannot answer this question with a yes, then you need to work toward acknowledging there is an issue. You have a problem. You are alive, but you are NOT living.

Nobody can uncover your life purpose for you. Only you can do that. So do not put pressure on finding the actual purpose, or purposes, at this stage. That will come with time.

Do not be hard on yourself for not living with purpose up until now. It happens to most of us throughout our lives. You cannot fix or live in the past. You are here in the now. Opening your mind to the concept of living with purpose is already a huge breakthrough. It should excite you as to the possibilities that will become available to you.

Before you can discover and travel the roads ahead for you, your first step will be to locate your compass and check what direction you should travel. Your purpose being the compass. And if you do not have that purpose, then you need to put in the time and energy to find it.

To open and clear your mind, I heavily encourage you to try different activities at various locations. Mix it up! But I will caution you, as I have before, that simply showing up physically and doing the activities will not guarantee results, especially early on. You need to practice, show up, and consistently work at finding your life's meaning.

For example, flying to Costa Rica sounds wonderful. I am sure it is a beautiful area from what I hear. Practicing yoga in Costa Rica is magical, I'm sure. But doing so for five days will not likely give you any quick fixes. You can benefit just as much by practicing yoga in your hometown or going to a studio three days a week!

Ultimately, the location is a placebo. If you believe and convince yourself that you need to temporarily change your location to gain a better understanding of yourself, then all the power to you. Even a partial reset serves a purpose. In the end, it comes down to the same *mindset*. You are going to find that you may still be trapped in the same thoughts, regardless of where you are. Most people don't want to talk to themselves and be stuck in their minds, so they get distracted and jump on a plane to search for freedom, yet they can't escape themselves. That's the paradox.

When you close and open your eyes and flow through a yoga practice, you can be anywhere in the world. You are wearing the same outfit, lying on the same yoga mat, and drinking the same water. The physical location in the world may change, but the mental location stays the same.

The same principle applies if you are attempting meditation or attending a service at a temple of your religious designation. The activity and even the location can shift, but your mind will not. You cannot escape your mind and thoughts. Getting into a car, bus, or plane and moving around will not change the mind that is attached to you. The shifting of the mind can happen anywhere and everywhere. So, once you know and accept that you need a life purpose to guide you, then focus on the opening and clearing of the mind.

Pick as many different activities and locations as you wish and find the combination that works for you. But make sure it is consistent as you practice your mental opening. As more time comes along, you will find your purpose and be able to work toward great enlightenment.

In any activity you do, especially in training your mind, you need to make sure that you follow through by *repetition*. Starting and stopping inconsistently gains no momentum in improving yourself. If you pause between repeated attempts, you will constantly return to the start. Whether it is daily or regularly scheduled intervals each week, you know that to succeed you must develop a routine to keep practicing over and over.

Inconsistency is the excuse for failure. Success comes with consistency and repetition. Remember that.

I have great news for you. Once you discover your life purpose, the work does not stop. Oh no, it is only the beginning! Now you get to work toward fulfilling that purpose and growing. This means that the work you originally put in to discover your purpose will continue as you work toward accomplishments and life successes. You may add, amend, and delete activities as you go along. Sometimes you need to try new things and hear new voices. Completely understandable! Your job at this time is to plan and then show up to these activities and locations. Outcomes are not guaranteed, and you never know what you will learn and experience each time.

Sometimes the effects of what you receive are not known to you immediately. You may only appreciate the time you are putting in now several years later. Simply allow yourself to experience it all, and know that purpose will come if your mind is focused on it.

* * *

It is now time for you to do more deep searching within yourself. Take a look at your life and world in the present moment. What forms of religion and/or spirituality do you have in your world?

I believe there are many reasons why people stay away from religion and/or spirituality. There are many taboos when it comes to these areas. Much has to do with the labels and lack of information available to people when it comes to both.

I would say that if you consider yourself an atheist or a non-believer, that's fine. Great, in fact. If that works for you, all the power to you, my friend! You do not need to convert or conform to some standard out there that doesn't work for you. So, let's shift the focus and the narrative surrounding religion and/or spirituality.

Consider dropping the labels. If you choose to attend a service with any group or at any facility/temple, that does not automatically make you a member there. You are not going against your beliefs, principles, and identity. You are simply exploring avenues to help open and clear your mind to allow YOU to discover your roads and journeys. Wild, isn't it?

Part of our lack of spirituality can come from past experiences. Bad things happen, which can create the cynicism we feel looking toward our future. Remember, though, that our past does not define us. The past simply represents life lessons that we utilize to learn and grow as people.

If we study our past and learn our life lessons, we can let go of the feelings attached to the past while having better knowledge and experience to make decisions when future situations arise. But if we do not let go of the past in terms of feeling, this can lead to resentment and hurt, which clouds the mind and closes our soul. A clouded mind and closed soul will lack spirituality, which leads to a life without purpose. Worse, such a blocked connection between the mind and soul can lead to a life lived with negativity, to the point that you will not live life with purpose and instead, with failure. Such a scary word that we try to avoid, but yet, we can easily embrace failure as a lifestyle if we live with a negative mindset.

Take Buddhism, for example. We can sit and debate all day about whether it is a religion or a spiritual movement. Does it matter? By being a JewBu, I consider myself Jewish by religion and spirituality, as well as Buddhist by spirituality. It's irrelevant that I don't consider Buddhism to be my religion. It is a label and mindset that I am comfortable with that works for me. How I think and feel today could change in the future.

What I did see and feel for myself is that when I attended classes and meditation sessions at my Buddhist temple, I gained an even deeper love and appreciation for my Jewish roots and religion.

Buddhism helped open my eyes and see my life and activities in a whole different light. Again, the shift was the mindset.

It's about not being closed and stuck in the past or distracted by the future. But rather, living in the present and in the moment. Yoga led me to meditation, which led me to Buddhism and back to Judaism. I was back at square one, but certainly feeling and thinking differently. My mindset evolved and attending different religious and spiritual activities helped free my mind of its limits and constraints. This certainly did not happen overnight and is still an ongoing process.

As long as I'm alive, I accept that I will evolve and change. The setting and events are almost irrelevant. It comes down to my mind and how I see things. My open mind fueled my soul to release, and the passion to grow and help others came from there. I put in the work and years later, I can tangibly see and smile at the results. Now I want to help you do the same.

Purpose, to me, connects with a higher power. To connect to a deeper meaning, we need to see life for the big picture that it is. Is there a G-d? Powers to be in the universe? If you have a current religious connection and affiliation, I encourage you to explore that. Reading books, watching videos, and attending religious services is a beautiful thing, if it works for you.

In surveying the religious landscape around you, keep in mind that you will come across many people who have a variety of religious beliefs. They may not be the same as yours. Sometimes, our instinct is to be afraid or skeptical of views that are not our own. A healthier way to live is to recognize that we can choose to have different religious affiliations and that is okay. This is NOT a competition!

Let's say you have a religious background in Hinduism. I would attend Hindu services at your temple if you invited me. I would invite you to my Jewish synagogue or Buddhist temple if you wanted to go. It's fascinating to experience religion through the eyes of others. If anything, it can help you connect even stronger with your own religious affiliation. But at the very least, you have nothing to lose by exploring it.

Consider finding local temples, reach out and attend services. These outings are not about labeling you in a religious way; it is about opening your mind and exploring who you are through your own eyes. Religious services can serve as a means to a destination. It still comes down to your mind and how you will think and perceive your life.

If you have a deeper resistance to religions as a whole and do not feel any desire or passion to look down this road, fear not. You are also not alone in this mindset. We are in an age where people look away from religion, rather than toward it, in greater numbers than ever before. Whether it relates to disenchantment with the religions themselves, or the state of the world, politics, and people overall, there are those who feel that religion is not part of them. If that is the case, there are many activities and locations for you to attend that do not have religious affiliations. Consider for yourself then, regardless of your religious radar, as to the concept of spirituality and lifestyle.

For me, spirituality begins with the soul; the inner being who cannot be measured or quantified. But we cannot deny that it is there within us and in the universe. There is an energy, when ignited, that fuels and drives us. We can connect with ourselves and others through means that are not physical or mental. We come together through spirituality. By doing this, we can better embrace the idea of who we are; why we are here; how we connect; and bigger pictures for ourselves, others, and our world. That can include a higher power, G-d, and/or the universe. The concepts of belief and faith, on whatever levels YOU see fit, would be part of your existence going forward.

At some point in your life, you will need to determine if spirituality is within you and if you want to channel it. Again, for you it can be similar or different from religion based on the labels and outlook you see for yourself. But the essence is there, no matter how you slice and dice it.

If spirituality is not within you, then your soul will be unable to open and you will be unable to find purpose. I know that this is a hard realization, but it's true. If you want your life to have purpose, you must be open to spirituality in whatever shape and form you can find it.

There is nothing wrong with being cynical and questioning the world. In fact, it's better to see the world with all of its flaws instead of through rose-colored glasses. You should never conform or do as you are told by a third party simply on blind faith or being ordered around. Your mind is your own and you should have reason and logic in order to proceed with any actions in your life that you are comfortable with. But being cynical works to a degree when you utilize it to OPEN your mind, not CLOSE it. When cynicism becomes a lifestyle and you choose to disregard the ideas of hope and belief, then you are hurting yourself more than you are helping yourself. Don't let cynicism and negativity hold you back from achieving and living the best life possible. Belief is the fuel that flows between your mind and spirit, which will drive you to your Chosen Life.

Life's purpose, as a bigger-picture view of your existence, is fueled by spirituality. For spirituality to enter your life, you will need to consider your beliefs and values. At its core, it almost doesn't matter what you believe, as long as you HAVE belief. To even the biggest so-called non-believer, I would challenge you to open your mind and your heart, rather than close them for no reason.

Having beliefs and values will result in you having faith in yourself. You will then start to believe there are reasons for the things that you do. And you will believe that there is a purpose for your existence, life, and actions. Some may call it blind faith, while I call it fueling your mind and heart with hope. Even if you do not know what it is you believe in, allow yourself to believe in something. If nothing else, believe in yourself and your life.

* * *

Religion is a fantastic gateway to spirituality, as religion is built on the concepts of belief and faith. If you have religion in your life, chances are that you have the tools available to you for belief and to grow the spirituality within you.

If you truly do not believe in anything from a universal perspective, consider taking the time to seek out religious or spiritual leaders in your community. Make an appointment and sit down with them. Discuss your views and why you feel the way you do. Do not worry about holding back; these advocates will appreciate your honesty and being approached. Listen to what responses you receive and ponder how you feel. If you keep an open mind, I am willing to bet that you are told that you should consider attending services and reading/watching the associated materials. Consider that such advice is not about the religion or view itself, but rather opening your mind to learning about your value system. Religion and spirituality are not the end result; they are the gateway for your mind, soul, and life. Religion and spirituality exist in our lives and world for a reason. The biggest reason is to help us understand better who we are and why we are here.

While different faiths have their own unique books and texts, the message is fairly consistent. It is about developing your understanding and knowledge of yourself and the world around you. So whatever negative connotations you may harbor against religion or spirituality, recognize that they are there for a reason. It is YOUR choice whether what they entail becomes part of your world to any degree. But regardless of your affiliation and choice, know that spirituality is part of religion but is NOT a religion in itself.

Religion, while it can help guide you down a spiritual path, is not the be-all and end-all when it comes to spirituality. You can discover and embrace spirituality in any form, through any activity and location that you choose. Spirituality is not created externally. It comes from within. External sources can introduce you and help grow your spirituality with you. But spirituality is born and grows within YOUR mind and soul. The key to spirituality is to find your belief and values. From there, you will ultimately find your path and be able to live your life with purpose.

One of the most rewarding experiences in life is to help others. For many, they have made this their life purpose. They see needs in the world and make it their mission to perform actions that help others. But consider this again if you haven't already: how can you assist other people if you can't help yourself? The best way to assist others is to utilize the tools and experiences that you use to solidify your own life and discover your paths to a happy and fulfilling existence that works for you. Practice what you preach!

As love has taught us, we are best equipped to give unconditional love to others if we first give ourselves the same. Do not neglect your life and forget that you are a priority. Your responsibility is to take care of yourself before assisting others. Your life purpose can be to help others while still making sure that you are receiving what you need so you can be the best version of yourself beyond what you could have ever imagined.

This is when it comes down to the 6 Commandments of the Chosen Life: to take care of the necessities and make sure we are functioning at our best at all times. From there, it is about physically, mentally, and spiritually living the life we seek. If you are taking care of yourself in that respect and finding your life path, then you will be able to better assist others on their journeys. Simply do not allow yourself to neglect your needs and have your past hold you back in any possible way.

To open your life and live with purpose, you will need to take an additional step. When you consider utilizing spirituality to seek a purpose for your existence, it is much easier to shift your mind to positivity. It means that you are ready to embrace the belief that there is purpose in why you are alive and in the actions you take. This will then involve shifting your relationship with negativity and the concept of failure.

Many people who have very little belief and faith in life have allowed failure to become a lifestyle or a future outlook for themselves. This is a scary way to think and live. If you can recognize that your mind is stuck in this realm, it is time to put an immediate halt to this cycle.

If you are going to have a purpose, then you will need to accept that failure happens throughout the course of our lives. What will change is how you view failures when they arise. You can choose to punish yourself and believe that future failures will continue to the point that you identify yourself as a failure. Or you can decide to embrace failure and use it as a teaching tool on the road to reinventing your life. The choice is yours.

Once you have made your selection, get ready to explore why failure is not your enemy. Rather, failure is your ally on the road to enlightenment and building your Chosen Life with the belief that there is purpose in all that you do.

TWENTY

Embrace Failure

"**Hello failure, my** old friend. I've come to talk with you again."

The universe will kick you in the teeth and then send you a dental bill on top of it. It is going to happen many times over the course of your life. Use it to your advantage.

The greatest successes come from the biggest failures. Consider that Apple and Tesla were once both near financial collapse. Now these are two of the most successful companies in the history of business. Similarly, IBM was originally known for producing computer hardware and chose to evolve into business consulting before the core segment of their business faltered. Today, when we mention all three companies, the focus will mainly be on their massive successes as a benchmark for others. But without embracing and understanding their failures, none of these companies could have evolved into the powerhouses they are today. Apple, Tesla, and IBM all learned from their experiences. So can you!

It may not feel like it, but you can elevate yourself from what feels like the gutter to the penthouse overnight. When you reach a low point in your life, know that this is not a death sentence. It is a learning experience. Life can change in a moment—as long as you keep perspective and do not let failures define you or hold you back.

Do not beat yourself up for losing. Smile, for you are wiser for the experiences and knowledge that you possess from being on the other end. And at some point, you will end up ahead for it, either by learning and growing from failed attempts or devoting your energy to future pursuits that work for you.

A wise man (Wayne Gretzky) once said, "You miss 100 percent of the shots you don't take." The only true failure is to never even try.

Failure can be defined in many ways. For some people, it entails actions that do not result in success. But missed opportunities and inaction can be considered failed results, as well. Such failure is even harder to swallow, knowing that taking the chance would have increased the probability of success if one had simply made the attempt. Whether you win or lose, succeed or fail, know that it always comes down to trying your best and making the best decisions in the moment. Do not be afraid of failure. Be afraid of not even trying!

We spend far too much of our lives trying to escape from failure. Do not hate failure and ask it to go away. Embrace failure for the lessons it brings into your life.

You have likely been viewing failure negatively. We are going to explore why that is and how you should have been viewing failure all along.

I hate failure. You hate failure. We all hate failure. Hate is a VERY strong word. One that we try to avoid, but sometimes our mind simply gives in to the heat of the emotion. We have known failure since birth. Failure has been part of our whole lives. Failure has been there for us through crawling, walking, talking, riding a bicycle, graduating from each level of school, driving, relationships, childbirth... You name it—failure has been there. No matter whether it is our first or tenth attempt at something, no matter how hard we try, failure appears time and time again, with that sly smirk on its face, telling us we CAN'T do it.

We try to push failure away, telling it that it's NOT wanted or needed. Yet failure keeps returning uninvited. It can make us feel bad about ourselves, seemingly chanting at us, "YOU SUCK!" The battle can feel hopeless each time. When failure wins out, the world feels so negative. You walk away feeling deflated. Depression, failure's cousin, would inevitably join the party and suck you further down the rabbit hole. Few people can win when that tag team has the upper hand. It's a terrible feeling—one that I have endured many times. I am sure you have, too.

Are you surprised to learn that failure and depression are related? They are first cousins, in fact! Growing up together, they ballooned into their own enterprises, but are cut from the same cloth. Failure and depression's lifeline is negative energy. They feed off it. They thrive off it. Failure says, "I knew you wouldn't get it done." Depression then moves into your mind and takes up space in the penthouse, squatting indefinitely. It reminds you daily of your experiences with failure, that you are sad, and regret that failure won out.

For some of us, depression can reside in our minds for days, weeks, months, and even years. We almost welcome depression at some point and develop a Stockholm syndrome-type relationship with depression. It is hurting us, yet we embrace and accept it. It is not our friend, but rather our enemy. Its sole purpose in life is to hurt us and we allow it to do that. It is a vicious cycle that feels like it will never end. Depression's hold on us becomes so powerful that many of us need medications and/or therapy to release the power that it has over us.

Yet, for all our battles with depression, we seemingly ignore the root of the problem. Depression can show up because of our interactions with failure. If only we had a better relationship with failure, perhaps we could avoid depression altogether!

When prolonged sadness and depression kick in, yet another cousin can show up as well: anxiety! We know it very well. When we accept failure into our lives on a prolonged basis, we start to worry about the future. Anxiety, just like depression, can move into our minds—sometimes next door to depression, other times replacing it.

Anxiety also likes to remind you of failure and its victories over you. But anxiety's power lies in its ability to use failure to create worries about the future. While your mind SHOULD always be in the present moment, anxiety only lives in the future. If failure has taught you that something couldn't get done, then anxiety tries to make you believe that the same act will not get done in the future, as well.

Anxiety has no proof of its claims. All it can do is plant seeds of doubt and make you believe that the future is bleak and has no hope. Without concrete proof of what will happen, you would think that anxiety would be weak and disappear rapidly. And it does, on occasion. When we live in the moment and do not put pressure on future results, then anxiety's words cannot hurt us. But much like depression, once our mind is hypnotized by anxiety's spell, we can become severely limited in how we think and act. It can become so bad that we don't even want to attempt something in the future because anxiety has convinced us that there is no hope and it is not worth it.

Think about it. It's one thing to try something and not succeed. But not even trying leads to 100 percent failure. Anxiety is a master at making failure return yet again, which then invites depression. They feed off one another. They must be stopped. But the issue is not anxiety, depression, or even failure. The problem is YOU!

The negative mind is a breeding ground for failure, depression, and anxiety. On the other hand, a positive mindset repels them. The three cousins, as I call them, do not fit in well when the people around them are happy and living in the moment.

Depression lives in the past. Anxiety lives in the future. They have no time or space in the present moment. Shifting your mind to the present helps instantly to give depression and anxiety their eviction papers. Your mind does not live in the past. It does not live in the future. You are a mindful person. You live in the present. You enjoy the present moment and each moment as they come. You have learned to say these words. Through mindfulness, you can help combat depression and anxiety. The most powerful tool that you have is your mind.

Yes, in times of extreme hardship, you have other tools such as medications and therapy when you need an outside stimulant or support to help shift your mind. I get it. I have been there before and it is never a weakness to ask for help. It makes you stronger by recognizing the issues and looking to be happier is a good thing.

In times of need, however, recognize that you are stronger than you think. The mind, as powerful as it is, can fix you as much as it hurts you. The same mind that invited depression and anxiety to be part of your life can also help eradicate them. Trust in your mind and work with it to shift to living in the present.

But mindfulness will only work for so long if you keep having a bad relationship with failure. The cycle will continue to compound itself with depression and/or anxiety until you begin at the foundation of the issue. It always comes back to failure. It's time to revisit our relationship with failure and how we view it in our lives.

Depression and anxiety have a terrible reputation which is well deserved. But if we truly do not want to live with them, we need to stop looking to blame them for our issues. Depression and anxiety would not show up and stay in our lives if we didn't let them. They exist when our mind opens the door for them. One cannot have a healthy relationship with either depression or anxiety. They only exist to hurt us. We have to choose to not let them.

Failure, on the other hand, is a different creature. It is much different than its cousins. By embracing failure and really getting to know it, I have learned how failure can exist in my life without depression or anxiety.

The hate all of us have for failure is unfounded. By learning to love failure, we can learn to love ourselves even deeper. It is time to get to know failure for what it really is. Failure is not here to hurt you. Failure is your teacher when you open yourself to it.

I started all of this by telling you I hate failure. That was a lie. I hat-*ed* failure. That was in the past. The feelings of hate that I had for failure have been buried, together with my relationship with depression and anxiety.

As I developed a strong and loving relationship with failure, I stopped seeing depression and haven't heard a peep from it for many years. Anxiety likes to come visit on occasion, but I use the tools of the Chosen Commandments to see that anxiety has no place in my life. I nourish my body, mind, and soul. I live in the present moment. I love myself. Life is a journey for me and a consistent opportunity to practice rather than compete. By living my life in this manner, anxiety feels unwelcome and quietly goes away.

My relationship with failure was a strained one for my whole life. Failure, either through my thinking or those around me, served as a reminder of what I could not do. It felt like failure was being thrown in my face at every turn. I found failure to be humiliating and oftentimes debilitating. As hard as I would work and attempt to succeed, failure would punish me and tell me that I was not good enough. Especially when I heard this from others, it would convince me that I was weak and a failure.

Think about that word. Failure. Derived from a failed act, the concept of failure can become part of our identity. We witness ourselves failing to complete a task and then label ourselves by the very term itself. Failure is the incompleteness of the act and then we become the failure ourselves. "I am a failure."

When I hated failure, in many ways, I morphed into it. I allowed failure to define me and become my identity, so much so that my hatred of failure became a hatred for myself. By allowing my mind to hate failure, and then become part of my identity, I was allowing myself to become what I hated. This then allowed me to hate myself.

That is so sad when I think about it, but looking back, at the time it all seemed okay. Nobody was going to wake me up from my crisis. I wish that I would have been able to spot the giant red flag earlier. By identifying myself as a failure, alarm bells should have gone off. But they did not. And in spite of my suffering and pain, I somehow justified my state of mind and convinced myself to continue functioning. I still went to school, graduated, moved on to two levels of postsecondary, and became a successful lawyer. But all that time, no matter what I accomplished for much of my life, I could not shake the feeling of seeing myself as a failure.

I was focusing on what I did *not* do, rather than being happy with my present moments. I had a terrible relationship with failure and as a result an unhappy existence. Antidepressants and therapy allowed me to shake depression and keep anxiety at bay. But until I could recognize my view on failure, I could never truly love myself and evolve into a better state of being. The solution? Yoga and meditation.

Funny how it seems to always come back to yoga and meditation. Surprised? You shouldn't be. As you learned early on, incorporating the initial Chosen Commandments of sleep, water, nutrition, and physical activity as part of your lifestyle creates the foundation of your existence. To complete the process, yoga and meditation are the drivers that bring it home.

Yoga and meditation were strong teachers in opening my mind and heart. During these practices, I learned to develop a relationship with myself. Instead of hurting myself mentally and focusing on my perceived negative reality, I came to embrace peace and happiness in the present. It took time and I continue to work on it in the present day.

In developing a relationship with myself, I also came to know failure. Failure would come up often in my mind during yoga and meditation. In quiet rooms with nowhere to run or hide, I had no choice but to acknowledge and be alone with my thoughts. Especially in the darkest moments, failure would creep in time and time again. My most hated rival that made so much of my life miserable was now in front of me. I lashed out at it many times. I would blame it for holding me back and wanted to punish it for my shortcomings. Yet, no matter how much I yelled and screamed at failure, it was silent. It never said a word.

Then a realization hit me: Failure has NO voice. It cannot speak. All the negative energy and advice that I had received for all these years was not from failure, it was from myself. Failure had never wronged me. It did not attempt to hurt or help me. Failure was simply there. It was there all along. How I perceived it was up to me. I saw failure in the wrong light all this time. Now it was time to shift perspective.

Once the dawning of reality hit me, I apologized to failure. I got it all wrong. I had chosen to make failure my enemy. I chose to allow failure to be painted in a negative light. By viewing failure as a punisher, I enabled depression and anxiety to follow and wreak havoc on my mind and life. Failure never invited them. Failure did nothing at all. I chose to make failure my foe.

The whole time, I was not fighting failure. I was fighting myself. Failure was whatever form I assigned it. Failure only represented an attempt at something that did not succeed for me. But that did not need to be an indicator of negativity. Failing at previous attempts did not make me a failure in the present moment. Nor did it mean that I would not succeed in the future.

The entire time I started to see failure in a new light, it never said a word. Failure listened, but did not respond. I embraced failure. I invited it to the dinner table. I let it know that it was my teacher. I acknowledged that failure was not looking to directly hurt me. Failure was teaching me lessons.

I could take each lesson as a painful reminder of what I could not do, wallow in misery, and choose to hold myself back. Or I could thank failure for the opportunity to try and educate me. I could then shift my mind to appreciate the lessons and devote fresh energy to other tasks as they arose.

True failure, I decided, was not to make the attempt and fail to succeed, but rather to fail to make the attempt at all.

Failure began to show me a new side of myself. Yes, I took many chances and risks in life. Some concluded successfully, while others were setbacks. At least I never held back in life. Failing to act would have caused me to miss out on as many hits as possible misses. What I previously viewed as failures were truly not failures at all. They were life lessons that showed me more possible opportunities in the future if I was open to them.

The only true failures were the missed opportunities that would have succeeded had I attempted them, but chose to not even try due to a fear of the unknown. Seeing failure in this new light gave me new hope and perspective. Each time failure and I visited each other during yoga and meditation practices, I told failure that I was excited about the life that was awaiting me. I committed to living in the present and appreciating where I was at. The past served as life lessons and the future began to represent opportunities that awaited me, once I was ready to see and attempt them. As I thanked failure for my awakening, it smiled and continued to not say a word.

As you read my experiences with failure, consider your own relationship with it. The likelihood is that failure has held you back in many instances. How much has failure punished you for your setbacks? Be honest with yourself. Think about how easy it has been to blame failure as a third party that has wronged you. The natural instinct is to despise failure and feel anger toward it, given how much it has supposedly cost you in lost opportunities and accomplishments over time. But it wasn't failure that hurt you. It was you.

It is mind-blowing when you realize that looking at failure in a negative light is, in reality, looking at yourself in the mirror. You CHOOSE how to view yourself when you view failure. If you hate failure, then you are directing hate toward yourself. If you are blaming failure for the negatives in your life, you are choosing to blame yourself.

All of the talk of failure and its effects on your life is in YOUR mind. You are choosing how to view your life. It is your decision to look to the past in regret or to the future in worry. You can choose to see failure negatively and invite their cousins—depression and anxiety—into your mind and allow them to reside there indefinitely. Or you can choose to live in the present moment and embrace failure as one of the greatest teachers you can ever have.

The next time failure comes into your mind and life, take the time to sort out your relationship. Rather than drive failure away from you, try inviting it in. Speak to it. The failed moment or event that took place is not negative. It is positive. You won simply by making the attempt. The result was irrelevant. If things didn't go your way, then more opportunities await you in the future. You can try again. And again. And again. Perhaps you will make the attempt in a different manner, having seen what happened during previous attempts. The next time you might be more successful. Or perhaps not. The outcome doesn't matter. It is the energy and positivity that you release as part of your actions that really measure your success.

You could also decide that you need to focus your energy on other activities and move on. This is not called quitting; it is called making optimal use of your energies. If insanity is doing the same thing over and over and expecting a different result, then rationality is taking failed attempts as learning experiences, cutting your losses, and moving on.

Seeing failed attempts as learning experiences rather than punishments is a profound mind shift. It is showing yourself love and gratitude rather than punishment and hurt. Failure is not in your life to hurt you. Failure does not define you. *You* define you. How you choose to view your experiences is on you. When you view failure from a different perspective, you will see yourself in a whole new light. If many things in your life have gone wrong, that is fine. They were life lessons that you needed to learn.

Your life has not been a competition. It is practice. You have the chance at a reset every day. Each morning you wake up is a fresh opportunity to be the best you can be. Failure is a wonderful teacher, as are victories.

When you fail at something, you can label yourself a failure. When you achieve a victory, you can call yourself victorious. The attempts are the same, the only difference being what you perceive to be the result.

We have one more member of failure's family to meet. Their twin sibling, victory. They are similar in many ways. They both never say a word—but one represents positivity and one represents negativity.

We are so quick to accept failure, yet we do not do the same for victory. Do you know what makes champions great? Do you think that they replay failed attempts in their minds? Do they picture and manifest their lives as failing to accomplish tasks? Of course not. Champions replay victories over and over in their minds. They focus on positivity. They take failures as life lessons and determine what they need to do in the future to achieve better results.

When champions see themselves in their minds, all they can see is the task being accomplished in the best possible manner with the highest chance of success. Champions manifest victories, not failures.

Consider yourself and your mind. What do you replay in your mind? The things that you have done right, or wrong? Many of us get caught in the spiral of focusing solely on failures. Why? We work hard and make numerous attempts each day. Think of how different life could be if we focused more on our victories rather than our defeats. The mind, for some reason, wants to gravitate to negativity. You are the captain of your ship. You can steer it in any direction you want. Victory is the best route to go. Do not ignore failure. But there is no reason to dwell on it.

The life that you live and want is based on how you shape yourself in the present and how you create your reality. Failure does not define you. It teaches you. Remember that as you look ahead to what is to come.

The next time you meet up with failure, it's time to give it a second chance. By understanding the role it plays in your life, the hate should be gone. There should be love and compassion for failure. It is one of the most important relationships you will ever have.

Failure is not your identity or lifelong partner. It is a teacher that pops in and out of your life, to remind you of lessons when needed. Rather than get upset at failure, thank it. By failing at a task, you are learning and considering better possible strategies for future attempts, or to steer completely ahead in new directions altogether. If you consider these life lessons in a positive light, then failure may not even be part of your life at all! If true failure is not even making the attempt—you did not fail by trying and not succeeding! You learned and grew. How mind-blowing is that? What you considered to be failure for so many years was nothing more than practice and growth. A subtle mind shift, but one that can completely turn on your energy and passion.

The mind that is present in positivity ignites fire within the soul. This, in turn, will make you work even harder to have your mind and soul work together. When you see a failed attempt as failure, the negative outlook toward the future dims the passion within your soul. The result is a mind that rests in the negative and has to work even harder since the soul has no energy to assist.

When you label yourself as a failure for not succeeding at an attempt, you exhaust your mind from overworking in negativity and you disconnect from your soul at an alarming rate. Why does the mind do that? Because we let it. We allow our minds to focus on the negative or the ten things we did wrong that day instead of the ninety things we did right. We have a need to shift our mind to negativity. This is how many of us are programmed, but it can change if we program ourselves to positivity.

We know the mind is a powerful tool. Let's make it work for us instead of against us. The mind works best when it is connected fully with the soul. To make that connection work, live in the NOW in a positive manner.

If someone tells you that to live in the present you will need to ignore your past and future, they are lying to you. The human mind is not capable of that. It is impossible to live 100 percent of the time in the present. We cannot and should not ignore our pasts, for they are teachers of our history and experiences. We need our past to help shape our present and future selves.

When a situation does come up in the future, your natural first instinct to deal with it is based on your previous interactions. If it is something that you have done before (and well), you will do your best to repeat your past actions. If your past actions did not succeed, then you will now consider an alternative route to achieve possible success. But the past and future only need to arise as they come. The danger is to live in one or the other, rather than in the present.

To keep replaying the past or worrying about what is to come in the future is exhausting. We are not equipped to handle situations as they arise with tired minds. As you have learned, tired minds do not ignite the passion within the soul. If you are going to build the life you want and be the best you can be, you will be in a much better position for success with an inspired soul.

To get the soul to its maximum level, it needs to be fed with energy from your mind. Your mind is able to fuel the soul when it is in its most relaxed state, which is the present. Remember this as perceived failures come into your mind. Say it to yourself or out loud if you have to. Thank past experiences for teaching you lessons. You are better for them.

But you are not *living* in the past. And failure does not define you. You are living in the present. When you do see the future, you manifest the things that you do RIGHT, not the things you do WRONG. Shifting to the present mode and taking on opportunities as they come is the healthiest mindset for you.

Situations will be what they will be. You will choose how they affect you going forward.

So the next time you fail at something, smile. Give yourself a huge hug. Feel proud of yourself. You have *tried*! There was never any pressure. No expectations. You did not sit on the sidelines. The result is secondary. All that matters is that you were passionate and you tried your best at what you attempted. The journey is the best part, not the destination.

Remember, life is an ongoing series of journeys. It is much more fun when we buckle in and enjoy the ride rather than regret or worry about what is to come. Understanding the role that failure plays in our lives means that we have wonderful teachers at our side, helping us along the way. We can focus on victories just as much, if not more, than failure. Each experience in itself is a guide.

We are learning how to live each and every day. Now that you have learned how to embrace failure, it is time to dig deep and make life even easier and more successful for ourselves. It is time to shift to the gifts that the universe has provided you and to channel them to being the best *you* that you can be.

TWENTY-ONE

Channel Your Gifts

⟞⟋⟍⟞

A common issue we have as a society is that we tend to focus on the negative. We look for what is "wrong" with a person and try to fix them. It is too rare that we focus on the positives and what is "right" within that same person. In this seemingly never-ending journey to improve and further ourselves, we can often lose focus on the greatness within us. As you discover your Chosen Life and work toward evolving yourself to the highest possible being you can be, never lose sight of who you are. There are special gifts within you, which are G-d-given gifts.

Throughout our journey together in *The Bible 3.0*, we discussed the creation and implementation of systems within your life. The 6 Commandments of the Chosen Life, together with additional steps helping you toward enlightenment, will come differently to every person who reads and utilizes them.

In your case, you may have already been adhering to some of the Chosen Commandments for many years. While for others, most, if not all, of the steps may be new. Whichever stage you are at, remember: *it is not a race or competition*. Any improvements you make today will bring you further ahead than you were yesterday.

Focus on how far you have come, not how much time and energy you need to still get ahead. By focusing on the positives, and shining a bright light on yourself and your journey, you will feel better about yourself and the work you are putting in. The results will come quicker, and you will feel so much happier as you build your life systems.

As you proceed on this path, you must keep a key piece of information in mind. Don't ever forget this. Ready? Here it goes…

YOU ARE SPECIAL. Say this to yourself, "I AM SPECIAL." Again and again and again if you have to. How does that feel? Exhilarating, I'm sure. Perhaps you have heard this before—from a parent, teacher, mentor, or colleague. If you did, I am happy for you. It is a great feeling. But for a lot of us, including myself, we have never heard this before. This is an affirmation that we are unique, that we have purpose, and that people admire and look up to us.

It is okay if we do not receive this form of inspiration from third parties. We will receive it from ourselves. As we have discussed, true love starts from within. Once we receive unconditional love from ourselves, we are fully fulfilled. We do not need to seek love from others. In fact, when we feel whole and complete, we are then equipped to provide unconditional love to others without requiring anything back. Please remember the self-love you require and need to function at your highest level. It can and should begin with you telling yourself that you are special.

I feel your next question coming on: "What makes ME special?" If we were conversing right now, you would likely be turning to me and waiting for my response.

Here is the reality: I don't know you. Reasonably, that would make you question how I can make that statement so confidently and boldly. For emphasis, then, I will say it again: YOU ARE SPECIAL! It is easy for me to say this because there are gifts within you that make you unique. If you look within yourself, ponder who you are and how you've lived your life, you will find them.

At this time, please prepare a list of all your gifts, in any format you would like. Seeing it visually will help drive the point home. You can make a point-form list or a spreadsheet. Are there certain types of activities that you have always naturally gravitated to? Are there specific tasks that you accomplish fairly rapidly and well because you are good at them? Take the time to think about it.

Gifts can come in many shapes and sizes. Consider all the special abilities a person could conceivably have:

- Musical talent
- Artistic talent
- Athletic talent
- The ability to build things
- Being able to fix things
- Having a green thumb
- Being able to understand animals

The list of potential gifts a person can have is endless. Some are very easy to spot, such as a person who sits at a piano and can instantly play without learning or can pick it up quickly.

Then there's the champion chess player who's been gifted from a young age, and the artist painting beautiful works of art. What about the star athlete or the gifted mechanic? These are skills and traits a person finds within themselves and is able to hone and craft to a high level.

It is a great feeling when we find a gift within ourselves and are able to recognize and utilize them to better ourselves and our lives. While it is tremendous to be a star in a particular area or field, not all of us are so blessed. For many, they can succeed in a chosen area not because they have talent or natural gifts, but because of hard work.

There is an expression that hard work beats talent every day of the week. But imagine you have a gift, *and* you work hard at the same time. Then you would be unstoppable! That is a fact.

While you can certainly look to work hard in any area that you wish and seek success, some things may come harder to us simply because we are not naturally inclined to do them. You are fully encouraged to build goals and dreams and work toward them. Nobody will stop you—but it's up to you to make it happen. But not everything has to come with difficulty. In anything and everything you do, it's important to recognize your gifts.

To acknowledge and utilize your gifts allows you to reach your full potential. While it is not always easy to spot the gifts, they are there. They have always been there over the course of your life. Now it is up to you to finally see and embrace them for what they are. Appreciate your gifts and utilize them toward the best you possible!

Let's fully acknowledge that the definition of a "G-d-given gift" is very subjective. For the purpose of self-analysis and growth, I want you to think of a gift as an ability to do something that comes either easily or naturally to you; an activity in which you are very strong and consistent over a great length of time. Ponder that for a while. Gifts can come in all forms, shapes, and sizes. There are so many potential gifts within you that you may not be seeing. They are there, but we must recognize them.

On a personal note, finding my gifts is an area I struggled with for some time. It was not easy to discover them, but I finally did.

I knew at a young age that I was born with three gifts. I knew how to speak well. This skill came with time, as I needed to learn how to listen before I could express myself verbally. Secondly, I had a photographic memory which, for the most part, faded over time. I am not sad nor do I miss it, as I simply felt lucky to have it for as long as I possessed it. But most of all, I could write.

I am fortunate to possess a writing style where the words flow through my fingers without thought or hesitation. It is hard to teach somebody to write when the skill is a G-d-given gift. This is how I have seen writing throughout my life, and the honor of being able to write out my words and have people read them is a gift unto itself.

As closed as my mind and heart were over the course of my life, I could not deny that I had this gift. I did not always see and understand my ability to express myself verbally or comprehend and accept my memory abilities, but I knew that I would write. Sadly, though, I didn't see that this was a gift for many years. To me, I did not think that I had any gifts for much of my childhood. I was not strong athletically, nor artistically, and I lacked construction abilities. I could not play a musical instrument. In all the extra-curricular activities during my childhood, I never performed well at any— so I told myself I lacked gifts and talents.

While I thought at points that not having any gifts or talents was extremely unfair, I learned to accept this as truth. As a result, I made the determination to work harder in life. In whatever I wanted to accomplish, I would have to work ten times harder than the average person to make it happen—but I would do it. This drive helped me build a successful career and life, but it certainly would have come easier and smoother had I embraced my strengths earlier on my path.

A key point to remember is: no matter what stage you are at in life, it is NEVER too late to adapt and grow. It all comes down to *mindset*. For myself, I began to grow even stronger once I felt and utilized my gifts in life. And certainly, you are able to do the same anytime.

* * *

Let's look back now at the list you produced. What did you write? If the page is blank, don't despair. It is likely because you still have a narrow view of what a "gift" means. Remember our definition. There are so many aspects of life in which we could see that we have very strong gifts within us:

- Organized
- A leader
- Cook
- Clean well
- Safe driver with a clean record
- Parent with motherly/fatherly instincts
- Organize and assist with charity work
- Travel and explore the world
- Enjoy and identify music
- Blog/create content on the internet
- Photograph/video
- Converse well on the telephone

Imagine that these are but some of many potential examples of gifts YOU could have.

Now that you completed one list, I would like you to prepare another of all the various activities you performed over the course of one week, from Monday to Sunday. Record every place you went and every task you attempted or completed during that time. Once you have prepared this second list, I want you to think it over. For each task you attempted, how often did you successfully complete them? How much time did you invest in each task? How much effort or strain did it take to work on each of these tasks?

Based on the second list, you will be able to assess what you could accomplish in one week, with minimal effort and time invested. Consider why that happened. It is the result of having gifts within you. From there, take a look at your first list again. Are you able to add more gifts?

In my world, cooking was an example of an activity that made me reassess my gifts. I have really liked to cook for several years. I never considered myself to be a professional by any means, but I certainly knew my way around the kitchen. I enjoy grocery shopping. I can locate, assemble, and purchase my required groceries in good timing. I keep my kitchen very organized and have cooked meals on a daily or weekly basis consistently for over twenty years. I received a crash course on cooking when I was seventeen and have excelled at it ever since. Cooking did not come naturally to me; I only grew with my abilities in the kitchen through hard work over the years.

After talking to many people about keeping a kitchen in a home, I realized that not every person is able to do that. Many people have a very difficult time keeping a kitchen organized and functioning. No matter how much effort they put in, cooking is simply not a skill they are able to master. For me, cooking does not feel like hard work. I very much enjoy it and succeed at it. As a result, I feel it is another gift I have.

From your list of tasks you recorded during one week, consider what comes naturally or quite easily to you. It may seem like a trivial or meaningless exercise, but even the smallest abilities can be gifts.

The reality, though, is that we can't be strong at everything we do. For example, not everyone is a good driver. For some, driving will never come naturally, no matter how hard they try. Not everyone can go to an opera and appreciate a performance, or attend a soup kitchen and display kindness and empathy to those in need. There are those who struggle their whole lives to communicate and relate to children. Many never travel and if they do, they have a hard time adapting to new countries and environments. Even taking a nice, focused picture is an impossibility for many. There is nothing wrong with admitting our weaknesses. In fact, we should embrace them. None of us are "perfect."

The problem arises when we focus on our weaknesses. We either pursue our lives endlessly trying to fix them, or give up in despair and label ourselves as failures. It is time to stop that cycle. Imagine a life where we focus on our gifts and strengths. We will be much happier, and our self-confidence will grow by the day.

The pursuit of perfection is a road to nowhere. As hard as you think you can try, you will never be perfect at everything. Your mind works best when it is focused and pursues what works for you. It's not that you need to give up on things; rather, it's that your life will be easier if you accept that certain activities simply do not need to be part of your life. There are particular tasks we have to do because they are required to maintain a lifestyle. You can still certainly work hard at them and get them done the best you can—but there is no need to see them in a negative light. You will be able to view your weaknesses in a compassionate light and give yourself a break because you did the best you could, and that is more than enough.

Simply do not put any more energy or thought into something that doesn't serve you. Focus instead on what comes more naturally to you and gets you the best results. By focusing your mind on your gifts, your soul will kick it into the next gear, rather than hold you back if it focuses on negatives. Remember that there is no shame in asking for help or outsourcing any functions which could be completed faster and more efficiently by someone else who is strong in that field. This will result in more productivity in your life and less wasted time and effort for you.

To get to the highest point in your life and be the best *you* that you can be, remember that your mind cannot do it alone. The mind works best when it functions in unison with your soul. Once your mind accepts a gift you have, it communicates this to your soul. From there, your heart and spirit become inspired to embrace this gift and work even stronger to develop it. Which, in turn, your soul communicates to your mind, and makes things easier on your body.

Picture your mind and soul as a well-oiled machine. Your mind thinks positively and inspires your soul to ignite passion. This passion then creates more positivity and works more focused and harder at the given task. With your soul and mind in overdrive, your body will combine as the third part to perform the task on a consistent and successful basis.

No matter how strong and well cared for your body is, it will be unable to consistently perform and succeed with the demands of completing given tasks if it is not fueled by the motivation given through your mind and soul. Working through gifts is the highest motivation your mind and soul can channel to elevate your body to function at its peak. Channeling your gifts is not a one-off thought. Rather, it is a pipeline for a lifetime of continued success and self-betterment.

The notion of gifts doesn't take away from the idea of setting goals and manifesting results. But now that you have learned all these skills, imagine being able to make them happen FASTER and BETTER. You CAN make this happen by focusing your mind on what you are good at.

When you turn your attention to what comes easiest and best to you, and when your mind and soul are focused on your present-day strengths, your future success is built on a foundation of power. You will look toward goals within your gifts. You will manifest a life that focuses on your gifts. As you channel your gifts, the future only looks brighter. When you truly love and embrace the person you are today, your evolution moves at a much more productive pace. The lesson? Know and embrace who you are and what you are capable of. Build upon the strongest you for the brightest road ahead.

* * *

Remember when I told you I once thought I didn't have any gifts? Then, slowly, as I entered my teenage years, I embraced my ability to write. I then began to manifest the idea of writing a book. It seemed like an impossible dream, yet one I felt comfortable envisioning knowing that I COULD write it. The only issue I needed to solve was whether I could get past my own mental limits and actually write it.

As I manifested a future as a published author, I set myself the goal of creating a blog website and writing consistently for it. From there, I eventually started the blog and published hundreds of articles. That site grew into additional sites, where I wrote many articles on topics of interest and passion. By setting my goals and furthering my gift, I started creeping closer and closer to my manifested dream.

From the time I embraced my writing gift and manifested a published book successfully, over thirty years had passed. Everything happens in its time and place. Simply having the gift in itself was not going to write a book for me. I still had to work at my craft.

Over time, I learned to practice and get better at it. But the work sure came easier because I enjoyed writing. I was motivated to work harder at it because it was a strength for me. My mind and soul fueled my passion and positivity toward writing, which allowed my body to sit at my computer and successfully complete a book hundreds of hours later. Channeling my gifts worked for me. Now I want you to find YOUR gifts to channel YOUR success.

Working on your mindset takes time. For many of us, we have focused on negativity our whole lives. The result is that it may take a lifetime to switch the focus back to our gifts instead. The good news is, once you do develop the ability to focus your mind on your gifts, then you should be able to develop the ability to switch your mind quickly through practice and repetition.

We are not born with mindsets. They are created and evolved throughout our lifetime. Know that when you are thinking negatively and can recognize it, half the battle is already won. The secret from there is to learn how to shift to the positive and maintain that mindset without shifting back and forth. Do not pressure yourself or place a timeframe on having to learn this mode of thinking. It will come when you allow your mind to be ready for it. Positivity comes from openness and clarity only.

I have seen and met far too many folks who have chosen to view their lives as a failure. They choose to focus on their misses and defeats, rather than victories and successes. This is, in most cases, a result of faulty programming of the mind, where people allow themselves to channel negativity and justify a lack of activity and effort due to what is perceived to be a low probability of success. This can be done in every aspect of life, both professionally and personally.

Think about something in your life that is making you unhappy. Is it your job, for instance? *Why* is it making you unhappy? Are you performing tasks you are good at and excite you, or do you find your job very difficult and unfulfilling on a daily basis? If your mind is telling you that you are not good at your job or that there is no reward in what you do, then your mind will close your soul from the tasks at hand. Your soul will be unable to channel passion for your job, and you will continue the negative cycle indefinitely.

If a negative mindset is you at the moment—or at any point in your life—take solace that you are not alone. Most, if not all of us have been there. It is normal to go through this process. But if you want to break out of the cycle, then you need to put your focus where it counts. Do not blame others for your dissatisfaction. Most of all, do not blame yourself. You are not purposely trying to harm yourself.

Your cycle begins and ends with your thought process. If an aspect of your life (such as your job) is draining rather than exciting you, then it is time to shift the mindset.

No matter how old you are and where you're at in life, it is never too late to create change. It will not shift overnight, but once you make the conscious decision for positivity and improvement, you are well on your way.

When thinking about a negative state in your life such as your job, compare your job to your list of gifts. Are they in line with one another? Part of our issue with roles is that we focus on what we think we are SUPPOSED to do, rather than what we are STRONG at doing. It is time to refocus our mindset. The key is not the gifts themselves, but how we are channeling them.

If you are able to evolve your role or even transfer to a different position at your company which better utilizes your gifts, consider it. You will be creating a much better chance for yourself for present and future success, as well as happiness. A win-win.

Companies are far more open today than ever before when it comes to utilizing the skillsets of their labor force to grow their organizations. If you are a stronger speaker than a writer, evolve your role to one that relies more on your voice than your writing. If customer service or teamwork is not your strength, consider a role that is more independent in nature. Whatever your gifts are, think of how they can slot within your job. Talk openly and frankly with your employer about creating short- and long-term goals for your position based on your gifts.

Channeling your gifts does not and should not be done in isolation. The more people who are part of your life who can understand and appreciate your strengths, the more they can help you shift your life and mindset toward a positive path. And if the people around you cannot or will not help you on that path, then it might be time to consider a different environment that rewards and encourages the best you. The example about your job can be transferred to every aspect of your life. In everything you do, you can make the decision to focus on what you are best at. If a role can be tweaked to embrace your gift, take it. If any role can be replaced or foregone because it does not play up to your strengths, own that. Do not consider your shift giving up or failure, it's an evolution toward positivity.

There is an expression that one should not throw good money after bad. Meaning, if you have already sunk resources into a losing proposition, then throwing more money and time into it will not necessarily make it better. Write off the investment as a learning experience. Devote your present and future resources toward areas that work better with your gifts, for you will be far happier and increase your chances at success.

For some reason it is easier for most of us to stay stagnant and accept our position in life, even if it is not our best. Is that the life you really want to live? Consider that as you look ahead. You should want and need more from your life. Make the decision to always work toward the best version of you. With this strong and positive mindset, you will be unstoppable—as long as you commit to yourself and the Chosen Life you can live.

Ultimately, you need to sit down and really ponder life. Why are you on this Earth? What are you supposed to accomplish? From the moment we came into existence as humans, people have tried to reason and solve the mystery of life. Why are we here? What does all of this mean? What are we supposed to do? Is life predetermined for us by a higher force, or do we control our own destiny? As you ponder questions of this nature, start taking an inventory of your existence. What goals have you set for yourself? Have you achieved them to date? Are you actively working toward a better tomorrow? Do you feel fulfilled in what you do and who you are? Do you truly understand and utilize your gifts on a consistent basis? Do you live a life of meaning and purpose, or are you drifting aimlessly without direction and focus? These questions are some of the hardest we will ever ask ourselves. If the answers come back negatively, then we open ourselves to the realization that we may be ALIVE, but we are not LIVING.

It is a very different notion to drift rather than to live. If your mind is present in the current moment and you are fueled by the inspiration of the wonderful possibilities that will come in the future, then you are on the road to living. If you are weighed down by regret and hurt from the past which disconnects your ability to live and strive ahead, you are drifting.

But *drifting* can quickly turn into *living* when the mind and soul are shifted to the present in a positive manner. It is never too late. You do not need to punish yourself anymore for areas of weakness or past mistakes. You can be the best you can be at this exact moment and every day to come.

You can hit the reset button. You can begin to live the life you *want*—not the life anyone expects of you. You need to live *for you*. It is *your life*. Take control of it.

* * *

Creating an existence that focuses on your strengths rather than your weaknesses will take you down the path to understanding the concept of LIFE overall. At some point in your existence, especially as you get older, you will begin to question the meaning of life more and more. You came into the world from nothing, and you will leave this world as nothing. Somehow, through the wonder of the universe, procreation made you. From there, one day, at a time that is unknown to you, life as you know it will end. You will no longer exist. From life comes death. Knowing and understanding that this existence you know is temporary, consider how precious the time is that you have while you are alive.

If we all know that we will die one day, then why do we bother to do what we do? Why do we work and build a life for ourselves? Why do we need to have strong bodies, minds, and souls if we know it will all end eventually? Do we really need to love ourselves and others if those we love—including ourselves—will not be around one day?

You need to make a choice. You must decide whether to live a life of meaning and work toward the best life for yourself, or give up and drift since none of this matters anyway.

What is THE MEANING OF LIFE? Let's get ready to explore and answer the question that brings all of your work and efforts together. I am not going to sugarcoat it or deny you a clear and concise response. There is a very simple meaning to life, and it has been under our noses the whole time.

TWENTY-TWO

The Meaning of Life

⸻ ⟨∞⟩ ⸻

From the moment Adam walked around the Garden of Eden, people have asked themselves one key question: What is the meaning of life? Why were we put on Earth? Why am I here? And what happens to me after I'm gone?

I have good news for you. I have saved the best for last. You have put in the work to recreate your life systems through the 6 Commandments of the Chosen Life. From there, you have done the work toward enlightenment by introducing more key steps. With all the work you have done, isn't it only fair that you figure out what the purpose of all this is? It is.

And so, I introduce to you the grand finale of *The Bible 3.0*. This is the encore, where we sit down and discuss the meaning and purpose of this writing. Grab a coffee, tea, a glass of water, or any beverage you wish. Get ready for one last ride as we uncover the meaning of life. To do this, we must begin with stories, of course.

Growing up, I was a huge fan of the rock band the Doors. I remember vividly listening to "Light My Fire" as a six-year-old and being absolutely captivated by their music and lyrics. Going into first grade, my favorite music was Sesame Street Live and the Doors. An eclectic mix, to say the least. When I received my first CD player as a gift on my twelfth birthday, I went out right away and bought three CDs: REM's *Out of Time*, *The Best of Jimi Hendrix*, and *The*

Doors, a self-titled album. I must have listened to *The Doors* over a thousand times.

I will insert a disclaimer here that for the longest time, I was convinced that I was a reincarnation of Jim Morrison; that his spirit and soul were within me. Parts of me still believe that. I had a few reasons for these beliefs. We both share the same astrological sign of Sagittarius, with similar birthdays. Jim passed away in 1971, so perhaps it took his spirit five years to follow into my body. I was drawn to the Doors from a young age, in the sense that the music spoke so vividly to me. Most of all, writing followed us throughout our lives.

I never made that last connection until the moment I sat down to write this chapter. I went to sleep in a calm and meditative state, and the universe spoke to me. It told me that I needed to sit down and write the words I am telling you today.

As I sat free and clear to express my thoughts, I understood yet a deeper connection to Jim Morrison. Many call him a rock star. From everything I read about the man, I think he would consider himself a poet and an artist. I would agree. That inspired my writing, as well.

Furthermore, while we have no evidence that Jim Morrison practiced yoga in his lifetime, he did find it fitting to write a poem about it in 1969. In many ways, my life journey took off when I adopted my regular yoga practice. Yoga gave me the power to take control of my thoughts and mind. Jim was onto something there.

When I think of Jim Morrison, I do not think of a traditional religious person, but rather, a man with a deep soul and energized spirit. The music of Jim Morrison and the Doors is timeless. Considering how long it takes most bands to come up with a second album following their debut, it blows my mind each time when I think about how many albums the Doors created in such a short amount of time. The Doors' self-titled album released in 1965. Their final album, *L.A. Woman*, released in 1971. They released two studio albums in their first year and then another album each year until Jim's passing. Six albums in five years. That, my friends, is what you call talent, determination, and productivity.

Until this day, the Doors' fans debate which of their albums is the best one. There are arguments to be made for each one of the six. That is how good the music and the writing are.

My mind and soul were shaped partially over the years by Jim Morrison. Maybe because a part of him resides within me, or that we shared similar souls and energies. Whatever the reason, I would not be the person I am today if not for the words of Jim Morrison. I honor and thank him for that. I thought for many years that Jim Morrison and the Doors had mostly ignited a passion within me that helped breathe life into my spirit. It turns out that this was only a small aspect of that. Jim actually helped me have a deeper understanding about life and death and helped shape balance in my thinking. This was done through, in my mind, his masterpiece of a song titled, "The End." This song is the basis for the final chapter of *The Bible 3.0.*

Music fans, especially those of the Doors, have a love-hate relationship with the song "The End." Some believe it is one of the greatest pieces of music ever created. Others believe it is dim, gloomy, and terrible. I would argue that to truly appreciate "The End," you need to have an open mind and soul to hear and understand the lyrics and feel the energy it creates within you. I would make the argument that your level of acceptance of life and death can be seen based on how you react to listening to "The End." Stop what you are doing right now and take a listen if you can. Whether it is your first or your hundredth time listening to it, go put it on. Stop reading. Close your eyes. And then return to reading for the discussion.

* * *

You are back. How do you feel? I would say one of two ways: happy or sad. Do you feel uplifted from the song or are you deflated? This feeling has more to do with your reaction to death rather than life.

When you think about death, are you fearful of it? Does the thought of not living absolutely frighten you? Don't worry; if you do, you are not alone.

Many people on Earth are absolutely afraid to die. Death is the one concept we cannot comprehend. We don't know what happens to us when we pass away from this Earth. We know our bodies decompose. Our brains shut off. But what happens to our souls? Are we ghosts who travel the Earth? Do we reincarnate into new bodies and minds? Or do we fully disappear from this planet without a trace? We actually do not know. So we look for answers. Many of us turn to religion for those answers. But do we ever find those answers?

Depending on your faith, or quest for faith, you may find different mediums that will help you find answers. Perhaps try different facilities or temples, or attend different gatherings with friends of different faiths. Mix things up! But if you are going to look for the answer to your life in a religious book, then you may be waiting for a long time. The answer does not reside in a nice clear manner written on a page. It is within YOU!

Religious and spiritual books, when it comes to the matter of life and death, are facilitators to open your soul and mind—for you to search within yourself. You actually have all your answers to life. You simply have to find them again.

If life is constructed from a series of experiences and events, then there are three events in my life that took place which shaped how I thought and felt about my existence. These occurrences were going to happen regardless. It was my reaction and feelings toward them which would really help shape my soul and outlook on life. I want to share them with you now.

1. FATHER PASSING AT AGE ELEVEN

It's the strangest thing when you lose a parent at a young age. I remember coming home from school one afternoon. It was a Thursday. I asked my mother where my father was. He was in bed for a couple of weeks not feeling really good. She responded that he had gone to the hospital but would be back, so I did not think anything of it.

I went to school on Friday and then came home. That night, my mother let me stay up and watch TV in her room while she hosted company. I thought it was strange that she was having a party unannounced. But I enjoyed the TV time and fell asleep in her bed.

When I woke up the next morning, I went to the kitchen. I announced to everyone that I slept great; that maybe it was the best sleep I ever had. My mother and brother looked at me and my mom told me that my brother had something he wanted to talk to me about.

I had no idea what he was going to say. He came right out with it: our father had passed away and he was not coming back.

I was more in a state of shock and disbelief than anything else. Life became a whirlwind. All of a sudden, family came to see us from Israel. We had a funeral (the first one I had ever attended) and we sat shiva for seven days to mourn my father's passing. This is a Jewish tradition whereby the family of the deceased says dedicated prayers for that one-week period, usually in the home of the departed. They are joined by people who come to pay their respects and celebrate the life of the person they recently lost.

It all felt like a strange dream—none of it felt real. I did not go to school during this period. Once the shiva was over, I went back to school the following Monday.

I cannot remember much of anything from the funeral or shiva. Those memories are gone. But I do remember one thing from that experience.

Standing in the schoolyard before school began, I realized that the week I was gone, school had gone on as usual. Whether I attended school or not, life would go on without me.

I realized at the age of eleven that in many ways, my existence did not matter. All of it was meaningless. Life and the Earth would function with or without me. It's a very deep realization to have at any age, but especially at eleven years old.

This did not deflate me. Rather, I felt much less pressure after that. I started to take life and myself a little less seriously. I knew that death would come for me one day and that life would continue on regardless of whether I lived or died. I took comfort in that.

This was my first and main spiritual awakening. My father passed regardless of how I would react to it. And it was up to me how I chose to view this and feel afterward. I did not take his death as a negative; I took this as a lesson for myself. This was my first brush with the true meaning of life.

2. MIRACLE INTERVENTION CAR ACCIDENT

Fast-forward to many years later. It was a Saturday morning in February. I had dropped off my girlfriend at the time at her job and took the highway back home. It was a really snowy day—so bad, in fact, that I could not see the lanes at all in front of me.

I was in the far-right lane of a three-lane highway. I did not have snow tires and did not feel comfortable during my drive. I had driven for about fifteen minutes already and it was not getting better. The truck in front of me was spitting snow and slush toward me at a rapid pace. So I decided to change lanes.

As I moved to the middle lane, my car began to do something very disturbing. The car was having a hard time moving along the tire grooves in the snow and slush buildups, and it started to spin. My steering wheel was out of control, spinning in all sorts of directions. My car started to slide across to the far-left lane and then back into the middle lane. I knew at this moment that I was going to die.

I had been in car accidents before, but here was a case where I lost complete control of my car and it was sliding across three lanes of a highway. There were cars coming toward me in all three lanes. I figured that I was about to be hit by multiple cars and that I was done for. I did not cry. Rather, I let go of the wheel and closed my eyes. I told myself, "I am now ready to die." I was at peace as I knew the end was there.

But clearly, I did not die. Unless I passed and all of my current existence is a dream within my mind—I survived. I opened my eyes. My car was on the far-right shoulder of the highway. Parked.

I have no idea to this day how I got there. It was almost like angels had picked up my car and set it safely on the shoulder of the highway. I went to check the damage. Not a scratch!

There was a wire fence on the shoulder that my back bumper hit, which caused it to become loose. That wire fence saved my life. If not for that fence, my car would have toppled over down a hill and been smashed. The fence dislodged my bumper, but other than that, no cars had hit me. It was a miracle!

I called my mom and told her the story. She made me make an appointment to see the rabbi and put on tefillin to connect to and thank G-d for the miracle that had occurred. I did that. I was twenty-four at the time.

This was the first time I put on tefillin since my bar mitzvah at thirteen years old. Tefillin are two leather boxes which contain Bible scrolls. Jewish men place the boxes on their heads and arms and wrap the leather straps attached to one of the boxes around their left arm and fingers. It is a custom that is considered very important and holy in the Jewish faith. I did not feel a deep religious connection when I first used tefillin, but I knew in my heart that a higher power was looking after me. It was clearly not my time to pass.

Before that miracle accident, I would say I had a fear of death. This deep fear was connected to my fear of heights and my related fear to fly. Those fears of death were so strong that they affected my ability to live and function. The accident woke me up in some sense because I truly thought I was going to die at that moment. This experience showed me that I, in fact, suffered from a fear of life.

That was when I knew I was not actually living. I was alive, as I had breath in my body, but I wasn't truly living. I was simply going through all the motions.

I could go at any time—including in that accident—but I did not. I was given a second chance at life.

I had the chance to continue, but now to truly LIVE. I took this miracle accident as a positive, for the universe and a higher power showed me how precious life is and that I was not enjoying or seeing it on any level. I knew that my frame of mind would not change overnight, but whenever life got very difficult or not worth living, I thought back to this accident and how lucky I was to be alive. Now it was up to me to figure out how to live!

3. REALIZATION OF DEATH IN ŚAVĀSANA

My last deep awakening event occurred at a yoga class (of course). The year was 2014 and I was in the middle of a consecutive streak of days spent practicing yoga that reached 395! But that streak almost did not happen and could have easily broken in the middle; not from injury, but from being unable to continue spiritually.

I was at the studio lying down in śavāsana, waiting for class to begin. I felt good and at ease. My body, mind, and soul were all refreshed and energized. I was at peace.

All of a sudden, my spirit left my body. I was watching myself lie still from up above. I could literally see myself.

And then I saw my same self in a box. In a coffin. It hit me like a ton of bricks: I WILL die one day. This will all be over. It is actually going to happen.

The realization overwhelmed me. I started to cry uncontrollably. I did not think that I would be able to continue with the class that day. I thought about quitting; getting up; going home—and either practicing yoga later in the day or calling off the streak altogether. But I decided to stay.

A yoga practice is not about the actual practice itself. It is about showing up. It's about being there. I did that—and anything I would do from there on was a bonus! So, I calmed myself down and stayed for the whole class. I did what I could; I finished, showered, went home, and reflected. A huge shift occurred within me that day and I acknowledged it.

While the reality of death was within me before, it was not until this one śavāsana that I truly realized that I would pass one day. It terrified me at the beginning. And then it soothed me.

I came to realize that much of my existence was meaningless. All the little details that stress and worry me—for what? I would die one day. And nobody would care about all the things that were worrying me. My fears and doubts—they lived in my mind. They bothered *me* and nobody else. Therefore, what was the point of carrying those burdens any further?

The unhelpful thoughts were bringing me down and did not serve me at all. If I was to pass the next day, my most imminent stress points were my own. It was time to let them go.

I wanted to get rid of all that wasn't serving me. It was time to no longer just *exist*; it was time to LIVE!

* * *

After experiencing all three of my awakening moments, the song "The End" came full circle to me. As I listen to the song today with older and more experienced ears, I hear it even clearer.

Jim Morrison was at peace with the concept of death. He knew the end was going to come. It would be the same for everyone. While living, it is important to live your life. It is most beneficial to celebrate the life that you most want—knowing and accepting that it will be gone one day.

To me, the song is more about a celebration of life rather than a fear of death. We know the end will come, so let's celebrate each moment like it is our last.

Ask yourself these key questions: Are you scared to die? Or are you scared to live?

I feel that people are too stuck on looking for the meaning behind their existence. Why are they on Earth? What is their purpose? I will then turn and ask you: Why put this much pressure on life? Why does life *have* to be about what you accomplish? Imagine a life where you have no pressure. You do not have to produce anything. If you do—great. But that will not define you.

When I accepted my JewBu identity, I felt more at ease. I didn't have to be what others expected of me. I could simply be. I could be me.

You are going to die one day. Accept it. Embrace it. For it means that while you are alive, you have life. Know that simply being alive is the meaning. It is your gift.

There are many people who have passed or are dying right now who wish they had your life. Your body, mind, and soul. *Your* existence. You have been given a gift: the gift of life. Every moment you are living is the meaning. Stop looking beyond the walls of your existence and simply look within. You are you. You exist. You are alive. The meaning of life is to live. Enjoy each day. Each moment. Live with love and you will have purpose in your existence. It is not about legacy; it is about enjoying it while we have it.

You have now discovered the meaning of life. Congratulations!

With this realization, you are now ready to enjoy each day. Each moment. Live with love, and you will have purpose in your existence.

When we all pass on, we will all follow the same path. No matter what job titles we have, education, money, power—we all die the same way. So why are we in such a rush to accumulate and prove our worth while we are here? We will pass on regardless.

I have seen millionaires with seemingly complete lives (mansions, cars, money, a beautiful spouse, and children) and yet they are completely miserable. On the other side of the coin, I have seen people with seemingly no material possessions who are completely happy. What we make and own does not define us. We define ourselves!

It is time to stop looking for material goods to satisfy you. Job promotions, an accumulation of wealth, love, attention, and admiration of others—those may all be nice things, but they will not make you happy. Only you can make yourself happy!

We started off *The Bible 3.0* with Chapter 1, "Love Is a Lifestyle." That love is the foundation of existence. Remember, it is not the love from others that will complete you. It is self-love. Once you have built a foundation of love, then you can prepare your life and incorporate the 6 Commandments of the Chosen Life into your world. Only from there can you work on the additional steps to help guide you toward enlightenment. There is a cycle to the process. Follow and utilize it to work toward YOUR Chosen Life and existence.

But, you are human. You will try to do the work. Yet there will be times you will fail and may want to give up. You will have a bad day, a bad week, or a bad month. Things may not always go your way. You will say to yourself, "What is the point of this? What am I working toward? Why am I bothering?" When you reach these crossroads, this is where you need meaning the most in your life.

For me, as a JewBu, it becomes clear: I am alive. I am lucky and fortunate. I am grateful to exist. All of these things that are worrying me are irrelevant. I will focus on being positive and appreciating that I do have life rather than worrying about what I am lacking and missing. Those other things may come and go, but as long as I have life, I have a purpose.

As you go through the exercises and homework I have given you in *The Bible 3.0*, remember to nourish every part of your being.

We tend to work so hard on our bodies and minds that we neglect the key component of ourselves: the soul. When you have moments that you are down and out, that is when you most need to feed your soul. Ask yourself: Where is your spirit? What kind of energy are you putting out? What is motivating you most? Find that energy within and let your soul heal and flourish. Do not neglect or bury your spirit. Remember—your soul completes you. Without your soul, you will never truly know who you really are.

Along our journey together, I also hope that you have found your spiritual and/or religious connections, or at least invigorated them. I was fortunate because my body, mind, and soul were opened as I discovered who I was in the world. I embraced that I am a JewBu, a person who fits within different categories of the religious and spiritual worlds but does not slot perfectly into one category.

Whether you identify fully or partially with any particular religious or spiritual group, do not worry. There is no pressure for you to ever be confined or constrained under one label. You are you. You define yourself. Even if you identify with any particular group(s), this will not change you. Remember that as you follow your Chosen Life.

Do not give up on your spiritual and/or religious sides. They are important. They feed your soul, which in turn shapes who you are as a person. This can happen whether or not you feel that there is a higher power or you identify with a particular religion. Discover your energy source for spirituality. Experience as much as you can from a religion/spirituality point of view—to help shape the well-rounded you. Do not give up on your soul.

I can tell you with full certainty that becoming a JewBu fully shaped the rest of my life and helped me reach higher levels of enlightenment. I am a much happier and more peaceful person for having nourished my spirit. May you find your chosen path that works for you.

I appreciate fully from the bottom of my heart the time and commitment you have given me—and yourself—by reading *The Bible 3.0* and any work that you have put in as far as your life goes. The most precious and limited commodity you have is *time*. You have given that to yourself by reading *The Bible 3.0*. I honor and thank you for that gift, as it is valued to the highest degree.

I have given you my gift of time in return by writing *The Bible 3.0* and sharing with you my stories, experiences, and processes for helping you attain, maintain, and evolve your Chosen Life. I have given you this book with pure love, as a gift to you and the universe. You have given me back that love by reading this book and working through the exercises. We each have given ourselves the purest love. We then have given to one another that pure love as a gift, without expecting anything back. By producing love from within and exchanging pure love back, we have achieved the highest state of love—and thus life—that we can. May that love continue to burn strongly in your heart. From today, tomorrow, and until the end of time. Namaste.

Acknowledgments

—∽∽∽—

There are so many people I have met over the years who have touched my life in one way or another. From family, teachers, co-workers, and friends in and out of the gym, I appreciate each and every one of you and the energy you brought into my world.

First and foremost, to my son, Jeremiah Hacohen. I selected your name way before you were born. Your grandmother asked me at your bris how I could give such a big important name to such a little baby. Well, you certainly grew into it and became a man I admire, respect, and love. From cottage weekends to our never-ending road trips, every day with you is an adventure and fun. You are not just my son. You are my best friend. I only wish you happiness in everything you do. Never stop believing in yourself. EVER! The life changes I made which became the foundation of this book were done so that I can be alive, healthy, and be here for you as your dad. Being your father gave me purpose and strength to travel our common journey together. Thank you for being an incredible son. I love you. I love you. And I love you.

They say that a dog is man's best friend. Well, Ollie, my Shih Tzu, is living proof of this statement. I know she can't read this. But if I read it to her, I know she would understand. Ollie, you came into our lives when I least expected to have a pet. And you filled a void and beyond that I didn't know existed. You are the smartest, most loyal, friendly, and empathetic dog I have ever met. Your grandma is convinced that you are a person trapped in a dog's body. I agree. No matter how rough my day may be, you are always waiting for me with kisses and snuggles. My doggy is truly an emotional support pet. She uplifts everyone who comes into contact with her. Thank you to the universe for bringing Ollie to our family. She is truly the G.O.A.T.

Thank you to my sister-in-law, Rivi. You are the glue that keeps us together. You devote your life to taking care of your family. It may feel like a thankless job at times (trust me, I get it). I wanted to take this moment to acknowledge all the sacrifices you made to make sure that everyone else was looked after. Your thirst for knowledge on health and nutrition constantly inspired me. You made me into a cook. You led me down many roads for a healthy lifestyle. *The Bible 3.0* does not happen without your words of guidance and encouragement. I love you and thank you.

To my nieces and nephew: Being your uncle is one of my favorite roles of all time. I have shared so many great times with each of you and love you so much.

Rachel—the original designer for my blogging logos. You are so creative and passionate. Plus, a big sister to all your siblings. Never change, please.

Michelle—my baseball buddy. We loved watching our Tigers and going to games together. I look back at those days and smile! I'm looking forward to our next one.

Dani—my gym buddy. I am so proud of the hard work you put in the gym and discovered your own path in life. You aren't afraid to take risks and I commend you for your strength and determination.

David—my favorite (and only) nephew. I can't even begin to thank you for everything you brought into my life. From getting me into Jordan 1 High OG sneakers, producing all my podcasts, designing the Chosen Championship Belt, and our many adventures together as the three amigos—thank you. You are Jeremiah's older brother by actions, and you are lucky to have each other. Thank you for always believing in me and the many hours you put in behind the scenes. None of this is possible without you.

Thank you to Sara, my mom. When I was young, you encouraged me to read a book per day. I guess all that reading paid off. As a single mother, the efforts you put into my development are simply remarkable. You programmed me to always strive for perfection. When people marvel at my work ethic and dedication, I can trace it all back to your teachings. It was painful and difficult at times to put in the extra energy and squeeze out every ounce of my potential. But I tell you today: thank you. It was all worth it. You are also the most devoted reader I know. I'm glad that I could add another book to your collection.

To one of my closest and dearest friends on the planet, Elan Weintraub: In addition to being one of the top mortgage brokers (shoutout to Mortgage Outlet), you are truly a kind, giving, and compassionate gentleman. My life is better in every way because you are part of it, and I am honored to call you my friend and brother. Thank you for being my golden goose and helping me build such a wonderful life, professionally and personally.

To Amir Ginzburg, my longest friendship: We were able to keep our bond since first grade, pretty much, which is remarkable in this day and age. Amir, if not for you and all your efforts, I don't think that I would be alive today. You have continually gone above and beyond for me and my loved ones. You are an absolute gift to medicine and society as a whole. You are the smartest person I know and set the bar very high for the rest of us. I would take a bullet for you. Yes, you are that damn special.

David Korman, you may be Mr. Korman to many people, but you are a brother to me. The universe blessed me with the greatest law partner a person could ask for. You are a true mensch. You make me want to be a better lawyer and person every single day. You never take the easy route out. I marvel at your level of logic, understanding, and passion for all that you do. Thank you for putting up with me and my shenanigans. Even when I raise ideas and goals that seem impossible, you are never surprised. You encourage me in all that I do and that means the world to me. You are my sounding board and devil's advocate. I always know that if you and I are on the same page for something, then it must be a good idea. I only wish that the world was filled with more David Kormans. It would be the point that we would reach a true utopia.

Mason Rush (you may know him as Jared Heft): professional wrestler, my trainer, and close friend, I could fill a book with the thanks I have for you. We have spent so many years and hours in the gym together. You believed in me and never gave up on my physical progressions. So many other trainers came and went during our time together. Yet you were the one constant in my gym world. I learned the difference between being skinny jacked and having true strength and endurance. You are a gifted teacher. You are patient. You always see the long-term progressions. All I had to do was show up and give it my all each time. But you are so much more than a trainer. From our sessions, so many ideas were born. There would have been no podcasts and theme song for The Chosen Lawyer if not for our talks. It was your idea to pull a funny flexing picture off my social media and blast the silhouette on a shirt. You inspire me to never settle for mediocrity. With you, there is always a higher ceiling to break through and achieve more. Now, as you progress in your wrestling career, I am grateful that I can be here for you as your manager and number one fan. The sky's the limit for our faction. Rushtourage 4 Life.

To the one and only Steve Karsay: The universe blessed me to have such a dear and amazing friend. You have accomplished so much in life and I marvel at how you stay humble and down-to-earth throughout. We bonded over baseball and it's our experiences as fathers that brings us even closer. One day, when I end up in Arizona full time, it will be all your fault. Thank you for our daily chats. Thank you for inspiring me to be the best dad that I can be. Kingston is lucky to have you. I wish you both only success in life and truly appreciate that you allow me to be part of your world.

To my music producer, as well as an artist/pianist/composer: THE Ron Lopata. We have known each other for most of our lives and I came to you half-jokingly to help me write and produce a theme song. You didn't blink an eye and before I knew it, The

Chosen Lawyer theme song was born. It is a song that fits and describes me perfectly. Whether I am walking down to the ring for a fight or to be interviewed in a studio, I would want that tune playing. From there, to put in the hours and effort to record and finalize our audiobook was magical. You are so talented in all that you do, and I am so grateful for the excitement and professionalism you brought to every project we worked on together. You helped shape my brand and image. This book is at its audible best because of your dedication. You are a modern-day Richard Clayderman to me, brother. Thank you for bringing beautiful music to our world and spreading positivity through the melodies you produce.

The Bible 3.0 was made possible through the talented geniuses at The Awakened Press, with a special shoutout to Lindsay Rose Allison Dierking and our editor Angela Heis. Lindsay: I honestly reached out to you originally to see if I was on the right track for my book vision. All I was expecting back was a "yes" or "no" and maybe two lines of comments. I did not expect your enthusiasm and drive to make *The Bible 3.0* a reality. Once we committed to one another to have me write this book, we never looked back. I am so grateful that the universe brought us together. Through blood, sweat, and tears—we did it. I was determined to write the greatest book ever. You brought out the best in me. I know how lucky I am to have you and your team by my side. We brought a book to life. Hugs and kisses always!

Finally, I want to take this opportunity to truly acknowledge and thank G-d and the universe. I was blessed from an early age to realize and shape a talent for writing. You gave me the gift. It was up to me to ask you to show me the available roads to use it. In some ways, I thought that I would have traveled this path long ago and written a series of books by now. In other ways, I did consider that I may never write a book at all. I'm glad that *The Bible 3.0* came today and not ten years from now. It took this time and life experiences for me to express my thoughts and share my life work with the world. All of this happened because G-d made the roads in my life available. If it came too early and easy, I would have never appreciated it. At last reflection, I wouldn't change anything. You have been with me from day one and always seen me through. My hope is that *The Bible 3.0* helps people and can make the world a better place. I have tried my best to use my talents for good. Thank you for making my opportunities possible. Amen.

Jonathan A. Hacohen

Jonathan A. Hacohen, AKA, "The Chosen Lawyer" and JewBu, is a speaker, author, and talk show host of "The Chosen Life Podcast." He completed a B.B.A. degree at the Schulich School of Business, was called to the Ontario bar as a lawyer in 2002, and is a partner at his law firm, Kormans LLP.

Jonathan is a seasoned lecturer and has spoken with many influential organizational groups, including the Ontario Bar Association. Known for his expertise, Jonathan is frequently sought after as a speaker at seminars, team meetings, and conferences. He puts his heart and soul into his work as he shares about mindfulness and productivity, organization, motivation, and work/life balance in his latest book, *The Bible 3.0: The 6 Commandments of the Chosen Life*, and on his podcast where he interviews brilliant minds for their personal development stories and encouraging and inspiring motivational experiences.

After yoga was revealed to him in 2009, Jonathan has since become an avid yogi and practiced thousands of hours of yoga and meditation. His yoga practice eventually resulted in his complete turn-around in mind, body, and spirit, allowing him the opportunity to train for two years toward becoming a professional boxer and compete in bodybuilding and fitness, where he became the winner of Silver and Bronze medals at an Ultimate Fitness Events championship in the physique category.

Jonathan was the former Vice President and Head of Brotherhood at Am Shalom Synagogue. In 2011, he visited Bali to meditate with Ketut Liyer, the Balinese medicine man featured in Elizabeth Gilbert's *Eat, Pray, Love*, who inspired him to make better possibilities that he could live longer than he initially assumed.

Many spiritual revelations compelled him to share his life experiences in the form of a roadmap to personal success called *The Bible 3.0: The 6 Commandments of the Chosen Life*. As his friends and colleagues describe him as an enlightened mind, Jonathan's charisma and enthusiasm for life cannot be matched.

visit
theBible3.com